My Kickstarter Backers:

Katherine Hughes
Hank Albarelli
Christina Richmond
Cynthia Goodman
Ray Del Papa
Dale Thorn
Leonard Steinberg
David O. Stewart
Bill & Lori Cowan
Adriana Adarve
Christine Casner
Joe McKee
Doug Valentine
Bill Tchakirides
Michael Drexler
James Pricer
John Colagioia
Shahid Buttar
Ray McGovern
David Swanson
Coleen Rowley
John Cristine
Peter J. Nickitas
*

Thank you!

To my daughters,
Sarah & Giselle

We shall not cease from exploration
And the end of all our exploring
Will be to arrive where we started
And know the place for the first time.
T. S. Eliot
Little Gidding

And for Aaron Burr

". . . Public, ye who like me not,
(God love you!) and will have your proper laugh
At the dark question, laugh it! I laugh first."
Robert Browning, *The Ring and the Book*
Book I, lines 410-12

Also by Jennifer Van Bergen

BOOKS

The Twilight of Democracy:
The Bush Plan for America (2004)

Archetypes for Writers:
Using the Power of Your Subconscious (2007)

Malice (the Musical Play) (Part One: © 2018)

The Unspoken Order:
Jesus, St. Joan, Lord Jim, Plato & Socrates
-- Prophets, Visionaries & Madmen (© 1980)

SCHOLARLY ARTICLES

Aaron Burr and the Electoral Tie of 1801:
Strict Constitutional Construction
1 Cardozo Pub. L., Policy & Ethics J. 91-130 (Spring 2003)

In the Absence of Democracy:
The Designation and Material Support Provisions
of the Anti-Terrorism Laws
2 Cardozo Pub. L., Policy & Ethics J. 107-160 (Fall 2003)

The Dangerous World of Indefinite Detentions:
From Vietnam to Abu Ghraib
(with Douglas Valentine)
37 Case West. J. Int'l L. 449-508 (Spring 2006)

Reconstructing Leonora Sansay:
Early 19th Century Novelist & Friend of Aaron Burr
A New World is Possible, January 3, 2010
(*See* https://en.wikipedia.org/wiki/Leonora_Sansay *and*
https://wikivisually.com/wiki/Leonora_Sansay)

MUSIC CD'S
(all songs © Jennifer Van Bergen)
Sand Songs (© 1978)
Black Hole (© 1998)[*]
Malice (© 2018)

---

[*] Black Hole available on iTunes & YouTube.

MALICE:

Thomas Jefferson's Conspiracy
to Destroy Aaron Burr

Jennifer Van Bergen

~Limited Privately Printed Edition~

BookBaby™
7905 North Route 130 • Pennsauken, NJ 08110
www.bookbaby.com • 877-961-6878

Printed in the United States of America
by Book Baby, Pennsauken, NJ, www.bookbaby.com

ISBN 978-1-54396-523-0

This volume is a first finished draft version
printed especially for my Kickstarter Backers.

Cover portraits:
Aaron Burr, 1802, by John Vanderlyn
New York Historical Society, New York, NY
Thomas Jefferson, circa 1797, by James Staples
Independence National Historical Park, Philadelphia, PA

Cover by Sarah Van Bergen

Preface to the Limited Edition

In his preface to the first (1963) printing of the remarkable *Jefferson and Civil Liberties: The Darker Side*, the author Leonard W. Levy wrote: "Historians and biographers have fixed a libertarian halo around the brow of Thomas Jefferson as if he were a plaster saint, a seraph, or a demigod." (Levy, vii.) The book received such criticism that when nine years later it came out in paperback, Levy wrote in that preface: "The reappearance of this book will doubtless disappoint some critics who would prefer to see it evaporate into oblivion . . ." (Id., xi.) He noted that "[w]ith few exceptions . . . most readers reacted [to his revelations about Jefferson] as if I had engaged in a sort of secularized blasphemy, like desecration of the flag. They felt hurt and angry, as if they had a personal stake in Jefferson's reputation as the apostle of liberty, and I had attacked an article of unquestionable faith." (Id.)

Levy spent 15 pages responding to the criticisms of his reviewers, among whom were the esteemed Dumas Malone, Jefferson's biographer, and Julian P. Boyd, the editor of TJ's papers.[1] Levy's reviews of their reviews are highly revealing about the level of denial existing in the minds of even the most eminent scholars about Jefferson.

The same is true in reverse about Burr. Anyone who speaks up for him in the slightest degree is subject to vicious attack. Both Jefferson and Burr were just men. Both were men of learning and talent. Both carried deep wounds from childhood. Both had great capacity to love and equal capacity to destroy others. They were very different men but the main difference was in this one thing: that Jefferson sought to kill Burr and Burr declined to respond in kind.

Burr was not corrupt or overly ambitious, a serpent in the garden, a defiler of women, a destroyer of democracy, or a would-be emperor. Those are projections of our own repressed personality parts, convenient dramatizations of our fears and unfulfilled wishes.

---

[1] Malone's "main objection, like that of other Jeffersonians, was to the very conception of the book." (Levy, xiii.) Boyd "took the position . . . that Jefferson cannot be measured except sympathetically and uncritically. He then alleged that my premises were unacceptable, my proofs unconvincing, and my standards often irrelevant and unfair." (Levy, xii.)

It was not even remotely true that Burr's "ambition [would] not suffer him to be second."[2] Other people put him first but history shows quite clearly that he was a collaborator and coalition-builder. It *is* true, however, that he was a natural leader who carried an irrepressible drive. That drive was not ambition in the way others interpreted it. His opponents believed the drive was for fame and glory to himself. But again, the historical record shows that the goal of Burr's drive was humanitarian, and that the wellspring from which it came was oriented to the realization of a form or structure that was probably not discernible to those who misjudged him or even fully to those who sided with him. (Burr's habitual mystique and secrecy was probably partly due to his awareness of these misjudgments.) People on both sides sensed a power in him but could not pinpoint what it was. This made him both magnetic and frightening.

Burr had the unique ability to make the best use of his world by aligning himself and his humanitarian pursuits for the continuous improvement and realization of human potential with the elements of that world. He cared about education, suffrage, freedom, and self-determination. But not only. He cared about self-improvement. But not only. Most importantly, he cared about the full appreciation and fulfillment of each individual. He wanted people in his ambit to become who they could be, to make use of all their abilities. He had the capacity to see latent and buried abilities in others. He wished to enable others to their higher selves and he did enable many, many people.

When Burr finally realized he could do nothing in the east and decided to move westward, he transplanted his vision to establish an elevated society there. His Bastrop settlement was to be that place and if he could liberate the Mexicans, his settlement could be a center of learning and achievement for them as well.

Burr's principles and life were exemplary and he used himself as an example to others. This has been viewed as arrogant and ambitious, but Burr was the only one who was able to fully grasp and envision the fundamental principles for this society and who could enable its realization. Nobody else could do this.

If Jefferson saw and understood this – and I believe he did – Burr's vision would have trumped Jefferson's; it would have shown his beloved "empire of liberty" as a mere fantasy. Jefferson, speaking for an entire nation, was the man who had with his words and ideals single-handedly eviscerated the tyrant King George. If Burr's society succeeded, Jefferson was no longer the savior of mankind, his rhetoric was empty, and he was nothing more than a scribbler.

Jefferson did not just destroy Burr. He destroyed the seeds of a mecca of learning and achievement in the heartland of America and he turned it back to the dark ages of slavery, corruption, graft, and fawning nationalism.   ~

---

[2]   R. Griswold to O. Wolcott, March 11, 1804, in Adams, *TJ Administrations*, 423.

"Our fates remain the same."

Theodosia (Burr's daughter) to Burr
Written to him in exile, 18 months after his trial.

*Eighteen days have elapsed since the above was written and there is no
news to add. Nothing has occurred, nothing altered. Shall it always be so
with us? All nature changes. Day has followed night. There have been
revolutions in the seasons; but our fates, which appear ever like black
impending clouds ready to burst, still threaten, and still remain the same.*

***

*Your acquaintance, Mr. Smith [Samuel Swartwout], arrived a few days
since, out of spirits and disappointed. He has left us again with new
courage. He has not contributed to enliven me. Already anxious and
distressed about you, he has rendered me doubly so by the addition of
unavailing regrets, and the dreadful conviction that I have been the cause
of real injury to you by the delay my illness occasioned. This I had felt
before, but it never appeared to me in its full extent till after my
conversation with him. The poignant sufferings this idea has occasioned me
are indescribable; and though my life has been saved by it, I cannot rejoice
at it, from a belief that your happiness will greatly depend on my existence.
And can I then remunerate you for such sacrifices merely by living? Under
every sort of misery, this reflection would make me careful of life, as of a
treasure which I have in keeping for you, to be spent in your service.*

**Theodosia Burr Alston (Burr's daughter) to Aaron Burr,
February 10, 1809 (February 1 – March 8),**
Davis, *Private Journal of AB*, 1:162-3

Nag's Head Portrait[3]

---

[3] For the "Mystery of the Nag's Head Portrait," see Richard N. Côté, *Theodosia
Burr Alston: Portrait of a Prodigy* (Corinthian Books, 2003), Chapter 12 (pp.
307-27).

These scenes will be deemed fables

I want an independent and discerning witness to my conduct and to that of the government. The scenes which have passed and those about to be transacted will exceed all reasonable credibility, and will hereafter be deemed fables, unless attested by very high authority.

Aaron Burr to Theodosia Burr Alston, July 24, 1807
Davis, *Burr Memoirs*, 3:410 (written in prison)

Burr's Trial

How long is it since the government began to digest all the information it collected by the most illicit means from the most foul sources, not of our acts but of our designs, before we did any act?
Harman Blennerhassett's Journal, September 18, 1807
Fitch, *Breaking with Burr*, 94

Mr. Burr observed that he meant by persecution, the harassment of any individual contrary to the forms of law; and that his case, unfortunately, presented too many instances of this description. He would merely state a few of them. He said that his friends had been everywhere seized by the military authority, a practice truly consonant with European despotisms.
He said that persons had been dragged by compulsory process before particular tribunals and compelled to give testimony against him. His papers, too, had been seized. And yet, in England, where we say they know nothing of liberty, a gentleman, who had been seized and detained two hours, in a back parlour, had obtained damages to the amount of one thousand guineas.
He said, that an order had been issued to kill him, as he was descending the Mississippi, and seize his property. And yet, they could only have killed his person, if he had been formally condemned for treason.
He said, that even post-offices had been broken open and robbed of his papers; that, in the Mississippi Territory, even an indictment was about to be laid against the [local] postmaster; that he had always taken this for a felony; but nothing seemed too extravagant to be forgiven by the amiable morality of this government.
Aaron Burr at trial, May 25, 1807
Robertson 1:77-78.

Table of Contents

– Because this book is not indexed, I have provided more information in the Table of Contents to assist the reader in locating material. Chapter titles (in caps) are followed by a short quote from that chapter. An asterisk before a lower-case title indicates a page containing images *or* quoted material, or both. Front material page numbers are identified in the Contents by roman numerals, starting at the Preface, but, due to formatting problems, are not numbered on the pages. –

Images

*[O]ur little world as you say is pregnant, but the gestation will be longer & the
parturition more remote, probably, more critical, than you seem aware.*
-Aaron Burr to Robert Goodloe Harper, May 29, 1804; Kline 2:870

~~~~~

*The history of the times to which these memorandums and documents relate are
enveloped in thick darkness. Whether the period has yet arrived when an effort
should be made to dispel that darkness is problematical.*
-Matthew L. Davis to Aaron Burr, April 22, 1830
Kline 2:1202 (on 1801 electoral tie)

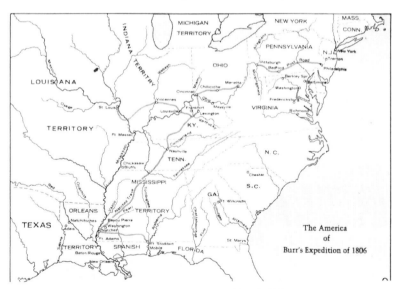

Map borrowed from Kline 2:599.

Secrecy

Everything secret degenerates, even the administration of justice; nothing is safe that does not show how it can bear discussion and publicity.
Lord Acton
(John Emerich Edward Dalberg Acton, 1st Baron Acton)
Letter, 23 January 1861,
Abbot Gasquet, *Lord Acton and his Circle* (1906), Letter 74

Never has there been an administration like the one in power today – so disciplined in secrecy, so precisely in lockstep in keeping information from the people at large and, in defiance of the Constitution, from their representatives in Congress.
Bill Moyers, September 14, 2004
(About the G.W. Bush Administration)

Democracy dies behind closed doors . . . The First Amendment, through a free press, protects the people's right to know that their government acts fairly, lawfully and accurately . . . When government begins closing doors, it selectively controls information rightfully belonging to the people.
Selective information is misinformation.
Judge Keith, *North Jersey Media Group v. Ashcroft*, 308 F.3d 198 (3d Cir. 2002)

[S]ecret persons [are] like the great rivers, whose bottoms we cannot see, and which make no noise."
John Adams to Benjamin Rush, January 25, 1806

When unprincipled men acquire the ascendancy, they act in concert and are silent.
John Randolph, Speech in Congress, Spring 1805
(on Jeffersonians in Congress)
Henry Adams, *Administrations of TJ*, 446-7.

Forward

What this book is and is not.

If [Burr's] guilt is as clear as the noonday sun, the first magistrate ought not to have pronounced it so before a jury had tried him. * * *The whole thing is a kind of waterspout, a terrible whirlpool, threatening to engulf everything. But it may be, as the fable says, that a single bullet shot through it will quell it all at once to the level of the sea . . .* **- John Adams to Benjamin Rush, February 2, 1807**
Schutz, *Spur of Fame*, 83.

[Our] contingent plans or operations against Spain . . . whilst kept secret, government would not disapprove, but when exposed, [they] would be obliged to frustrate. **Harman Blennerhassett, Brief,** Fitch, *Breaking with Burr*, 196.

This book is about the *Jefferson Conspiracy* to destroy Aaron Burr. It does *not* tell any version of the so-called *Burr Conspiracy*. Nor does this book make any attempt to write another Burr biography or history of the time. I assume readers know the history. My focus is on the development and enactment of Jefferson's conspiracy against Burr, the characters of the individuals involved, and their relationships. I write for the general reader but this is a scholarly work, though it is also unlike other scholarly works in a number of ways. Rather than telling a story or laying things out chronologically, I go at the facts in a number of different ways. There are, in fact, many characters and many stories in this telling.

In addition, I make no effort in this book to be balanced, objective, or impartial. This does not mean I am unfair. I use the evidence and I make logical inferences but I am advocating for Burr against Jefferson. I am not a Jefferson-hater or a Burr-lover. I am an admirer and critic of both men but if I am hard on Jefferson and sympathetic to Burr, it is because of what TJ did to Burr, and because Burr has had it hard enough. He has had no genuine advocate, no one to speak for him, in all the years since Jefferson took him down.[4] So, in order to best understand what happened from Burr's perspective – which is history as much as anything else -- I construe events and actions in a light most favorable to him and least favorable to Jefferson. I make no apology for this.

Further, I do not claim this work to be definitive or

---

[4]   Burr has had what might be called quasi-defenders (McCaleb, Lomask, Isenberg, Kline), authors purporting to be "objective," not quite willing to take his side, and always within the context of the fictitious Burr Conspiracy.

exhaustive. On the contrary, as deeply as I may have delved into many things and as strong as my assertions and conclusions may be, I consider this work exploratory, preliminary, incomplete. I am able only to touch upon much that deserves further and deeper investigation.

I am not focused here, either, on defending Burr against Jefferson's charges. The facts I set forth herein, I think, suggest that Jefferson (with the help of Wilkinson, mostly) *fabricated those charges*. Engaging in a defense against fabricated charges is, well, quarreling with phantoms, as Burr put it. Rather, I show the sources of the charges in Jefferson and suggest reasons why he brought them.

Although I have culled, there is necessarily some degree of redundancy and repetition in the narrative from one chapter to the next, partly because I am arguing a case from many angles, partly due to the structure of the conspiracy itself (circling around a common center, Jefferson, who, however, informs and utilizes each co-conspirator differently and depending on public conditions at the time), and partly due to the need to fill in legal premises and historical background, and to reinforce critical details.

Other than my loyal Kickstarter backers, who funded this limited edition from their pockets, and my friend Don DeBar, who covered printing costs, I have had no financial or scholarly support from any person, group, association, or institution, including the Aaron Burr Association, or any academic, corporate, or other organization.

In truth, the public lack of support for my "theory of the case" has been disheartening. As an independent scholar, my work – not my academic affiliation – speaks for me. One would think there would be more interest in a work like this one but not even the appearance of Lin-Manuel Miranda's wonderful musical "Hamilton" seems to have changed America's reception to any effort on behalf of Burr.

This is hard on the spirit. But it may be seen as further proof of my thesis that the things Jefferson did affected the entire nation and still affect us. Americans went into denial during the second Jefferson Administration, in part due to Jefferson's confounding behavior during the Burr episode and partly due to his later destructive policies. We are still in deep denial. We want to believe America is good, even if we think our politicians and leaders might be bad. We think our founding is pure and the Founders are unalloyed embodiments of the noble American Dream. Advocating for Burr or questioning Jefferson's status or character challenge those ideas and are literally seen as treason.

Perhaps this is because Jefferson – not Burr – was the one who betrayed this country. Indeed, what TJ did in colluding with Wilkinson may well have constituted actual treason. But he also damaged both the judiciary and the executive, and subverted the ideals and doctrines on which he had come into office. Henry Adams sums it up in his chapter on "The Costs of the Embargo 1808":

> The Republican party by a supreme effort kept itself in office, but no one could fail to see that if nine months of embargo had so shattered Jefferson's power, another such year would shake the Union itself. The cost of this 'engine for national purposes' exceeded all calculation. Financially, it emptied the Treasury, bankrupted the mercantile and agricultural class, and ground the poor beyond endurance. Constitutionally, it overrode every specified limit on arbitrary power and made Congress despotic, while it left no bounds to the authority, which might be vested by Congess in the President. Morally, it sapped the nation's vital force, lowering its courage, paralyzing its energy, corrupting its principles, and arraying all the active elements of society in factious opposition to government or in secret paths of treason. Politically, it cost Jefferson the fruits of eight years painful labor for popularity, and brought the Union to the edge of a precipice.

(Adams, *TJ Administrations*, 1125.) This is what Jefferson did by his well-intentioned policies that followed directly after his take-down of Burr. The facts of his ill-intentioned conspiracy against Burr are far worse. They provide decisive evidence of high crimes and misdemeanors, crimes of moral turpitude, on Jefferson's part that, at the very least, should have resulted in his impeachment, if not his prosecution and punishment for those crimes.[5]

---

[5] One small example of unlawful activity that Jefferson encouraged and applauded: Burr's counsel spoke at trial about "the plunder of the post-offices . . . [and that] officers of the government [had] broken opens letters from Colonel Burr," that "[i]f the post-office was robbed, the possession of the paper was gained feloniously. The constitution has provided against the seizure of papers; and the act of congress has fixed the offence of stealing from the post-offices . . . It is impossible that this most detestable vice of the most infamous of European courts can have been patronized by the government. By a familiarity of our rulers with such hateful practices the people would be demoralized." (Mr. Botts, June 17 & 16, 1807, Robertson, *Trial of AB,* 1:235, 213-14.) Burr offered to provide proof but was not afforded the opportunity. In 1814, Jefferson shamelessly confirmed in a letter to his former post-master general Gideon Granger that Granger had indeed "seen that the mails were expedited" in New Orleans, had removed those postal employees "whose fidelity could be justly doubted" during the crisis, and that these actions were "taken with my

But the failure by Burr's peers to grasp that their President had engaged in grievously unlawful behavior, their acceptance of Jefferson's lies, and their eagerness to throw blame on Burr is another matter. Professors Michael Drexler and Ed White posit that Burr simply filled an empty slot in American's thinking that needed filling because of the collective guilt about the institution of slavery. (This is particularly apt with respect to Jefferson's motives.) In other words, it was not what Burr did; it was the empty spaces that his persona left that allowed Burr to be saddled with the American public's psychological projection of its own terrible crimes against blacks.

I think this is true but whether it is or not would not have mattered to Burr. As clearly and cogently as he spoke, he was not heard and has not been since his downfall. Although I acknowledge that my efforts here are surely inadequate to the task of remedying this void, I hope at least that this book may open Americans' ears to hear Burr's voice again and learn from his experiences.

I trust and believe in my work. I believe this work has meaning beyond that which it represents to me or Burr alone, or to those who associate or have associated in Burr's name, or to historians and history buffs in general. The meaning of the Jefferson conspiracy to destroy Burr extends far beyond the subject itself into the psyches of all Americans, all of whom are descended from and/or follow the legacies of those who either participated in the heinous conspiracy to destroy him, stood by and watched (remained "neutral"), turned away, or simply failed to speak out, stand by him, or come to his aid or defense - continuing to the present day and to my work. This is *our* legacy. We allowed this to happen.

That Burr was *not* a villain -- that he was a man of decency, integrity, honor, intelligence, merit, and ability -- *matters*. That Jefferson did all he could to destroy this man *matters*. It is a taint on all of us because it is not just about Burr; it is about *our* founding, *our* rearing, our maturation, *who and what we are*.

I believe that we must absorb what Jefferson did to Burr, all this, absorb and internalize its meaning, before we can become the nation we hoped to be (if that is still possible). And if it is too late for America to eradicate the malignancy, we, the people, can at least throw off some of our illusions, walk forward into the uncertain future, and find our way under the light of an essential truth we had hitherto lost.   ~

---

approbation." (TJ to GG, March 9, 1814; GG to TJ, February 22, 1814; TJ to JM, March 10, 1814, Founders Online.)

My Method

Scholarship & Character Work

A book in shape but, really, pure crude fact
Secreted from man's life when hearts beat hard,
And brains, high-blooded, ticked two centuries since.
Give it me back! The thing's restorative
I' the touch and sight.
Robert Browning, *The Ring and the Book*

As an independent scholar, I have been free to use any approach which suits me. However, this does not mean that my standards are lower than those used by scholars in academia. In some ways, my standards are more stringent; in some ways less so. I think it is important that I enumerate these.

I rely heavily on primary source material – letters and documents in each person's own words. Sometimes, I quote secondary sources -- other authors – because their opinions support mine or they explain something well.

For use and citation of source material, I apply general standards of scholarship (though I use my own citation system).[6] Where possible, I try to view the original document or a verified typewritten transcript of it. If I cannot view the original (or an official copy of the) document or work to which another author cites, I cite the work in which I found the material and include the source to which they cite. For example: (Kennedy, 123, citing to writer, recipient, date, source).

Where I have accessed a primary document through a published collection, I cite to the document and the collection, in that order. Where a primary source is quoted in an editorial note, I cite the editorial note first, followed by the word "quoting" followed by the document quoted from. Where a letter is found in an authoritative collection, I cite the letter first and then the collection: (TJ to AB, December 18, 1800 in Kline 2:200). Where I have been unable to view an original or verified transcription, I use the best source available to me.

The bibliography includes all book sources I have used

---

[6]   *See* Bibliographic Note.

directly. Many letters and documents from published collections or otherwise are now available online. I do not cite to specific URL's for these, since they are generally easy to find by googling the author, recipient, and date.

Where possible, I keep in mind legal standards of proof for assessment and application of evidence. Since I am writing for educated readers and not lawyers specifically, I assume most readers will not have a full understanding of legal and evidentiary standards. Thus, I introduce and discuss some of these standards. For the most part, however, I do not explicitly state legal standards but simply engage in a discussion and weighing of the evidence.

I may critique or discredit evidence Jefferson relied on (as rumor or hearsay, for example) but rely on similar evidence when it benefits Burr, such as Swartwout's account of what he knew of Burr's intentions or Blennerhassett's brief on his discussions with Burr (both hearsay about Burr's intentions but important as to what he conveyed to them). I think the reason for my doing this is obvious. Jefferson was the one who prosecuted Burr and it is important to know that many if not most of Jefferson's premises were derived from rumor or hearsay – that he relied on those to charge his former running mate with a hanging offense. It is equally important to know what Burr's own close associates knew and thought, if not more so, since Burr's side has never been sufficiently told.

This does not mean, however, that my evidence against Jefferson rests solely on hearsay. The evidence showing that Jefferson wanted to destroy and even kill Burr is direct. He admitted it. That he had no case is obvious. The evidence that he was using public funds to outfit expeditions in order to illegally enter Spanish territory and acquire "intelligence" is well-established.

Co-conspirators' participation is largely a matter of documentary record. The connections between them and the damage they did to Burr is well-documented. Most of the members of what Burr called "the knot of knaves" had a record of conspiratorial "intrigues" both before and after their attacks on Burr. It is important to know the characters of these men but proof of their involvement in the campaign to destroy Burr is not based on prior or later record but on evidence of their direct involvement. The involvement of Cabinet members is also quite clear.

In some ways, my research approach is less systematic but more in-depth than that which scholars or lawyers are trained to use. This is due in part, I think, to my focus on extracting and utilizing action-principles. This is the process of discovering core operating principles within the words and actions of individuals.[7]

    This approach requires, as it were, going outside one's own conscious processes (that is, using one's subconscious), to gather and assemble information that is relevant to the particular pursuit of understanding the actors and their actions in context.[8] There is a reason for working this way and there is a trick to it, as well. More importantly, "thinking in principles" enables one to discover the *form of what actually happened*, rather than relying on pre-existing narrative structures or creating derivatives (in other words, retelling the same story, if with a new slant, or some "newly discovered facts"). The existence of an operating principle and its form are internally dictated by the material itself.[9]

    The practice of unearthing and applying action-principles is what enabled me to discover the Jefferson Conspiracy. In essence, I listened to Jefferson and Burr: they led me to it. Doing this, however, required that I read every book I could on the subject, absorb (to my capacity) all the known facts, then *set aside* all those versions as I tried to isolate each piece, allow them to assemble themselves into natural groupings, searched for corroboration or disaffirmation, and then began to reconstruct a picture based on what I found. This is an extensive process and it took years.

    The picture that emerged was an inversion of the known one. It is a straightforward enough story – you'd think it would be easy enough to tell – but it not a mere opposite. It is a separate story of its own, a long-lost one. Recreating that story from the disintegrated, wind-blown ashes (particularly when everybody else denies its existence) was a task that could only be completed had I possessed some innate internal principle that grasped it and was able to hold it together: a centripital force within my own being. Without that, it all would have crumbled between my fingers and been swept away into

---

[7]   This is what I call "archetypal thinking." Archetypes are, according to Carl Jung, "patterns of human behavior." However, because the word "archetypes" is so often misconstrued and misused by people, I have found it better to talk of "thinking in principles" and more specifically thinking in action-principles or operating principles.

[8]   Subconscious processes involve what has been called "trance logic" or "both/and thinking," in which contradictory facts can be accepted and utilized. *See* Stephen G. Gilligan, *Therapeutic Trances: The Cooperation Principle in Ericksonian Hypnotherapy* (Brunner/Mazel, 1987).

[9]   The *form of what happened*, in this case, is Jefferson's conspiracy. That, however, is not the same as *the form of this book*, which is, of course, structured to elucidate the conspiracy but must also consider what readers are expected to know and what must be explained – and how best to do that. The form of the conspiracy is created by the characters. The form of the book is dictated by the subject matter, the author's purpose, and the intended audience.

swirling dust. How many times did it feel like that! Writing this thus became an act beyond reconstruction that required an almost supernatural energy. But these things are also why the material belongs to me.

There are several premises upon which I rely in this work of character analysis. The first one I have borrowed from an early mentor of mine. It is this rule: *Everything means all it can mean. Everything is multiply determined and serves multiple ends.*[10] This means that a more socially, culturally, or academically acceptable meaning does not trump or erase a less acceptable one. They co-exist, even if contradictory.

My second premise comes from the law. In law, you are said to intend the consequence of your actions. (The intenion is imputed by the consequence.) Thus, whether consciously or not, something you do once is something that you may do again. The person thus becomes identified as "the person who does that thing" and with any intended consequences and meanings of that action. Intended consequences can be inferred from the nature of the action within the context. Thus, Jefferson prosecuted Burr for treason. We can infer that he wanted Burr to be convicted and hung for that crime.

The meaning of the action may not always be clear in a single instance. Thus, Jefferson was "the man who prosecuted Burr." Does that mean Jefferson acted with malice? No. If he had a reasonable belief that Burr had engaged in treason against the United States, it was not malice to prosecute him.

Another method is to search for comparable examples that clarify meaning. So to parse out the meaning of the prosecution, we search for other examples (isotypes) of Jefferson's actions that resemble "prosecuting a man." We ascertain the meaning of "prosecution" then through groupings of similar behavior, as when Luther Martin called Jefferson "a hunter of men" or when Jefferson told Hay that he wanted to impeach the Chief Justice for acquitting Burr. We ask: is prosecuting a man the same or similar to hunting a man? Is it the same as impeaching a chief justice? In what ways, if any, are these the same or similar – or related?

The third premise on which I rely is to attempt always to see things from the perspective of each individual in any given exchange. This requires imagining oneself in that person's shoes. Each person is a universe unto himself. We must go into that universe and discover its "laws" to understand the actions of that person. How do things "work" in his universe and how does he

---

[10]   This rule or law was formulated by theoretical scientist, Bettina Olivier of New York City, NY.

experience them?

Fourth, I rely on many principles of psychology – such as the understanding of the stages child development, repression, denial, dissociation, and projection of disliked or prohibited parts of ourselves, and so on. This will probably be the most controversial aspect of my work, but the application of principles of psychology is critical to character analysis.

As part of my reliance on psychology, there is another premise I have developed: in figuring out what a behavior, situation, relationship, or event means to and about an individual, we need to view it in its earliest form, at the earliest point it could have occurred in that person's life. We assume, with or without corroboration or admission, that what Jefferson or Burr did at, say, age 50 or 60 (or any age)[11] reflects something he experienced in at a certain stage in his childhood. (The content of the action usually gives clues to the stage of development.) What happens at each particular stage of development has lifelong effects on the individual.

This is character work. Character work is normally identified with what novelists and actors do and is viewed as unacceptable for historians or biographers. But this type of work is essential to an understanding of what happened between these two men. It requires great discipline; an ability to retain and organize a large amount of apparently random facts and principles out of any order, the meaning of which is not always immediately clear; great patience and tenacity, as well as a high level of curiosity, while those facts float around in one's head and simmer; and finally an ability to discover hidden commonalities between disparate and distant sets of facts, derive principles from them and apply principles to them, and finally to ascertain the meaning of such doings by these comparisons and juxtapositions.

~

---

[11] The age at which one "re-enacts" a childhood event matters as well but depends on context. We explore this idea below at various points.

PART ONE:

BACKGROUND

The human mind does not acquire knowledge by intuition, but by experience. The march of understanding in the investigation of truth is slow. In cases of jurisprudence, as well as in every other intellectual research, the advances toward truth are gradual. Case after case must be studiously considered, judgment after judgment must be rendered and revised, and consequence after consequence traced to their terminations. In such a course of proceeding, it might happen, according to the amount of business which occurred, that generation might follow generation, and age succeed to age, before the summa ratio, the high result of reason on the subject, could be attained.
– Speech of Senator Samuel L. Mitchell,
Annals of Congress, Senate Journal, 10th Congress, 1st Session
[February 1808]

To select from a thousand thoughts that which is best and most seasonable; of the variety of attitudes of which every object is susceptible, to determine on that which is most suitable for the thing and the occasion; of all possible modes of expression and language, to discern the most appropriate, hic labor, hoc opus est.
Aaron Burr to Theodosia Burr (Alston)
January 26, 1800; Davis, *AB Memoirs* 1:401

Story & Character

You can go to incredible lengths, on an enormously circuitous,
serpentine journey to arrive at an understanding of someone else's life.
You can do that. You can also look at someone and, in a moment,
understand what it feels like to look through that face.
Daniel Day-Lewis, actor
quoted in Richard B. Woodward,
The Intensely Imagined Life of Daniel Day-Lewis,
New York Times Magazine [Spring, 1992].

History books teach us that Thomas Jefferson was a great man. Flawed perhaps but great. History books further teach us that Aaron Burr was a very bad man – a man with great qualities and potentials but ultimately a bad man.

Now let us step through the looking glass, for history has it all backwards. The truth is almost the exact opposite of what history has taught. It was not Burr who tried to steal the presidency, overthrow Jefferson, illegally filibustered against Spain, tried to separate the states, or committed treason on the United States. It was Jefferson who grabbed power, robbed Burr of his titles and possessions, unlawfully invaded Spanish territories, tried to have Burr killed, and nearly destroyed the nation he had assisted in founding.

In our telling, the great man did some very bad things. He covered those things up so well that they have been lost to history for more than two hundred years. And in this story, the man that history tells us was the villain is here the hero, for he gave everything, permitting the total sacrifice of himself in service to his country.

Jefferson wanted to be seen as the embodiment of pure goodness. He could not permit his flaws to be seen, for he was deeply ashamed and embarrassed by them. Of course, many of Jefferson's contemporaries did see him as purely good. Many people still do. Others in his time (but few since), who knew human nature better, viewed Jefferson's image-making as intentionally deceptive and hypocritical. But Jefferson understood what today we call marketing and branding. He understood what celebrities do: they create an image of themselves for the public, a single image, persona, or "brand" that the public can grab hold of.

The real Jefferson, however -- the man I portray in this story, *the man whom Burr confronted* – although indisputably a man of many fine qualities and great abilities, *was a man with a hidden dark side.* He was not a nice or good man, at least not to Burr. Surely Jefferson believed, as every man does, that he was justified in doing the things he did. We know that he would have liked to have seen the end of slavery but he did not believe it wise simply to free slaves, for like most southerners, he knew of their oppression and feared their deep hatred and rage. He considered himself a benevolent slave owner and this seems to have been true, as far as it goes. It is now fairly well accepted that he had an ongoing sexual relationship with one of his slaves, Sally Hemings, and that she had at least four children by him. To what extent could his relations with her have been acts of benevolence? To what extent were they consensual? How can a slave be said to give consent to her master? Is it not rather obedience? And what does this really mean about the man, Jefferson?

We will grapple with questions like these in this book. This glimpse gives us some idea of at least one corner of Jefferson's private relationships. They all involved his use of power over others. Power that most of us would consider illegitimate, for it is without true consent, although Jefferson viewed it as legitimate because he intended it benevolently. What happens in this scenario to the idea of "consent of the governed"?

These kinds of contradictions have been observed by historians and biographers but when it comes to the episode known as the Burr Conspiracy, they are forgotten.

*

So here is how our story goes: Jefferson conspired to kill Aaron Burr. It started as dislike and grew slowly into a desire to be rid of Burr, finally developing into active plotting to destroy Burr's person forever.

Jefferson had developed ambitions that he may not have admitted even to himself. His close friend and collaborator, James Madison, had carefully nurtured those ambitions and continued to provide Jefferson with both the coddling and the grounding he needed. Without Madison, there would have been no great Jefferson. Theirs was one of the greatest and closest collaborations in history. It was, in fact, a well-hidden lifelong love affair.

This relationship contained elements within it that could be challenged only at great hazard. As a unit, the two men formed an impenetrable wall against those with whom they disagreed. That coldness often grew to cruelty in private discourse, where it generally manifested in communications between the two men but seeped invisibly into every relationship. Friends who were admitted into the inner circle of secret misanthropes were encouraged to heap abuse on outsiders; enemies were identified and discredited. It was an exclusive club.[12]

These behaviors had an agenda, which can be discerned by looking at what the two men actually sought to accomplish. They wanted the freedom to expand and command. It was, as Jefferson put it to Madison, an *empire* they sought.[13] It was, in fact, what they had accused Burr of seeking. Jefferson wanted nothing short of the entire continent under American rule. It was the beginning of America's doctrine of Manifest Destiny: the belief that the expansion of the U.S. throughout the North American continent was both justified and inevitable. Anyone who stood in the way of the men achieving their glittering goal became an enemy.

There are clues to the nature of that domination, as benevolent as Jefferson would have liked to believe it to be (an empire of *liberty*): the extension of slavery into the new territories, the reversal of the promise of civil liberties and self government to the citizens of Louisiana, the secret and unlawful reconnaissance missions by American "explorers" into the sovereign territory of Spain, using men for purposes other than stated ones (such as using citizen explorers to gather intelligence on the enemy and invade their territory), as well as using bad men for purposes known only to them and Jefferson (spies and assassins). And it included removing anyone who got in their way. By whatever means. Burr was not the only victim of this policy.

Does not every president face this situation? Perhaps. But it is important to recognize it is not benevolent. It is not the defense of liberties or freedoms. It is not synonymous with national security, nor necessary to the protection of the executive. It is not truth or goodness. It is dirty power politics.

It is important to see, also, that it was Jefferson, not Burr, who was so vastly ambitious. Or rather that if Burr was ambitious to liberate Mexico from its oppressors, he would have done so if there was war with Spain (which was expected by everyone and would

---

[12] *See,* Burstein & Isenberg, *Madison & Jefferson,* 95, 99-100, 11-113. *See also,* chapter below on "The Madison & Jefferson Bond."

[13] *See,* Koch, *Jefferson & Madison: The Great Collaboration,* pp. 243-46 ("It was to Jefferson's and Madison's eternal credit that they converted the unsolicited 'empire of circumstances' [of the Louisiana Purchase] into a political philosophy that retained the essential ideals of their earlier belief in the 'cause of liberty' [to formulate] an 'empire for liberty.'" Id. 243.) That Louisiana landed in TJ's lap does not mean it was unsought. Turning that into a theoretical "empire of liberty" was the least expected of them, but it was not even true.

have been well justified by the law of nations), and in order to give the oppressed the opportunity to create a democracy, while Jefferson, who was equally interested in seizing Spanish-held territories, had no such interest in "liberation" for civil liberties purposes but rather simply to expand the American domain, any way it could be done (but preferably without war): to have it be part of his beloved empire of liberty.

We can already see the conflict brewing between the two men. Jefferson could not tolerate what Burr wanted to do or that Burr would be the one to do it. If Burr liberated Mexico, he would be a hero. What would that make Jefferson? There was no room in Jefferson's world for any genuine competitor to his ideals.

Burr had adopted "the principles and spirit which gave birth to the revolution" as his own. (Kline 1:424, quoting the Burrite paper, March 26, 1800.) He was a true democrat. Jefferson was not a democrat; he was a southern Republican. Jefferson may have authored the Declaration of Independence and the two parties may have allied to win the 1800 election but Jefferson did not adhere to most of the northern democratic ideals. He mistrusted northerners. In essence, he allied with them to win the presidency, after which Jefferson removed the democrats he could not control (including Burr) and adopted those he could. (*See* chapters below on "Events" and "Character & Circumstance.")

Burr naively thought he and Jefferson shared ideals: equality of all men (and women), the importance of education, the right to self-determination, to choose one's own course in life, to come to one's own conclusions based on one's own judgment, to create one's own destiny through hard work and merit, and the belief that collaborating and finding common ground was key. Jefferson may have said those things when he was in opposition to King George but when he disagreed with his own countrymen, their rights quietly diminished.

Jefferson never liked Burr, per his own admission. From the get-go he mistrusted him. Burr was a tactician, a military and legal strategist. He had no need to prove his worth as a man. These were givens for him. He thought logically and strategically. Legal and military strategic thinking often involve thinking in alternatives. To Jefferson, such thinking -- along with practices that Jefferson abhorred (such as economic or land speculation, "jobbing," banking, campaigning for office) -- was deceptive and duplicitous. Perceiving deception in those around him, Jefferson, who had a overly-open and sensitive personality, buried himself and became deceptive.

When Burr began to intrude into Jefferson's political inner

circle -- befriending Gallatin, Dearborn, Monroe, and Madison (although Burr had known all these men for years, in some cases far longer than TJ had) – Jefferson viewed it as political maneuvering and perceived it as a deep personal threat. Burr's unwillingness to oppose the constitutional mandates for the electoral college or House of Representatives if they elected him president instead of Jefferson was not the first straw for Jefferson; it was the last. Burr's strict adherence to the letter of the Constitution did not matter to the author of the Declaration of Independence. What mattered was personal loyalty. It was a personal betrayal that had nothing to do with Burr's alleged lack of principle.[14]

To Jefferson, Burr's response to the electoral tie was proof of the opinions the Virginian had already formed: Burr was an enemy, not a friend. He needed to be driven out. From that point onward, we can see Jefferson taking steps to remove Burr; to destroy his reputation in his own state and nationally; to sow suspicion against him; to portray him as a Satan, a womanizer, a trickster, seducer and deceiver, a liar and cheat.

It was later on, after this, not because of this – after Jefferson had already sown seeds of suspicion widely against Burr and Burr still had not "become invisible" – that Jefferson determined he must be rid of Burr altogether.

That was not the first time in Jefferson's life that he had apparently felt compelled to make such a decision. There were others who had mysteriously fallen under his watchful eye. Others he had exposed to extreme danger and those who had died strange deaths under his employ. There were those who had been in his service and had strayed somehow – had perhaps discovered Jefferson's duplicity, his dark side, and had died trying to tell the truth.

And then there was General James Wilkinson. The history of Wilkinson's life apart from his involvement in the Burr episode: his many intrigues, treacheries, and involvement in plots and attempted and actual assassinations, would alone take volumes to tell. His involvement with Jefferson is naturally of great interest, for (what has hitherto not been recognized) he represents a type, a position, that was not exclusively occupied by Wilkinson in Jefferson's life.

Thus was Burr, the strategist, nudged by Jefferson's maneuverings and by his "friend," Jamey Wilkinson, into making a westward expedition. It wasn't only in Wilkinson's mind but he was the prime mover always of the idea of invading Mexico. (He proposed the idea to an excited Alexander Hamilton only a few years before Burr.) And Wilkinson was the one who "knew the way" to

---

[14]   *See,* Van Bergen, *Aaron Burr and the Electoral Tie of 1801.*

fabled Sante Fe and from thence to the city of gold, Mexico City.

Burr's close friend, Charles Williamson, a Scotsman who managed some land speculations in upstate New York, helped Burr to see the western adventure as a lucrative settlement of lands and shared Burr's belief in creating a protective military buffer in the West. He also showed Burr how to use foreign powers to promote American interests – raising funds to engage in what was then called, with a different meaning than it is today, *filibustering*: making an expedition, often using foreign funds, to invade and incite revolution in another foreign nation. Not that filibustering was a new idea but Burr and Williamson had a meeting of minds.

This point is where the proof of Burr's alleged treason is found by some scholars: that he suggested treason to foreign nations – that he was going to separate the western states and create his own empire; that he would turn Jefferson out of office – in order to raise funds for his filibuster. Burr repeatedly declared in writing that he had no interest in separating the states and his project was not illegal but would benefit the U.S. He *did* say that he thought separation was inevitable (but he had no interest in it) and he probably did express opinions of Jefferson's weakness.

But what Burr said to *foreign powers* was another matter. He may have been engaging in a classic Burr tactic of tricking an enemy into acting against its own best interests by encouraging it to do that which it had of its own accord offered to do. In this case, the great powers were all engaged in funding covert activities on the continent intended to subvert American interests. Burr intended to trick England and Spain into giving him funds for his expedition by offering to assist in their subversive activities. The funds, however, would be used against the interests of those nations to benefit the United States and would teach those powers not to meddle.

Wilkinson was but a player in Burr's mind – an important one, a motivated one, but Burr's intentions were not the same as Wilkinson's. Though Burr knew JW was suspected of taking money from Spain, JW probably assured Burr (whom he had known since the war) that he wished to do something similar to what Burr intended to do. JW reasoned that he would extract money from Spain (he already had done so) in order to march on them (so he would have told Burr), "liberate" their gold, and live forever after in wealth, ease, and glory. And sure, liberate the poor downtrodden, while we're at it. Burr wanted fame too, but not in the same sense. He wished to reclaim his high estimation in the eyes of his countrymen. And he truly wanted to help the Mexican peasants self-govern.[15] He

---

[15]   JW's goals are mentioned in most biographies and histories. For Burr's views, I

thought: Why could not all their needs be met?

In any event, Jefferson meanwhile had been slowly driving Burr out of his eastern power base and into a western channel, at the last by specifically sanctioning and encouraging his western expedition – probably both in private meetings with Burr and through Henry Dearborn's excited approbation.

Burr was primed, the old doors had been closed, and the new course had been opened to him. Burr, like most intelligent men of action, needed an outlet. He had been driven out of national politics. Having spent six years serving as U.S. Senator from New York, having made Jefferson's presidency possible, having served four years as vice president under Jefferson's first administration, he was ungratefully removed and replaced by George Clinton, an old man, the former longtime governor of New York, who had done nothing for Jefferson's cause (until TJ had begun colluding with his nephew to destroy Burr). Burr ran for the post of New York governor himself and lost. He had spent years working his way up the political ladder and he was not interested in starting all over again. Friends suggested he move to Kentucky or Tennessee and get elected to the U.S. House of Representatives. He thought about it and perhaps would have if the timing had been right but reportedly decided not to wait for another election cycle.

He determined to settle lands in lower Louisiana and start his own community – a place where men could build their own democratic society, which could be founded on Burr's core beliefs in the equality of all men and women, education, open discourse, and making one's way on self-discipline and merit. He'd maintain a protective buffer of military men between Spanish and American territories. And if war with Spain came, they'd be ready to go into their country's service once again. Burr would recruit and lead young men into battle, a place where his abilities had historically been best used and recognized, where his strategic bent was less readily misinterpreted. And maybe there would be a place for him in relation to Mexico, where he could free the oppressed and help them to establish their own democracy.[16]

Burr did not fully grasp the forces arrayed against him. He was aware that DeWitt Clinton and Alexander Hamilton were

---

have drawn from Kennedy and from the notes of Burr's meetings with Roux, the French employee, as well as a multitude of other sources.

[16] Burr's interest in liberating the Spanish colonies is visible in both Roux's notes of their meetings and in Burr's later correspondence. *See* Kline 2: 1099-1126 (Editorial Note: *Burr & Napoleon's Court* and Roux's Reports) and 2:1169-75 (Editorial Note: *Burr & Latin American Independence* and correspondence with John Alderson).

engaged in defamatory campaigns but it is uncertain whether he knew of Jefferson's direct involvement in Clinton's campaign. He surely suspected it. He knew he had other political opponents but probably never was sure how closely several individuals were working with Jefferson to destroy his political career. Nor did Burr anticipate Wilkinson's sudden about-face. And though he knew Jefferson was distancing him, there is no evidence that he suspected that Jefferson was setting a trap for him. Even after his arrest and removal, and through the trial, it seems that Burr did not fully grasp the extent of Jefferson's malice or his purposeful hand in the doings against him. It perplexed him, as it perplexed everyone else.

Had Burr known, he would have, he *could* have, he *should* have come out of the gates full force against Jefferson. He was fully capable of eviscerating his opponent. He could have shown Jefferson to be a president who was using the power and tools of his office unlawfully for his own personal and political ends. Although Burr mentioned these matters at his treason trial, he did nothing against the President. Burr never ceased showing deference and respect to the man who was doing all in his power to destroy him.

We know from the prosecution itself (and from Jefferson's incredible efforts to manage and control the prosecution) that Jefferson wanted Burr dead. It was, after all, a hanging offense that Jefferson was charging Burr with. It was, moreover, a very weak case, such that most prosecutors worth their salt would have dropped it. Jefferson's list of the proofs of overt acts is absurd.[17] Jefferson clearly was set on Burr's end.

Thus, any further evidence that points to Jefferson's hatred of Burr should not be surprising – nor should it be dismissed. Jefferson had motive and opportunity. He had malice towards Burr. He had what in legal terms is called "malice aforethought," which today we would call premeditation. Jefferson had long wanted to remove Burr. This wish had eventually formed into a full-blown need to have Burr permanently "disappeared." Or as he put it himself "become absolutely invisible." (TJ to George Hay, February 16, 1808, National Archives.)

Jefferson had the opportunity, he had the power, the funds, he had the means. And once he set things in motion, he never showed hestitation, second thoughts, or remorse. This is one of the most astonishing revelations about Jefferson: that even after he had proof of JW's treason, even after Burr was acquitted, and even though we can be sure he knew Burr was not guilty, he did not relent

---

[17]   *See* TJ to William B. Giles, April 20, 1807. The list is quoted in full and discussed below in the "Jefferson's Mirror, Part Two" chapter.

or show the least remorse, ever.

In Jefferson's extraordinary letter to Rep. William Branch Giles noted above, he remarked that he believed the people would wish to "amend the error in our constitution which makes any branch independent of the nation" by "setting itself in opposition to the other two, and to the common sense of the nation." *He was referring to "the error in our constitution" which gave the judicial branch independence from the executive,* and to Chief Justice John Marshall's refusal to fall into line with his persecution of Burr. For, according to Jefferson, Marshall "proclaims impunity to that class of offenders which endeavors to overturn the constitution." He meant that Marshall was proclaiming impunity to Burr. (How exactly Marshall was doing that is unclear. And how exactly Burr was eneavoring to "overturn the constitution"?) Jefferson concluded: "[I]f their protection of Burr produces this amendment it will do more good than his condemnation could have done. * * * [I]f his punishment can be commuted now for an useful amendment of the constitution, I shall rejoice in it." (TJ to WBG, April 20, 1807, Founders Online.)

Jefferson was thus suggesting that the condemnation of Burr was not meant to punish any supposed crime but to do good for the nation! And that his punishment was equivalent to a "useful amendment of the constitution" in which Jefferson could rejoice (presumably equally) – the useful amendment being to stop the independence of the judiciary!

This utter lack of remorse and lack of awareness of the full meaning of his words, the lack of willingness to own up to his own wrongs or admit the least error, or *to relent* are remarkable. What in God's name did he have to lose? He had already prostrated this innocent man whom he deemed his mortal enemy! What more did he want? He wanted to punish this man for some imagined good of the nation but was willing to exchange his life for a constitutional amendment that would put the judiciary under his thumb!

The Burr prosecution is but one example of this side of Jefferson. We will discuss more examples in the "Jefferson's Mirror" and "Jefferson's Layers" chapters. The Burr trial certainly marked a major turning point for the President. It would not be long before Jefferson himself was removed from office and almost drummed out of Washington. On a psychological level, the degradation and attempted killing of Burr anticipated Jefferson's fear of his own humiliating demise.

~

Burr: The Center of Union

New England Federalist George Cabot wrote in 1804 that his colleague "[Roger] Griswold rightly argued that nothing could be done in Congress [for the Federalist cause, that] the formation of a Northern interest must begin at home, and must find its centre of union in Burr." (Cabot to Pickering, February 14, 1804, Adams, 412-13 [citing Lodge's Cabot, 341].) Griswold agreed but believed that "[Burr's] ambition will not suffer him to be second, and his office will give him a claim to the first rank." (RG to Wolcott, March 11, 1804, id., 423.)

These two conjoined ideas – Burr as the "center" and Burr's selfishness or ambition – were found not only among the Federalists. His New York friends believed in his "generalship, perseverance, industry, and execution," his "management and industry," and saw him as capable of "bring[ing] about a concert in action" between NY factions by his "unceasing" efforts.[18]

Other Republicans believed that "no one else [could] do" what he could, that his "friends everywhere look to you."[19] But a former friend of Burr's wrote "we have, *as it were*, two chief magistrates, *one,* the governor, by the voice of God, and the people, an another the governor of Mr. Burr and the canvassers" and Republican "political intelligence agent" John Beckley told Madison that Burr's efforts were "more directed to himself than anybody else, mirroring Hamilton's thoughts ("Burr loves nothing but himself.")[20]

Burr's efforts, however, were never directed to himself but always to bringing about the best result in the judgment of himself and others whose opinions he trusted and to finding common ground between polarized groups. That he was on several occasions able to effect a coalition or joint action was viewed by both sides as nothing short of miraculous. This elevated him in the eyes of participants, made him seem superior to them. Thus, *he* must be first, selfish, ambitious.   ~

---

[18]   John Nicholson to Gallatin, May 6, 1800, Kline 1:425; Matthew L. Davis to Gallatin, May 5, 1800; MLD statement in Davis, *Memoirs of AB*, 2:55.

[19]   John Taylor, of Caroline to AB, n.d., Kline 1:170 (Davis, *Memoirs*, 1:407); Benjamin Rush to AB, September 24, 1792, Kline 1:137.

[20]   Robert Troup to John Jay, June 10, 1792, Isenberg, 111; Isenberg, 116 (agent), John Beckley to Madison, October 15, 1796, Kline 1:269; AH to Harrison Gray Otis, n.d., quoted in full in Kennedy, 65-66 (citing *Papers of AH*, 25:259-60, 271). *See also* Lomask, 1:281.

You, Judge & Jury

(With Some Legal Discussion & Examples from Our Case)

I was obliged to give an opinion, and I have not yet learned
to give any other than that which my judgment directs.
Burr to Jacob Delameter, June 15, 1792
Kline 1:126

Under different circumstances, I might think and act differently,
but the industry which has been used through this country to prejudice
my cause, leaves me very little chance, indeed, of an impartial jury.
Burr at trial, May 22, 1807
Robertson 1:44

The plain, palpable evidence has been looked on with an
indifference that has astonished me.
Daniel Clark, *Proofs of the Corruption of JW*, 115
(in reference to Wilkinson's originating "the plan")

In this book, we are not discussing the alleged guilt or innocence of Aaron Burr. Rather, we are charging Thomas Jefferson with a crime. This book intends to show the facts and participants of that crime. The crime was conspiracy to destroy Aaron Burr. By the time you are finished, you will have decided whether I have succeeded in proving beyond a reasonable doubt, or by a preponderance of the evidence, that Thomas Jefferson conspired with his cabinet and others to destroy, even to murder, Aaron Burr.[21]

You are the jury. In a colloquial sense, you will also be the judge, but in legal language, where there is a jury, the judge only tells the jury what the law is (which in this instance, the author will do); it is the jury that decides the meaning of the facts, applies the law to the facts, makes inferences, and

---

[21] The state applies "beyond a reasonable doubt" standard in criminal cases because the state can take away the freedom, or even the life, of that person if he is convicted. Individuals may also sue for harms to a person and there are two standards used in civil litigations: preponderance of evidence and clear and convincing evidence. In civil cases, there are only monetary damages, no jail time. O.J. Simpson was acquitted of murdering his wife but her family won in a wrongful death litigation against him.

determines innocence or guilt.

If this were a live prosecution, we would be in court and both sides would have the ability to subpoena witnesses and documents, to examine and cross-examine witnesses in order to establish the narrative we want to put before you and to put holes in the narrative of our opponent. We would engage in the process known as discovery, where we obtain documents and items from the other side. The parties on both sides would be required to produce all documents, letters, papers, or items relevant to the case and would be prohibited from destroying any.

It would also be possible, if this were a present-day prosecution, to retrieve or reconstitute erased or deleted electronic files. Before the time of email and the web, before modern-day methods of forensic analysis, it would have still been possible, if the prosecution were contemporaneous to the events, to find footprints, make tracings of and authenticate writing impressions, and take witness statements: to establish a course of events. But this is history. The actors and witnesses are long dead. Any destroyed documents are long decayed into dust and even those that were retained in archives or personal files may be missing or subject to mishap. We have only what we have.

Yet, there is a case to be discerned. There is still a trail to follow. We have discovered it and we will show it to you. We will connect the dots and engage in making fair and reasonable inferences from the facts.

In real trials, prosecutors and defense counsel haggle over who should sit on the jury. A prosecutor in a case such as this, where a well-known, beloved public figure – Thomas Jefferson – is being accused of a heinous crime, will want to find jurors who can keep an open mind and determine guilt or innocence on the facts. We will ask jurors if they have any biases for Thomas Jefferson or against Burr. Those who admit to either would be excluded.

The defense on behalf of Jefferson would want to strike jurors who are pro-Burr or anti-Jefferson.

The kind of jurors one might select for either side depends on the case one wants to make. For our case, we have a hard task to overcome a long-established tradition of reverence for the great man who authored the Declaration of Independence. We need to show the other side, the dark side of Jefferson, the man known to very few during his lifetime, who – by Jefferson's own intent – was buried and forgotten even by the time Jefferson was out of office. So, we need to find jurors who can handle that as a possibility, people who can see other human beings as both good and bad.

We do not wish to show that Jefferson did no good. That would be absurd. We wish to show simply that Jefferson not only did good but also did bad things.

We also want jurors who do not need to rest on authority or on accepted history, who are able to reconsider and come to fresh conclusions that might challenge or contradict the opinions of established authorities – people willing and able to think for themselves and come to their own conclusions based on facts presented to them.

The prosecution will want jurors who are not stuck in the well-established bias against Aaron Burr, who can view him afresh, as well, and be willing to reconsider the many particulars long held against him.

Jefferson's defense, on the other hand, will want jurors who are pro-Jefferson, those not willing to give up their association of the ideas of liberty and democracy with Jefferson, long established in the minds of his followers. Those who have strongly-held ideas of freedom and independence. Those who have read some history, perhaps, and have an idea of Jefferson's contributions, as well as those who accept the history about Burr as corrupt and ambitious.

In the legal analyses in this book, we hold ourselves as closely as possible to legal standards of proof and law. Lawyers and judges know there is no such thing as absolute proof, that direct witness testimony is unreliable and must be viewed in context, that not even positive forensic proof is ironclad. Fingerprints on a document show only that an individual held the document, not that he used or authored it or what he was doing with it.

There are two important concepts in this case that we need to know about. One is "standard of proof" and the other is "conspiracy." In the American criminal system, the standard of proof is "beyond a reasonable doubt." Guilt must be established beyond a reasonable doubt in order to convict someone of a crime. "Beyond a reasonable doubt" is a high standard but it does not require 100% proof. It does not mean "beyond *any* or *all* doubt." It does not require a smoking gun. It requires a chain of strong circumstantial evidence that points clearly to the defendant and no one else.

Preponderance of the evidence means more probable than not. Clear and convincing evidence is higher than preponderance: evidence leading to a firm belief.

Conspiracy law is a bit different than most other areas of law. Conspiracy is a crime that occurs mostly in the minds of those who engage in it. It is called "an inchoate crime." This means "anticipating a further illegal act."[22]

In conspiracy, while the acts of the underlying crime (which could be money laundering, murder, just simple theft – or even something legal, like flying a plane, by unlawful means, like hijacking) may be what we call "overt" – out in the open and observable, the *agreement* to carry out the crime or crimes by different persons remains hidden in the minds of those persons. And because of that, as well as because by nature conspiracies are purposefully hidden (because the conspiracy is a secret enterprise), the kinds of proof permitted are a bit broader than in regular criminal prosecutions. Courts may be more lenient in allowing hearsay testimony, character evidence, or other bad acts.

To prove conspiracy, we must show that the actors agreed to engage in the conspiracy to commit the crime and that they each carried out an "overt act" toward its fulfillment. To prove these things, we must first know what the unlawful end or ends of the conspiracy are. We distinguish between the goal and the means. Where, as here, the primary goal to which the conspirators agreed was to remove Aaron Burr from office and from politics and to destroy his chances of returning to power in any way, which in itself is not unlawful, the means

---

[22] The full legal definition is: an offense involving "conduct designed to culminate in the commission of a substantive offense but has either failed or has not yet achieved its culmination because there is something that the actor or another still must do." *Barron's Law Dictionary.*

might have been either lawful or unlawful. If, for example, Jefferson and his co-conspirators bribed officials, that would be unlawful, though even in that there are grey areas (what is a gift and what is a bribe?).

On the other hand, if Jefferson's goal was to kill Aaron Burr, the goal is patently unlawful. No matter what contribution made by a co-conspirator to this end, he would be liable for the result. The question then becomes whether others knew of and agreed with the goal and if so, at what point and under what pretext and to what extent? If the Secretary of War, Henry Dearborn, gave General James Wilkinson orders, at Jefferson's request, to hire assassins, Dearborn has agreed with the goal of murder and committed an overt act.

At Jefferson's request, Gallatin released the funds to pay for the prosecution of Burr. This means he knew the end result could be Burr's death. Does this mean he was guilty of conspiring to kill Burr? (No, he was paying for the prosecution, not an execution, and he would have had reason to believe that the trial would legitimately determine guilt or innocence, despite Jefferson's beliefs to the contrary.)

If Wilkinson told his hired assassins to "cut off" Burr, and Wilkinson's prior conduct shows that both he and they understood him to mean "kill," they are guilty of conspiracy to murder.

In interpreting the possible meanings of what was said, written, and done, past history and character become relevant. If for example, we know that Wilkinson was involved in a number of prior assassinations or assassination attempts, if we know he hired men previously to carry out such deeds, if we know that his language tended to underplay or overplay his meaning (so that "cut off" was intended to mean an act of violence), or if we know he previously used the phrase "cut off" to mean "stop dead in his tracks," or if he used those words previously to have two alternate meanings (put him in irons or kill him) and the choice was left up to the doers, those facts could help us to interpret what he intended in relation to Burr.[23]

---

[23] JW wrote Silas Dinsmore on December 4, 1806, offering him $5000 "to cut off the two principal leaders." (Kennedy, 320, quoting McCaleb, 230.) Senator Plumer wrote that John Randolph had seen a letter from Wilkinson that stated

Past crimes, past bad conduct, and past or present character generally, standing alone, are not permitted in courtroom evidence. Where we know that in another event closely related in both time and circumstance to Burr's enterprise, Jefferson ordered documents to be altered and references to particular topics or persons deleted, we cannot simply assume he did so in Burr's case. But where there is evidence that documents in relation to Burr went missing from official archives and where there is other evidence of a cover-up,[24] it would be unreasonable to assume the opposite either: that the missing documents went missing by chance or that Jefferson had nothing to do with it.

~

---

that "altho' Aaron Burr's treasonable plans are supprest – he will soon revive them – To prevent which, its best to *take him off* – & that he has provided 2 or 3 men who are well qualified to effect that laudable service for their country." Plumer adds: "The plain english of which is that Wilkinson has men in pay to *assassinate* Burr!" Plumer, *Memorandum,* 616. *See also* the chapter on Wilkinson below.

[24]   *See, for example,* Henry Dearborn's letter to "Judge Davis," April 4, 1807, discussed later ("Smoking Guns" chapter). David Chandler notes that there are documents missing from the Dept. of War archives, which relate to Wilkinson's activities in New Orleans in late 1806 - early 1807. (Chandler, *TJ Conspiracies,* 349n13, 350n4.)

Conspiracy Overview

When unprincipled men acquire the ascendancy, they act in concert and are silent.
-John Randolph, Speech in Congress, Spring 1805
(on Jeffersonians in Congress)
Henry Adams, *Administrations of TJ*, 446-7.

~~~

Burr said "[I]t would be found that he had been accused [to] cover and conceal the crimes of others, and this would be known and verified before long . . . he could say something before them of a high criminal nature that would show the iniquity of those who were persecuting him and would do it if he did not change his mind."
-Burr before Judge Thomas Rodney,
Mississippi Supreme Court, February 2 and 4, 1806; Kline 2:1019.

Jefferson's conspiracy against Burr is harder to prove in some ways because it is historical and because it is the creature of long-forgotten characters and context. The characters we know as Jefferson and Burr are not the ones that acted out the drama of 1806-07. We no longer know and understand the background, which contains all the context for the playing out of that drama. No matter how much filling in historians or biographers may do, background remains elusive without an organizing principle. In this case, the background is everything, because it is what Jefferson used, both to invent and to hide his conspiracy to destroy Burr, which makes its operative parts particularly difficult to see, because they were merely things going on "in the background" of their own accord.

The answer to the centuries-old question: "What was the Burr Conspiracy?" (or "What did Burr intend?") is actually not found in Burr at all. The mystery arises because the alleged Burr Conspiracy was actually Jefferson's fabrication, using background as the context. The context also contains the character of each man.[25] Both Jefferson's and Burr's characters have been grossly misread and misrepresented. History is told by the victors and Jefferson destroyed as much evidence of Burr's character and intentions as he could, muddying the

---

[25]   The characters lead to the context and the context informs the characters. As Elizabeth Barrett Browning wrote in her epic narrative poem "Aurora Leigh": "Inward evermore / To outward,– so in life, and so in art."

remaining waters with innuendo and outright lies.

Good men may conspire to do bad things to their supposed enemies and may believe their conspiratorial goals are lawful and justified. Such may be the case here. But law decides criminal intent based on actions and consequences, not reputation or belief.[26]

To be a criminal conspiracy, there must be an unlawful goal and an agreement by the parties to take actions to reach that goal. Was the effort to remove Burr from political power a conspiracy? Without a doubt, yes, but at the outset, that goal was not itself unlawful – not until the purpose changed to the destruction of Burr's person. And even throughout the conspiracy, even at the end, it is possible that not all of the participants considered it as unlawful or knew the end goal was not justice but murder.

Was the conspiracy generated by Jefferson? Yes it was, but he used the needs, drives and actions of others – so that, in a sense, it became everyone's conspiracy – those who participated, including those who initiated, those who carried out orders, those who fabricated or destroyed evidence, coerced witnesses, arrested suspects without warrant, rifled mails, those who suggested courses of action, those who ensured funding, those who went along, and those who let it happen. To be a criminal conspiracy, the participants would not need to believe it was unlawful. They might think they were just serving their president, doing their job or their patriotic duty. They might believe the ends or means were completely justified or lawful.

However, such excuses have no merit for the men who sought to hang Burr or see him dead in a ditch in reliance on rumor and their leader's orders. And for those who were close to Jefferson, were they so beguiled by their leader's distortions and fabrications that they really could not see the brazen falsities and gross missteps?

For Jefferson, having developed antipathy toward Burr, having fostered his dislike and permitted it to grow into malice, even having perhaps consciously nurtured the sentiment, he

---

[26] Belief matters, of course, since it informs intent, but an unreasonable belief is not justification or excuse.

cannot be excused for having allegedly acted under the necessity of a national crisis that he knew was an invention by him and Wilkinson. Indeed, even if the supposed Burr Conspiracy crisis had been real, it did not provide justification for Jefferson's actions and those actions he sanctioned (or ordered) in others. As Justice Story (a Madison appointee) noted only six years after Burr's trial, no president may "lawfully exercise powers or authorise proceedings which the civilized world repudiates and disclaims." (*Brown v. U.S.,* 12 U.S. (8 Cranch) 110 (1814).)

The conspiracy to destroy Burr may be divided into three periods. In the <u>first period</u>, only Madison and Jefferson colluded. In this period, as Jefferson later wrote, despite his dislike of Burr, because Burr "possessed the confidence of the nation, I thought it my duty to respect in him their confidence, & to treat him as if he deserved it." (TJ to William B. Giles, April 20, 1807, National Archives.) This is a pretty spiteful remark. It is beyond dislike – closer to contempt or hatred.[27] So, in this period, Madison and Jefferson treated Burr with respect, while sharing between each other their contempt for him[28] and agreeing to support him in national elections as the vice-presidential candidate while withdrawing votes from him at the last minute.[29] This period lasted from 1791 to early 1801.

The words Jefferson wrote in 1782 and 1784 to

---

[27] This is the same letter in which TJ says he "personally ... never had one hostile sentiment" toward Burr. Really?

[28] For TJ and JM's way of relating, *see* Burstein & Isenberg, 95, 99-100, 11-113. TJ wrote in his memoirs: "I habitually cautioned Mr. Madison against trusting him too much." (*TJ: Memorandum*, January 26 [1804], Kline 2:822.)

[29] Monroe proposed to mollify Burr "by the most soothing appearance of esteem & confidence on our part," resting their objections to his nomination "altogether on his youth &c." (Kline 1:139, n1, quoting letter from Monroe to Madison, October 9, 1792.) Burr had "no confidence in the Virginians; they once deceived him, and they are not to be trusted." (Kline 1:266, 269, *Editorial Note: The 1796 Presidential Election* [12 November 1796], quoting Hannah (Nicholson) Gallatin to Albert Gallatin, May 7, 1800.) Burr thought "no Arrangement could be made which would be observed to the Southw[ar]d[,] Alluding as I understood to the last Election, in which He was certainly Ill Used by Virga. & No. Carolina." (Kline 1:433, *Editorial Note: The Republican Vice Presidential Nomination* [13 June 1800], quoting James Nicholson to Albert Gallatin, May 7, 1800.) Burr wrote: "As to myself, after what happened at the last election (*et tu Brute!*) I was really averse to have my Name in question." (Burr to John Taylor of "Caroline," October 23, 1800, Kline 1:451.)

Madison about *Patrick Henry* mirror his later words about Burr. Henry was a man whose "schemes" were "crooked" and "[w]hile he lives . . . [w]hat we have to do I think is devoutly to pray for his death."[30] Whether or not TJ intended this as a joke, he used almost identical words to describe Burr to William Branch Giles in 1807: "crooked gun." And in 1808 he affirmed his wish for Burr to get "what he deserved" – meaning death. (TJ to Giles, cited above; TJ to James Brown, October 27, 1808, Founders Online.) So, TJ may already have wished for Burr's death, but the worst he did was try to publicly humiliate him and undermine his popularity.

The <u>second period</u> was after the electoral tie of February 1801 to late 1806. Jefferson began to actively seek the aid of the Clintons and others in New York to exclude Burr's followers from office and destroy Burr's reputation in the newspapers. Jefferson declined Burr's recommendations, excluded him from his counsels, finally secured his removal from the office of Vice President, ensured his exclusion from the New York governorship, and then permitted him to believe that he, Jefferson, sanctioned his removal westward.

It was in the second phase that Jefferson gathered the first group of co-conspirators. These were younger, ambitious men of lesser fame and ability than Burr, who had won no honors in the Revolution, who were seeking means of climbing the social and political ladder to make names for themselves. They also had a significantly lower moral compass.[31] Gideon Granger, John Armstrong, DeWitt Clinton, and James Cheetham comprised the most active participants. Jefferson supplied these men with reasons to dislike Burr and they in turn supplied him with evidence to support his reasons. It was a self-affirming circle. With his encouragement and gratitude, they gave him advice on who were Burr partisans (thus who should not be appointed to governmental offices, who should

---

[30] Burstein & Isenberg, at 99, 112, quoting TJ to George Rogers Clark, November 26, 1782 and TJ to Madison, December 8, 1784.

[31] Their biographers would disagree, of course. DeWitt Clinton, in particular, operated from an altruistic base of educational privilege and moral superiority, and "[b]y 1805 ... offered education as a significant means to guarantee an industrious attitude and preserve republican virtue among the urban poor" (Siry, 255.) But see what you think after you read about them below.

be shunned or viewed with suspicion), kept an eye on his doings, infiltrated Burrite groups, shared rumors, and alerted Jefferson to any activity on Burr's part that could be negatively construed in any way.

In this phase Jefferson also gathered other resources (adherents, evidence, rumors, corroboration, support). He was clearly preparing for something. If his actions in this period are looked at apart from his later actions, one may see only his efforts to counter Burr as a political threat. Looked at in the context of the whole, however, his activities are more ominous. We can see a determination and persistence to harm Burr that went beyond political ambition.

In this phase, the goal (political removal) was still probably lawful but at least some of the means used and actions taken probably were not. Jefferson's henchmen engaged in the continual publication of grossly false and defamatory statements about Burr. They undermined his long-standing and hard-earned popularity, damaging his political reputation and livelihood. Today these could constitute defamation, misrepresentation, tortious interference with business, mental/emotional distress, stalking, harassment, intimidation and assault. Economic and noneconomic harm, as well as punitive damages, could be found.

The third phase was the emergence of Jefferson's active and determined pursuit of the absolute eradication of Burr. In this phase, Jefferson in due course obtained the agreement and collusion of the members of his own cabinet, using their offices for every aspect of his pursuit, as well as the services of James Wilkinson and his minions. One could say these men – Madison, Gallatin, and Dearborn[32] – merely did their jobs by doing the President's bidding but it would surpass credulity to maintain they did so without knowing, at some point, that Jefferson had gone beyond the limits of rationality and legality. Their lack of judgment should be surprising. These were educated men of high intelligence, of sound mind and body, who had all been friends with Burr. Yet they followed a leader who was willing to exchange this man's life for a constitutional

---

[32] Neither Samuel Smith, the interim Secretary of the Navy, nor his brother, Robert Smith, who took over for Samuel, are considered in this narrative. Nor are the roles of Jefferson's several Attorney Generals.

amendment to deprive the judiciary of independence! A man's life in exchange for the executive's absolute power! And this was all for the nation's good! These men had gone through a war to end tyranny! Even if they didn't know Jefferson's faulty reasoning on this point, are we to believe they didn't know something was amiss?

Granger also falls into this category, since he was postmaster general, with access to post offices and postal workers nationwide. Granger, however, merits his own chapter, for he was much more proactive than the others. During this last period, Jefferson benefitted greatly from the services of both Granger and General James Wilkinson to "cut off" Burr – seize his things, arrest and detain his friends, cut off all avenues of escape, lock everything down, and finally capture or kill his person.

From this standpoint, if we look back at the two earlier phases, it is hard not to discern an underlying drive of great force and turpitude in Jefferson. A person does not so actively and persistently engage in protracted activities against another -- or operate to involve others to do them – over such a length of time without harboring a jealousy or hatred, a compulsion, and ultimately a dark purpose.

It was in the third phase – once he had JW in pocket – that Jefferson made clear that purpose: he wanted Burr dead. He declared Burr guilty and *then* charged him with a hanging offense. Again, if this phase is viewed in isolation from the earlier periods, one might excuse Jefferson's prejudices against Burr as the result of well-founded fears, as long as we think he had legitimate reasons to believe there was a national crisis. But we know he knew there was no crisis, or rather that any supposed crisis was actually created by him and his illegal incursions into Spanish territory. Moreover, his contempt for Burr and wish for his removal long preceded any such supposed crisis. Jefferson certainly wanted everyone to believe there was a crisis. He wanted people to think *he had good reason to believe* there was a crisis, but even as he declared Burr guilty and put the entire west on military alert, he was writing that Burr had not "yet" committed any overt acts.

~

Map of Burr's Locations in 1806-07

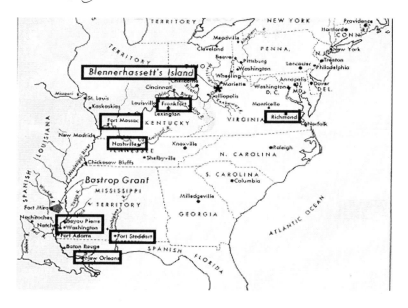

This is a peculiar case, sir. The president has undertaken to prejudge my client by declaring, that "Of his guilt there can be no doubt." He has assumed to himself the knowledge of the Supreme Being himself, and pretended to search the heart of my highly respected friend. He has proclaimed him a traitor in the face of that country, which has rewarded him. He has let slip the dogs of war, the hell-hounds of persecution, to hunt down my friend.

And would this president of the United States, who has raised all this absurd clamour, pretend to keep back the papers which are wanted for this trial, where life itself is at stake?

It is a sacred principle, that in all such cases, the accused has a right to all the evidence which is necessary for his defense. And whoever withholds, wilfully, information that would save the life of a person, charged with a capital offense, is substantially a murderer, and so recorded in the register of heaven.

-Luther Martin [counsel for Burr], June 10, 1807
Robertson, *Trial of Aaron Burr* 1:128.

Set-up & Take-Down

Wherein we outline the events
up to Burr's capture and trial

From any man, save one, if I cannot vanquish, I can escape. In the hands of that one, I am just what Theodosia is in mine. This was perceived after the first two hours; and seeing no retreat, nor anything better to be done, I surrendered, tame and unresisting, to be disarmed, stripped, hacked, hewed, dissected, skinned, turned inside out, at the will and mercy of the operator. Much good may it do him.
Aaron Burr to Jeremy Bentham, January 31, 1809, Edinburgh, Scotland
Davis, *Private Journal of Aaron Burr* 1:169.

As stated above, Jefferson formed his intent to actively destroy Burr during the electoral tie of 1801. It may not yet have taken the shape of murder but it did constitute malice. However, Jefferson did not form this hatred of his running mate because of Burr's purported attempt to steal the presidency from him. Burr let Jefferson know he could have but Jefferson knew he didn't. Rather, Jefferson formed this intent to destroy Burr when he himself determined to grab the presidency that he believed belonged to him, but to take it by illicit means since he believed that, after all, Burr and the evil Federalists were about to take it from him. Burr then became merged in his mind with the rabid Federalists.

It was at this point that Jefferson began to conspire with DeWitt Clinton, whose darker nature Jefferson seems to have conjured out of the muddy waters of New York politics, and with other men of poor character from the region, such as Gideon Granger, John Armstrong, and James Cheetham. These men were generally prone to vindictive activities and political intrigue. Jefferson not only capitalized on their bad propensities but encouraged and funded them, thus making permanent what before may have been only latent or in infancy. Jefferson actively engaged each of these men, elevated their standing, followed their recommendations, and rewarded them with government appointments for years to come.

Meanwhile, Jefferson shut Burr out of power, out of his administration, out of politics in every way possible and shut out his followers from every post he could. During this period, from 1801 to 1805, Jefferson did whatever he could to disable and paralyze Burr. Then he made sure Burr was removed from the vice presidency and even excluded from any political position in New York. Everywhere Burr turned, Jefferson made sure the doors were closed. When Burr finally turned away from his home state and looked westward, Jefferson sanctioned it (or permitted Burr to believe he did), allowing Dearborn to verbally encourage his Lousiana settlement and his gathering of a military force by providing Burr with blank muster forms.

While Burr was still in office as VP, Jefferson acquired the Louisiana Territory and began seeking ways to acquire the Floridas and the rest of the continent. Jefferson's true goal for having Congress fund his western explorations – the Lewis & Clark, Pike, and other expeditions – long preceded his serendipitous Purchase and was neither exclusively botanical nor geographical. Getting the lay of the land was merely one form of information-gathering. There were also "diplomatic" efforts to gain the allegiance of the Indian inhabitants, making physical incursions (establishing squatter's rights, as it were), and finding other grounds to claim territory (such as discovering a river's source and laying claim to it).

This was the doctrine of Manifest Destiny before it was so named. Roger Kennedy writes that "[t]hough these founders knew that the unity of the Great [Mississippi] Valley, with its water trunk spreading into two great limbs to the west and east, the Missouri and the Ohio [Rivers], could not be divided into parts without destroying all hope of a united and vigorous nation, none but Jefferson seems to have contemplated the extension of the Republic [westward] beyond that valley." (Kennedy, 408n20.)[33] It was not just TJ; most Americans felt this expansionist drive. Alexander Hamilton had written about New Orleans some years before: "The rapid increase of our Western country is such, that we must possess this outlet." (Kennedy 136.)

---

[33] Flores writes: "It is hardly surprising that for many years before his election as president ... Jefferson nurtured dreams of exploring the still unknown interior of North America. The fact that Spain controlled Louisiana did not deter him from attempting to convert those dreams into actions." (Flores, 5-6.) Flores lists the explorations TJ initiatedfrom as early as 1783, concluding: "Four times, then, Jefferson had attempted to have the West explored by private parties, and four times his plans had met with frustration." (Id., 6.)

On the other hand, the somewhat opposing concept of separatism was closely related to the expansionist drive. Many felt that "if a government should be formed beyond [the highest peak of the Rockies], that government should separate from the mother Empire as the child separates from the parent at the age of manhood." (Kennedy, 408n20, quoting from Frederick Merck, *History of the Westward Movement* (Knopf, 1980).) While Jefferson had himself earlier shown support for separation of the states east of the Allegheny mountains and those west of them, by the time he was in office, he had become purely expansionst and acquisitive – or perhaps it was the fortuitous acquisition of Louisiana that excited his expansionist sensibilities. An "empire of liberty," he told Madison. (*See* Koch, *Jefferson & Madison,* 243-47.)

The event, however, that prompted Jefferson's need for a fall guy was the near-disastrous 1806 Freeman/Custis Red River expedition, which resulted in an armed confrontation with a Spanish regiment and came near to starting a war with Spain. The news of this began showing up in newspapers in September and October of 1806. Burr had departed westward in mid-August 1806 and was in Ohio, Kentucky, and Tennessee through November.

With the news of the Freeman/Custis confrontation with the Spanish, two opposing things happened. First, the news would have confirmed Burr's belief that war with Spain was imminent and would have kept Burr on track to head southward, down the Mississippi to his Louisiana lands, and second, Jefferson had to figure out a way to *prevent* war and quiet the incident. Seeing the situation on the frontier with the Freeman/Custis expedition and hearing the absurd reports about Burr's activities, Jefferson only needed to put one hand together with the other. Burr's supposedly mysterious activities supplied the bandaid for the wound Jefferson's expedition had opened with Spain.

Burr's expedition, however, was delayed by the U.S. District Attorney in Kentucky, Joseph Daviess, a Federalist left in office by Jefferson, who began attempting to prosecute Burr. Henry Adams explains: "Burr's admirers were Republicans, so numerous that the President shrank from alienating them by denouncing Burr, while they in their turn would not desert Burr until the President denounced him. The Federalists saw here a chance to injure their opponents, and used it." (Adams, *TJ Administrations*, 788.)

Daveiss had begun writing to Jefferson the previous January, claiming a renewal of the old "Spanish conspiracy" to effect a "separation of the Union in favor of Spain ... *finally*." (Daveiss to TJ, January 10, 1806, quoted in Adams, at 789.) Adams claims it was "Burr's appearance on the Ohio and at St. Louis in Wilkinson's company during the summer of 1805 [that] called attention to the old Spanish conspiracy, and gave Daveiss the opportunity he wanted." (*Id.*)

In February, Daveiss again wrote Jefferson, "calling attention to Burr's movements during the previous summer, and charging both him and Wilkinson with conspiracy." (Id., 790.) It was around this time that Jefferson received another warning from General William Eaton, whom Burr had attempted to interest in joining his expedition, for Burr knew Eaton was a military man who had been snubbed by the Administration. Daveiss continued to write letter after letter to Jefferson, "without receiving answer or acknowledgment." (Id.)

Throughout November and into December, Daveiss kept issuing warrants for Burr's arrest or swearing out process against him. Adams observes: "The air was full of denunciations, waiting only for the President's leave to annihilate the conspirators under popular contempt. A word quietly written by Jefferson to one or two persons in the Western country would have stopped Burr short in his path, and would have brought Wilkinson abjectly on his knees." (Id.)

The confrontation with Spain happened and Jefferson did nothing. He did not stop Burr. He was waiting for Burr to take "overt action."[34] "Jefferson's persistent silence and inaction left the energetic district-attorney free to do what he liked." (Adams, 792.) Daveiss established a newspaper, "Western World," which first appeared in July 1806 and

---

[34]   These are the words in the treason clause of the Constitution and Jefferson repeatedly used these words when he told his correspondents that Burr had not done anything yet, and then later when he told William B. Giles what he alleged Burr's treasonous actions were. (*See* TJ to Giles, April 20, 1807, list quoted in "Jefferson's Mirror, Part 2" chapter.)

"seemed to have no other object for its existence than to drag the old Spanish conspiracy to light." (Id. at 791.) Adams observes that in striking at the members of the old Spanish conspiracy, who were by now presiding judges, "he threw consternation into the ranks of Burr's [western] friends." (Id.)

A letter from Gideon Granger conveyed Eaton's allegations of a separatist plot by Burr. (Lomask 2:176.)[35] By then Jefferson knew about the Freeman/Custis expedition's confrontation with the Spanish regiment. He put two and two together. He decided to foster the idea to the American public "that the Burr Conspiracy was actually responsible for the uproar in Texas." (Flores, 294.) That also enabled him to advise his minister to let the Spanish authorities know the absolute untruth that there was "no better proof of the good faith of the United States . . . than the vigor with which we acted ... in suppressing the enterprise meditated lately by Burr against Mexico." (TJ to James Bowdoin, minister in Madrid, April 2, 1807, quoted in Kennedy, 311.)[36]

On October 22, Jefferson and his cabinet resolved "unanimously . . . to have [Burr] strictly watched, and on his committing any overt act, to have him arrested and tried for treason, misdemeanor, or whatever other offence the act may amount to; and in like manner to arrest and try any of his followers committing acts against the laws." (Adams, at 795, quoting Cabinet Memoranda, Ford, *TJ Writings*, 1:318.) Already Jefferson was talking of treason, but only a separatist plot had been alleged. No proof of any unlawful activity had been shown.

In early December, Daveiss again forced Burr into court and on December 5, the grand jury again discharged him. However, on November 25, a dispatch was put in Jefferson's

---

[35] Lomask does not provide a source. Granger wrote Jefferson in 1814, reminding him that "in 1806[,] I communicated, by the first mail after I had gained knowledge of the fact, the supposed plans of Burr in his western expedition; upon which communication your Council was first called together to take measures in relation to that subject." (GG to TJ, February 22, 1814, Founder's Archives Online.) And TJ's cabinet memoranda note "information from Genl. Eaton, thro. . . . . Granger." (Lomask 2:177).

[36] According to Kennedy, this letter was one of the diplomatic dispatches that Jefferson later was unwilling to let the grand jury (or Burr) see as it considered whether to bring charges against Burr. (*See* Kennedy, id.)

hand from General Wilkinson, claiming there was "an expedition by sea against Vera Cruz." (Adams, 798, not citing source but clearly to Jefferson's Memoranda of the November 25 cabinet meeting.) The cabinet decided to issue a proclamation and orders for the arrest of all persons involved.

Adams notes: "A moment's thought should have satisfied the President that Wilkinson was deceiving him, and the city of New Orleans must be the real point of danger. In truth, Wilkinson's letters suppressed more than they told, and were more alarming than the warnings of Eaton or of Daveiss, for they proved that Wilkinson was playing a double part." (Adams, 799-800.)

But Jefferson was determined to wait for Burr to commit "an overt act" and charge him with treason, and by the way, whatever other offenses. Neither Daveiss's letters nor Wilkinson's nor Granger's pointed to treason. Eaton, who was trying to get his military expenditures reimbursed and was an alcoholic known to tell wild tales, only later claimed the absurdity that Burr was planning to march on Washington to throw Jefferson out of office. (Lomask 2:203, 264.)

On November 6, 1806, Jefferson wrote his son-in-law that Burr was "unquestionably very actively engaged" in a scheme to sever the Union, adding that "as yet we have no legal proof of any overt act which the law can lay hold of." (Lomask 2:198, quoting TJ to Thomas Mann Randoph, November 6, 1806.)

Jefferson's first proclamation of November 27, 1806 did not mention Burr by name but was the first denouncement of Burr's expedition, stating that "sundry persons" were conspiring against Spain, contrary to the laws. (Adams, 800; *see also* Lomask 2:180.) Still Jefferson was waiting for Burr to do something that would permit the President to lay blame on him. "Jefferson did nothing of consequence about the Burr problem," but "[h]is silence did not prevent the Philadelphia *Aurora*, the leading Democratic newspaper, from telling its readers that the Administration had 'penetrated to the bottom ... the projects of Mr. Burr.'" (Lomask 2:197, quoting *Aurora*, December 1, 1806.) Again focused on the claim of separatism, the editor wrote that Burr had but one "*Grand design . . .* that of *raising himself to a powerful station* over a separate government and an independent territory – to become himself the lawgiver and the founder of a new power." (Id.)[37]

Burr didn't get moving until mid-December. He left Frankfort to Nashville on the 10th and was at the mouth of the Cumberland River on the 28th. By New Year's Eve, he was at Ft. Massac and on January 1, 1807, he was on the Mississippi. On the 4th, he was at Chickasaw Bluffs (Memphis, TN) and at Bayou Pierre (30 miles north of Natchez) on the 10th, where he learned of Jefferson's proclamation, Wilkinson's betrayal, and the arrests of his friends. Burr "surrendered" and again was brought before a grand jury at Washington (in present-day Mississippi) in early February. Learning of orders to seize him and fearing assassination, Burr disappeared on February 5, the day before his 51st birthday.

On January 1, 1807, Jefferson had received a second letter from Wilkinson, the one in which he cited the alleged Burr cipher letter and "prophesied that the arch-conspirator would prove too wily for him, that the dagger of the assassin would terminate [Wilkinson's] struggle to save the nation." (Lomask 2:198.) Lomask writes: "The student of these events wonders how Jefferson managed to peruse the general's frenzies with a straight face. He read them earnestly, as a matter of fact." (Id.)

On the 22nd of January, 1807, Jefferson issued a message to Congress, in which he identified Burr as the "arch conspirator," whose guilt was "beyond question," and who was attempting to divide the nation, pretending to purchase land as a pretext, an allurement to followers, and a cover under which to retreat. (Lomask id. at 199, quoting from Jefferson's Message to Congress, *American State Papers*, Misc. 1:472.) Still no treason.

The take-down was fairly simple. Although Burr had been followed and harassed for some time, it wasn't until he allegedly jumped bail that local official reluctance to arrest him turned to active pursuit. But Burr did not in fact jump bail. He

---

[37] Again, Burr never proposed such a position for himself and his past record showed quite clearly his willingness to serve in secondary positions. As we shall see in the "Events" chapter, too, Burr engaged in many actions for which he never took credit.

had promised Mississippi Judge Rodney that if more charges were brought, he would appear. However, the agreement was not drawn up by Burr himself but between the judge and the state Attorney General, leaving each side with a different interpretation of it. (*See* Kline 2:1023-24n2, and *Editorial Note: Burr's Flight, id.* at 1017-21.) Thus, Rodney believed Burr was bound to appear from day to day and Burr believed he did not need to appear unless further charges were brought, and indeed Burr's interpretation is the more legally correct one, for a judge cannot simply bind a person over without charges (and Burr would never have agreed to that). (*See* "Declared a Fugitive" chapter below for full discussion of this event.)

But the storm had been brewing in everyone's minds and this broke it. Burr must be guilty if he jumped bail!

Given what we know of Wilkinson and his history of betrayal and murder, Burr was justified in fleeing. Given, too, that the civil authority had been widely suspended with Wilkinson's induction of martial law, leaving Wilkinson a free hand, Burr had legitimate reason to fear assassination. He told a prosecutor that he was deterred from meeting Governor Mead "by a belief that he would be assassinated were he seen passing through the Territory." ("Statement of George Poindexter," quoted in Kline 2:1015, citing to *American State Papers*, Misc. 1:568.)[38] Burr later at trial raised the fact that he had seen orders printed in the newspaper not just to capture him but to kill him. He had confirmed these orders with a naval officer.[39]

At this last state court hearing before Burr had flown, he showed his awareness of TJ's and JW's roles in the goings-

---

[38]   Poindexter also remarked that Burr seemed "particularly unwilling to fall into the hands of General Wilkinson" and he understood that an officer of the army was sent by Wilkinson to take Burr, having "heard a lieutenant of the army (but I had rather not mention his name) say that he was one of the persons employed for that purpose." (Poindexter's Testimony, Annals of Congress, 10th Congress, 1st Session, (Senate), 1807-08 (October 7, 1807) 585-87.)

[39]   Harman Blennerhassett also stated he feared assassination. He wrote in a brief to his lawyers during the Burr trial that until news of TJ's first proclamation arrived in Lexington, KY, "Burr's popularity [was] daily increasing [and HB] heard of no jealousy or suspicions." He then learned by an express messenger that the Woods County militia (where his home was in Marietta, OH) were going to burn his house and "in all probability" would shoot him and Burr if they returned there. (Fitch, *Breaking with Burr,* 197 [HB's Brief].)

on when he declared in open court that "he could say something before them of a high criminal nature that would show the iniquity of those who were persecuting him and would do it if he did not change his mind."[40]

Two weeks after Burr fled, he was recognized on horseback in the backwoods of Alabama (Mississippi Territory then) with a servant. He was thus captured and transported via military escort 1200 miles to Richmond, Virginia for trial. This was in late February 1806. The preliminary hearing began in late March.

The government brought charges of misdemeanor (for the alleged filibuster against Spain) and treason. In late August, Chief Justice John Marshall issued an opinion that voided the government's treason charges. (*See* Lomask 2:204-06; 279-82.) The trial for misdemeanor began in August 1806 and also ended in an acquittal.   ~

The Arrest of Aaron Burr

"The criminal [Burr] is preserved to become the rallying point of all the disaffected & the worthless of the US, and to be a pivot on which all the intrigues & conspiracies which foreign governments may wish to disturb us with, are to turn."
Jefferson to George Hay, September 4 1807
https://rotunda.upress.virginia.edu/founders.

---

[40]   Kline 2:1019-20, apparently quoting from William B. Hamilton, *Anglo-Amer. Law on the Frontier: Thomas Rodney and His Territorial Cases* (1953) 261-63.

Evidence

Wherein we discuss the rules of evidence (with examples from our case)

> *[W]hat he particularly wanted was that the great principles of evidence should be laid down which would be equally applicable to this and to all other affidavits.*
> **Burr at trial, May 27, 1807**
> Robertson, *Trial of AB*, 1:95.[41]

> *Hitherto my proofs have been presumptive, and such only as might be expected from the secret nature of the crime.*
> **Daniel Clark, Proofs of the Corruption of General James Wilkinson (1809), 14-15.**

When the state tries an individual for a crime, the prosecution must offer evidence at trial to prove the defendant's guilt. There are many different types of evidence, from eye-witness testimony to documents to other physical things. Courts have certain standards for admissibility of evidence. Not all evidence is admissible. Unreliable, prejudicial, irrelevant, and immaterial evidence is excludable.

A good deal of what has been written about Burr the past two hundred years would be inadmissible in a courtroom today (and would have been then, as well). Similarly, although the scholarship has been much higher in Jefferson's case, even many of the works critical of him give him benefits of the doubt that would not exist in a courtroom where both sides are fairly presented. Such things should matter to anyone who cares about truth or justice.

Many if not most people come to their conclusions about others rather casually. Much depends in these situations on social context and values, on being one of the group. These social standards accept a rumor conveyed by a friend above

---

[41] *Also,* Burr at trial, May 22, 1807, Robertson, *Trial of AB*, 1:46 ("Colonel Burr then addressed the court, and stated his wish that the court should instruct the grand jury on certain leading points as to the admissibility of certain evidence, which he supposed would be laid before the grand jury by the attorney for the United States.")

fact or logical inference that does not affirm social bonds or alliances. A prosecutor who works this way is not a good prosecutor. Since many, if not most, readers are likely to have little knowledge of standards of evidence and proof, I take time here to set forth the standards courts use.

Evidence Generally –
Relevance, Materiality, and Probative Value

Evidence introduced at trial must be relevant and material. Evidence is **relevant** if it tends to prove the existence of a fact at issue. If we were to produce the orders issued by Jefferson to capture or kill Burr (as Burr asserted at trial), they would be relevant to show Jefferson's intent to kill as well as to show that Jefferson performed an overt act towards the goal of the conspiracy to kill Burr.

Evidence is **material** if it is of consequence to the matter before the court. The evidence just set forth above is also material in our case against Jefferson.

Where the evidence is the same as the proposition to be proved, it is **direct evidence**. If the orders issued by Jefferson included the words "or kill," they are direct evidence of his intent to kill Burr.

When Jefferson himself writes that he had early formed a bad opinion of Burr, when he declares before Congress that Burr is guilty, and when several years after Burr's trial he affirms that he really did want to see Burr "get what he deserved," that is all direct evidence of Jefferson's state of mind relative to Burr. In murder, state of mind (malice or ill will) is an element of the crime to be proven at trial. (Of course, Jefferson also denied having any ill will towards Burr and that would also be admissible, along with other evidence that Jefferson did or did not exhibit ill will – such as his insistence on going after Burr even after Burr's acquittal, or his expressed desire to impeach Chief Justice John Marshall for not having convicted Burr.)

Where the factual proposition to be proved must be *inferred* from the evidence, the evidence is **circumstantial**.

Even if we can show directly that Jefferson had ill will towards Burr, that does not mean he had what is called the *mens rea*, the intention to commit the crime of murder. Thus, his expressed ill will may be used as circumstantial evidence of his *mens rea.*

Evidence must also be **probative**, that is it tends to make the existence of the factual proposition more likely than not. Without the phrase "or kill," the orders to capture Burr are not probative of an intent to kill Burr. However, if official copies of orders that included the words "or kill" were found or if someone testified he received such orders, they would be probative of Jefferson's intent to kill Burr.

Probative value depends generally on *how many inferences* must be made to arrive at the fact to be proved. The more inferences the less its probative value. If we wish to show that Jefferson intended to have Burr killed, the probative value of Jefferson's later wish to see Burr get what he deserved requires us to infer that he had felt the same during the prosecution as he did later, that Burr getting what he deserved meant being convicted of treason, that being convicted meant being hung, and so on.

Probative value also depends on the *strength of the inferences*. The stronger the logical relation between each inferential step or between the evidence and proposition, the more probative value it has. The strength of the inferences in the above paragraph is fairly strong. If you try someone for treason and then say you really did wish for them to get what they deserved, the inference is pretty strong that the wish is for his death.

Some inferences have more probative value when viewed together. This is what is often called "connecting the dots." Much of the case against Jefferson involves connecting the dots. We must be careful to not "pile inference on inference" to arrive at a conclusion.

However, especially in a conspiracy case, multiple connecting inferences are often necessary to seeing the whole picture, and oftentimes those connections are scattered in many directions.

Generally Inadmissable Evidence and When it May Be Admissible

There are some forms of evidence that are generally not admissible because of their unreliability or prejudicial quality, such as hearsay and character.

Biographers and historians, of course, do not use legal standards of evidence or proof when they draw conclusions from different types of historical factual material. Most historians will differentiate between primary (first-hand) and secondary (second-hand) source material and will avoid drawing conclusions from hearsay or assertions of character, but even well-respected scholars may use such evidence to make suggestions that perpetuate accepted viewpoints. Then other biographers or historians follow their lead. Overturning (deconstructing) such accepted history places a high burden on the writer.

It is also critical to recognize that the case against Jefferson is not fiction. Indeed, it is far less fiction than the accepted history and denigration of Burr. But the facts here have long been scattered and buried. Some evidence was removed, destroyed, and lost forever. This was intentionally done before Burr was even arrested or charged and it continued right through and long after his trial.[42]

This is not uncommon in conspiracies. Indeed, all trials require that the judge or jury make inferences and all cases contain circumstantial evidence. It is a common layman mistake to believe that eyewitness testimony is required to prove guilt. Eyewitness testimony is actually the least reliable. Forensic evidence (such as fingerprints, blood/DNA) may be the most reliable, where it can be found (and that depends on what is being proven), but forensic methods of analysis did not exist in Jefferson and Burr's time. Documentary evidence is critical and in this case is mostly all we have.

There are several types of evidence that are admissible only under certain circumstances.

---

[42] Granger, postmaster general, had Burr's papers seized and apparently destroyed. (See chapter below on Granger.) Chandler notes that there are documents missing from the Dept. of War archives. (*See* Chandler, *Jefferson Conspiracies,* 349 n.13, 350 n.4.) Flores notes that TJ had apparently instructed Nicholas King, who transcribed Freeman/Custis journals, to redact portions. Flores, 91-94, 100, 293. Clark, who in 1809 published several hundred pages of documents indicting JW, complains that critical parts of a letter he sent Madison "has been suppressed." (Clark, *Proofs of the Corruption of JW,* 143-44; 173 in "Notes" (Appendix) section [Note No. 88, Clark to Madison, March 8, 1803.)

Bad Character or Bad Prior Acts

Character evidence is labeling someone by some general opinion or commonly recognized characteristics. These are often biased and unreliable. He has a reputation as a womanizer, so therefore if he is accused of rape or other improper conduct towards a woman, it must be true.

Rule 404 (a) of the Federal Rules of Evidence ("FRE") states: "Evidence of a person's character or character trait is not admissible to prove that on a particular occasion the person acted in accordance with the character or trait."

It would not be permissible to show that Jefferson was a known liar in order to prove that he lied about Burr. This type of assertion uses the conclusion to prove the instance. It should be the other way around. You do not call someone a liar in order to prove he is lying. You prove he is lying and then conclude (or let the jury conclude) he is a liar – at least on that occasion.

Past acts to show character, too, are inadmissible. FRE Rule 404 (b) (1) states that evidence of a defendant's past crime, wrong, or other act "is not admissible to prove a person's character in order to show that on a particular occasion the person acted in accordance with the character."

So, just because Jefferson had previously made false statements about people he wanted to discredit does not mean that when he told Congress Burr was guilty, he was making a false statement – although it may make it more likely than not that he did. Or just because he ordered passages removed from documents on other occasions before publication or distorted the contents of such documents in an official statement doesn't mean he suppressed documents or distorted contents of documents in Burr's case.

FRE Rule 404 (b) (2), however, provides that evidence of a past crime, wrong, or other act "may be admissible for another purpose, such as proving motive, opportunity, intent, preparation, plan, knowledge, identity, absence of mistake, or lack of accident."

So, if we discover that in 1805 Jefferson gave instructions to suppress passages in an explorer's journal in 1804-5 before submitting it to Congress for publication, this does not prove that Jefferson instructed General Wilkinson or his postmaster general Gideon Granger to seize and remove or destroy letters from Burr and his cohorts from the postal offices in 1806-07.[43] But it is admissible to show what is sometimes called a "common scheme or plan" of Jefferson's. In other words, *modus operandi*: we know from the past bad act that Jefferson did work this way and so the past conduct is admissible to show that Jefferson previously used a similar scheme, plan, or practice as we see him using in Burr's case.

That evidence may also be admissible to show, if relevant, the content of what Jefferson wished removed from those documents, which was anything that would alert Spain to his actual intentions by having "explorers" wandering accidentally into Spanish territory. And again if relevant and probative, this may be used to show Jefferson's intentions relative to the Burr expedition. (E.g. Jefferson did not want Spain to know that Jefferson was conducting illegal intelligence-gathering incursions into Spanish territory. He could throw Spain off the trail by sanitizing the published explorer's journals and pointing the finger at Burr.) When offered in conjunction with Jefferson's remark after Burr's prosecution that Spain would now see how diligently his administration prosecuted Burr for having engaged in actions hostile to Spain, Jefferson's motives for suppressing the passages from the explorer's journals as well as for going after Burr with such avidity may be clarified.[44]

When we learn in addition that Jefferson distorted and suppressed certain passages from the written correspondence of Daniel Clark (a merchant in New Orleans, no relation to the explorer Clark brothers) relating to Wilkinson's "corrupt

---

[43]   The evidence shows that TJ approved of both JW's actions and Granger's. For Granger: *see e.g.,* Granger to TJ, February 22, 1814; TJ to Granger, March 9, 1814; TJ to Madison, March 10, 1814; Kennedy, 274-75, 292-93. (Discussed below in "Granger" chapter.). For JW, *see e.g.,* Clark, *Proofs of the Corruption of JW,* 7 (JW "is supported by the strongest marks of presidential favor"); Plumer, 544 (TJ said "That there was no room to doubt of the integrity, firmness & attachment of Wilkinson to our government."); John B. Colvin to TJ, September 14, 1810 (*TJ Papers,* Library of Congress) (requests TJ to clarify "the principles upon which you approved of Gen.Wilkinson's conduct at New-Orleans").

[44]   Jefferson instructions to James Bowdoin (U.S. minister to Spain), April 2, 1807 (Lipscomb 11:279, Lomask 2:201; Kennedy, 311).

receipt of money" from Spain, which Clark claimed "the President thinks ought to be forgotten,"[45] it is, again, not admissible to prove that Jefferson did anything similar in Burr's case, but it is admissible to show Jefferson's awareness of evidence of Wilkinson's corruption earlier than he claimed (and that Jefferson lied to Congress about this), Jefferson did not want the public to know how much he knew, that he had ulterior motives for refusing to acknowledge Wilkinson's corruption.

The Federal Rules of Evidence were not in existence when Jefferson was president but the common law provided parties with rules that were essentially the same, although as judge-made law, there was likely more leeway. (See for example, the famous speech by William Wirt at Burr's trial, in which he paints a vividly detailed picture of Burr as Satan. Although that speech was made during the prosecution's opening statement, where courts usually give greater latitude, courts today would be less likely to allow it even in opening without showing a strong factual basis.)

Hearsay

Another type of evidence that courts generally will not admit is hearsay. FRE Rule 801(c) defines hearsay as: "Any statement other than a statement made by the declarant while testifying at trial or hearing in which the statement is proffered, which is offered into evidence in order to prove the truth of the matter asserted."

What this means is that the person testifying (the declarant) is not permitted to testify to what was said by somebody else who is not in court (that is, who is not testifying himself), IF the declarant is testifying that what that person said proves the truth of the statement.

So, a witness would not be permitted to testify that Wilkinson told him he would pay him $5000 to kill Burr if that testimony was intended to prove that Wilkinson was guilty of soliciting murder. If, however, that testimony is intended to show the mental state of the witness, as for example, why the witness went out with his gun in search of Burr, it would not be hearsay.

---

[45]   Clark, *Proofs of the Corruption of JW,* 144.

Wilkinson could also testify to receiving verbal orders from Jefferson to hire someone to kill Burr because this would be offered to show why Wilkinson offered to pay someone to do it. It would not prove that Jefferson did issue such an order.

If Wilkinson could produce an authenticated copy of the order in Jefferson's hand or signed by him (and someone would have to authenticate it) or by a deputy of his (which would then require establishing whether the person who signed it had authority from the president to do so, and so on), Wilkinson would not be testifying to what Jefferson told him out of court.[46]

Many of Daniel Clark's remarks about the difficulties he had in obtaining the proofs of Wilkinson's corruption: "Witnesses are with difficulty persuaded to appear; documents are withheld; and in this country [Louisiana] particularly, where the laws have been so grossly violated by this very man [Wilkinson] with impunity, the fear of military execution has, I know, prevented my obtaining much evidence which would have supported a prosecution [against Wilkinson], carried on under the sanction of government" may be inadmissible as speculation or hearsay.[47] How does Clark know that witnesses were persuaded to appear only with difficulty, or that documents were withheld? What is the basis of his conclusion that the laws were so grossly violated by Wilkinson in Louisiana? How does he know that others' fear of military execution had prevented him from obtaining evidence? Was he told these things?

These assertions cannot be used to show that witnesses would not appear, that documents were withheld, or that people feared "military execution." Nor are they admissible to prove that Wilkinson ordered such goings on or that he ordered others to execute Burr. They can be admitted to show what Clark claims to have experienced, his difficulties in obtaining evidence.

They may also be used to corroborate the *existence of a*

---

[46] If the document was signed by Jefferson and someone who knew his signature could confirm it was his signature, or if it bore the presidential seal (and that seal could be authenticated), or if Jefferson himself or his attorney admitted that he had signed it, it would be authenticated.

[47] Clark, *Proofs,* 7.

common plan to intimidate witnesses, withhold documents, or threaten (or even carry out) military execution. (In other words, they corroborate what Burr told the court at trial.) When we learn that Wilkinson had on other occasions had witnesses secretly assassinated or openly executed – the sources of which, of course, we must also analyze and authenticate -- Clark's evidence gives us the picture and enables us to start to connect some dots, for not only does it show *modus operandi* (giving us a full range of doings) but it connects Jefferson to Wilkinson's doings. It is certainly not enough to say "these things were generally known." Clark's *bona fides*, his reputation for integrity on both sides of the conflict, his discretion, and his extensive knowledge of the entire region from New Orleans to Vera Cruz, matter as well.

Clark's assertion about the threat of military execution also corroborates the reason Burr gave as to why he disappeared into the wilderness for two weeks (commonly but mistakenly believed to have jumped bail) when he knew he was sought by authorities. Again, although it does not prove Wilkinson issued or carried out threats, it does show that at least one other man had a valid reason to *view Wilkinson* with fear and suspicion for the same reasons as Burr.

What happens in situations like this – where direct evidence is lacking – is that such evidence (testimony of out-of-court statements to prove things other than the truth of what was supposedly said or use of prior acts to show a common plan) may be used by the prosecution to create a chain of circumstantial evidence that requires the jury to connect the dots to come to a conclusion of guilt. It is not an easy way to make a case and it is demanding on the intellect of the jury, but it is valid.

~

Burr's Proposed Instructions to the
Grand Jury on Points of Evidence[48]

166   *TRIAL OF AARON BURR.*

First. That the grand jury can not, consistently with
their oath find a bill except on such testimony as would
justify a petit jury to find the prisoner guilty. *Foster,*
232, § 8; 3 *Institute,* 25; 2 *Id.,* 384; *Dalton,* 519; 2
Judge Wilson's Works, 364; 3 *St. Tr.,* 419, 420; and Sir
John Hawles' Observations, 4 *St. Tr.,* 133; 4 *Black.;* 302–
306; 2 *Hale,* ch. 8, 61, Wilson's edition with Wilson's
note; 2 *Hale,* ch. 22, 157, with Wilson's note; 2 *Euno-
mos' Dict.* § 39, 124, 5, 6,; 5 *St. Tr.* 3; *Foster,* 232,
§ 8.

Second. That no testimony or witness ought to go
to the grand jury, but what is legal and competent
to support the charge about which the inquiry is made.
Danby's case, *Leech,* 443. c. 187; Dodd's case, *Id.,* 59, c.
77; Commonwealth of Virginia *v.* Hopbam, *Warles &
Daws,* before the general court at Williamsburg.

Third. That the grand jury can not return a bill for
treason for levying war against the United States, unless
they have two witnesses who swear to the overt act of
the treason laid in the indictment; both which witnesses are believed by them. *East's Crown Law,* ch. 2,
§ 64.

That both must be believed. 3 *St. Tr.,* 56.

Fourth. That there must be two witnesses to the
grand jury of each overt act, follows also as a consequence from the former position, that they must have
such testimony as would be requisite for the petit
jury.

Fifth. That the grand jury can not find a bill for
treason in consequence of any confessions made, though
proved by two witnesses. *Foster,* 241; 4 *Black.;* Constitution of the United States, article 3, §3; *Graydon's
Digest,* 11; Judge Iredell's charge, *Fries's Trial,* 171,
172; *East's Crown Law,* 96, 97.

Sixth. That as the grand jury only hear evidence
on the part of the state, if upon that evidence they
entertain a doubt of the truth of the charge, they ought
not to find a bill; as the presumption is ever in favor of
innocence. 1 *Mac N.,* 2· 6.

Seventh. No act of a third person can be given in
evidence against the accused to prove him guilty of
treason or of a misdemeanor under the law of the 5th

Burr "*requested [Chief Justice John Marshall] to inspect the list of
propositions, and the authorities referred to in support of them [so that] he
might then determine which of those points would admit of the delivery of
his opinion, and which would not.*" Robertson, *Trial of AB*, 1:172-73.[49]

---

[48]   This is 7 of his 8 points. This image is from another edition than my copy. The
citation (and page numbers) I provide is to my copy.

[49]   The prosecutor "contended that the court had no right to give specific
instructions to the grand jury after they had been once generally charged by the
court." (Id., 173.) Marshall nonetheless had "no difficulty in giving his opinions
at this time on certain points" and did draw up a supplemental charge. (Id., 175.)

Smoking Guns:

Blennerhassett's Brief & Dearborn's Letter

Burr stated many times both before and at trial that he had the Administration's sanction for his expedition. He wrote to Henry Clay, the attorney who represented him at several grand jury inquests in Kentucky, that "my views have been fully explained to . . . several principal officers of the government [and] are well considered by the administration & seen by it with complacency." (AB to HC, December 1, 1806, quoted in Lomask 2:96.)[50] At trial, Burr stated that "his designs were honorable and would have been useful to the United States." (Robertson, 1:7.)

There are two documents that corroborate Burr's claims of the Administration's knowledge and approval of his plans – not just his settlement plans but his filibuster against Spain. One is a statement made by Burr's associate, Harman Blennerhassett, in a document known as "Blennerhassett's Brief," which he wrote for his lawyers' use at trial. It was never used because HB was not tried; he was detained until Burr's acquittal. In this document, HB told his lawyers that Burr and

---

[50]   In November 1806, Burr wrote to Edward W. Tupper, a commander of the Ohio militia: "I am authorized in saying that it is the wish of [the] government that American settlers should go to the country west of the Mississippi in the Orleans Territory." Burr added: "Indeed, a man high in office, & in the confidence of the President told me that I should render a very great service to the public and afford pleasure to the administration, if I should take ten thousand men to that country." (AB to EWT, [November 18, 1806], Kline 2:1002.)

Burr wrote similarly to William Henry Harrison, governor of Indiana, that he was "engaged in an extensive speculation . . . [t]he objects [of which] are such as every man of honor and every good citizen must approve – They have been communicated to several of the principal officers of our government[,] particularly to one high in the confidence of the administration – He has assured me that my views would be grateful to the administration." (AB to WHH, November 27, 1806, Kline 2:1005.)

Kline notes that "Most contemporary reports indicate that AB and his associates hinted that their friend 'high in office' was Henry Dearborn." Kline, 2:1004; *see also,* id., 2:993. We know that Burr also communicated about the Bastrop lands with Gallatin. (*See* AB to AG, July 31, 1806, Kline 2:992.)

his associates had "contingent plans . . . against Spain . . . which, whilst kept secret, government would not disapprove, but when exposed, [they] would be obliged to frustrate, as [they] had done at New York in the case of Ogden and Smith."[51]

HB's statement reveals an explicit but secret understanding between Burr and the Jefferson Administration and is highly credible because HB told it to his attorneys in a private record for purposes of his defense. It was never made public. Though Burr repeatedly stated he had the approbation of the Administration, this secret agreement was never raised in court and there is no mention of it (to my knowledge) in any public or private correspondence.

HB's statement sheds a different light on Jefferson's prosecution of Burr and his associates, suggesting that the cause of TJ's sudden vindictive turn was as much about his fear of being found out by the Spanish as about the fortuitous opportunity to take down Burr. His loud denunciations of Burr were, in essence, disavowals of this secret alliance. Burr was the sacrificial lamb.

The second document that corroborates Burr's claim is a letter from Secretary of War, Henry Dearborn. This letter also shows Jefferson's early efforts to cover his tracks once Burr's "contingent plans" had been outed. It was written on April 3, 1807 to Judge Thomas T. Davis of Indiana. I quote Dearborn's carefully worded letter in full:

> It has been asserted by a certain Davis Floyd or a man by the name of Ralston[52] or by both of these, that Judge

---

[51]   HB wrote that he had published several essays in the Ohio Gazette in August or September 1806 "setting forth motives of right and expediency which should induce the country west of the mountains to seek a separation from the Atlantic states" with a view "to prepare the [western] country ... for a crisis sooner or later ... not from the views or operations of Col. Burr, but from the state of things," and "to divert public attention from scrutiny into contingent plans or operations against Spain, which, whilst kept secret, government would not disapprove, but when exposed, [they] would be obliged to frustrate." (Fitch, *Breaking with Burr*, 196 [HB's Brief].)

[52]   Major Davis Floyd and Alexander Ralston had warrants drawn up against them along with Burr and Blennerhassett, by a Judge Harry Toulmin of the Tombigbee District of Mississippi, who "thought it was time for me to act, especially as Judge Rodney appeared unwilling." (Kline 2:1020, citing Toulmin to Schuyler, 7 Feb., DLC: Burr Conspiracy.) (*See* chapter on "Jumping Bail.")

Davis had seen a letter from the Secretary of War countenancing Burr's expedition and indicating that it had the secret approbation of the government, I take the liberty of requesting you to state to me whether either of those persons or any other persons have received from you any indications of the existence of such communications from me, either in my private or public capacity, and if so will you be so obliging as to inform me of the source from which you derived your information. I am confident that you have not given any such information to any persons, but if you have you will have no objections to a compliance with my foregoing request. It is with regret that I take the liberty of asking this favor but I am sure you will excuse the trouble all _____.[53]

This letter is a clear threat to a local judge from the Secretary of War of the United States: "You'd better not have told anyone!" Dearborn does not deny the Administration secretly approved of Burr's expedition. If the Administration had not approved, he could easily have said so. But his concern is not whether Judge Davis thinks the Administration approved but whether *others* had received "any indications" from Davis of "the existence of such a communication from me, either in my private or public capacity." His main interest is to stop the circulation of the *idea* that the Administration had approved Burr's expedition.

Meanwhile, Jefferson was telling people that *Burr* "has been able to decoy a great proportion of his people by making them believe the government secretly approved of this expedition against the Spanish territories." (TJ to William C.C. Claiborne, Governor of New Orleans Territory, December 20, 1806, *Papers of TJ*, Library of Congress.) If the world knew Jefferson had secretly approved of Burr's expedition, the treason case would fall apart. People would question Jefferson's reasons for prosecuting Burr.[54]

---

[53] Henry Dearborn to "Judge Davis," April 4, 1807 (handwritten) in Dearborn letters and documents. Manuscripts and Archives. The New York Public Library. Astor, Lenox, and Tilden Foundations.

[54] It is unlikely that Dearborn approved of Burr's expedition without TJ's approval. In every other instance, HD did nothing without orders from TJ and followed his

Lomask states that <u>Burr</u> was the person who showed the judge the letter from Dearborn, which "according to some sources" Burr had forged. (Lomask, 2:106, citing to Isaac J. Cox "The Burr Conspiracy in Indiana," *Indiana Mag. Of Hist.,* XXV (Dec. 1929), 257, 263.) While it is possible that Burr showed Davis a letter from Dearborn approving of the expedition, that he would have forged it is not consistent with Burr's character, with Dearborn's letter, or with HB's brief. If Dearborn had not sanctioned Burr's expedition, all he had to do was say: "I didn't write that. It's a forgery." He didn't say that. Instead, he twisted and turned all around the question, avoiding it like the plague, which suggests he was covering his tracks.

Did Jefferson use his secret approbation to lead Burr into a trap? After 15 years of hating Burr, wishing he were dead, and trying to find a way to get rid of him? It is possible, even probable.

In any case, the President was actively misleading people when he said that Burr was "decoy[ing] a great proportion of his people by making them believe the government secretly approved of this expedition against the Spanish territories." Jefferson was the one decoying people.

In fact, even if Dearborn never said that the Administration secretly approved of such a filibuster, wasn't it true that Jefferson <u>did</u> approve of such an endeavor? After all, he had always secretly supported many such expeditions. (See Kennedy, chapters 8 and 9.) But he surely didn't want Spain to know that. Jefferson was creating as big a distance between himself and Burr as possible, and the easiest way to do that was to throw back onto Burr what the President's intentions were. He was willing to fabricate "facts." He was willing to fabricate a conspiracy (with Wilkinson's help). He was willing to sacrifice Burr, hang him, break his neck or choke the life out of him, just to keep Spain from finding out the truth.

That is, if the story had started here. But it didn't. It started 15 years before this when Jefferson formed his dislike of Burr. Whether Jefferson premeditated trapping this man he hated or simply took advantage of the moment, his intention to sacrifice Burr's life, no matter what, is clear. It was not about

---

orders to the T.

Spain. That was just a good excuse.

Dearborn's letter was from an Administration official. It shows that the Administration was covering its tracks. Both TJ and Dearborn knew what they were doing, tacitly or explicitly agreed to do it, and whatever other ends they were working towards, the end of Burr was not questioned.

Dearborn perhaps thought he was covering his own tracks and saving himself from a charge of perjury by not specifically denying he had written such a letter or given Burr approval, but this does not save him from the charge of conspiracy to murder. On the contrary, it implicates him. He *knew* that he and Jefferson had encouraged Burr to go west, recruit militia, and settle lands. He knew that they had led Burr to believe the administration supported a filibuster. Did Dearborn have any qualms now about throwing his old friend under the cart? Had he now really come to believe (on what basis? Jefferson's word? Burr had not been tried yet) that Burr -- a longtime friend, a man of honor, "a fellow traveler through the wilderness"[55] and renowned soldier, a champion for the republican cause and a longstanding public servant -- was committing treason?

It is astounding that Dearborn seems to have had none of these qualms but was worried that he should not be found openly lying. But both the President and the Secretary of War were lying to cover their tracks. This was not just any lie. This was a lie that would likely result in Burr's death.

~

---

[55] AB to John Coats, February 23, 1803, Davis, *Memoirs of AB,* 2:220. (Burr's fond words about Dearborn on the famous March to Quebec.) Note the contrast between Jefferson's attitude in his remark to Giles that he had treated Burr "as if he deserved respect" – an incredibly mean-spirited remark – and Burr's gentle and fond "fellow traveler in the wilderness" remark about Dearborn. Or the one he made about Gallatin, a year after the Treasury Secretary had participated in the attempt to hang him, being the "best head" in the nation (Kennedy 156; Parton 2:168-69). Or his continuous efforts to show respect to Jefferson's person and status, both in his personal encounters (as in his remark to Jefferson that he had always found him fascinating and wished to support him) and even at trial. (*See,* Robertson, *Trial of AB,* 1:77, 171, *385-86.*) (Burr "urged [his counsel] that the government should be treated with the utmost delicacy, though there was great provocation.") Even after all these men betrayed him, Burr never spoke ill of any of them until years later.

Dearborn's Letter to Judge Davis

Henry Dearborn letters and documents. Manuscripts and Archives.
The New York Public Library. Astor, Lenox, and Tilden Foundations.

Declared a Fugitive

The effect of Jefferson's Proclamation

[T]he prosecution against me [is] beyond
all example & in defiance of all law.
Burr to Charles Biddle, February 22, 1807
Kline 2:1025.

After Jefferson had declared Burr guilty, one of the events that convinced the public of his guilt was his allegedly having jumped bail and disappeared into the wilderness. Burr, who had worked long and hard for decades to attain a high reputation in his public life, had a right to expect a better assessment by his friends and associates, as well as by the public at large. Having appeared to meet all charges against him up to that point, in four separate grand jury inquests, he did not suddenly turn on his heel and run because of another inquest. He ran because he feared for his life.

But it was an oddity of Burr's life that at critical moments such as the one I am about to discuss, a miscommunication led to his actions being misinterpreted. Furthermore, the fears and prejudices that Jefferson and Wilkinson had aroused in the public mind made the unfavorable interpretation the compelled one. Jefferson's determination to portray Burr in a negative light created conditions that no one could have overcome.

Burr summed things up in a short letter to his old friend, Charles Biddle:

I was arrested a few days since by a party of the UStates Troops, near this place [Ft. Stoddert] and am now moving towards the City of Washington under Military escort. [T]his proceeding is the more extraordinary as the Grand Jury summoned for the purpose before the Supreme Court in Adams County [Natchez] the day before my departure from that place acquitted me in the Compleatest manner of all unlawful practices *or designs*. The report of this Grand Jury who censured the Conduct of Government in some particulars concerning me & for this reason I am told that the printers have not thought it discreet to publish that report entire – the pretence of my having forfeited a recognizance though sanctioned by the proclamation of Govr: Williams is utterly false. [T]he details of the prosecution against me cannot now be given – [T]hey are beyond all example & in defiance of all law – please to communicate this to my friends in N.Y. What I write must be inspected by the officer of the guard.

(AB to CB, February 22, 1807, Kline 2:1025.)(Original spelling, punctuation, and capitalization retained, except where bracketed.)

Kline gives a full and detailed account of the events that led to Burr's decision to withdraw from public view, as he put it, but Kline missed the opportunity in her editorial notes to show how the prejudices excited by TJ and JW affected official interpretations of Burr's actions, leading them to treat Burr as a guilty man even though he was "not offending against any law and [was] avowing a lawful object of [his] pursuits." (Fitch, *Breaking with Burr*, 204 [HB's Brief].)

On January 22, 1807, after another acquittal by another grand jury, Burr, the Mississippi Attorney General (Lyman Harding), and Judge Thomas Rodney (the father of the U.S. Attorney General Caesar Rodney) entered into a "special form" of recognizance (bail) in which Burr agreed that he "was bound on condition that I should appear *in case of indictment should be found against me* and not otherwise." (AB to Robert Williams, Governor of Mississippi, February 12, 1807, Kline 2:1022-23.) Burr told Williams that this form "was agreed to by Judge Rodney after nearly half an hour's discussion between him, Mr. Harding and myself – drawn up at his request by Mr. Harding and signed by the judge in our presence . . . and will be found in the hand writing of Mr. Harding . . . unless for fraudulent purposes the judge shall have destroyed it." (Id.)

But Kline notes that the dispute "stemmed from misunderstanding, not fraud." (Id.) When Burr's disappearance was reported to the court on February 7, Rodney read aloud a recognizance that required Burr to be present "to answer bills of indictment that might be found against him, and to continue to appear from day to day, until dismissed by said court." (Kline 2:1023, citing Mississippi Archives, *3d Annual Report*, p. 73.) Harding (who was one of Burr's sureties) objected, saying that was not the form taken, insisting that "Burr was only bound to answer any bills of indictment found against him, and as none was found he was clear of his recognizance." (Id.)

Kline remarks that the judge's "own notes solves the mystery," for at Rodney's request, Harding had begun to draft the recognizance, "wrote a few lines more and threw down his pen, saying it was not necessary to write the recognizance at large they would acknowledge and then Judge Rodney could write it at large and in form at his lazure – which I assented to and then took their acknowledgement respectively to the respective sums, 'To be levied ... if Aron Burr failed to attend at the Supreme Court . . . to answer such accusations as might be made against him on the part of the U.S. and not depart without leave of said court . . .'" Rodney added that they "replied content to" and he "did not even read anything wrote by Mr. Harding." (Id., capitalization modernized but original punctuation and spelling retained. Poindexter's testimony confirms both accounts.) Neither Burr nor Harding apparently inspected Rodney's version. Poindexter stated Burr had already departed.[56]

After Burr failed to appear, Harding insisted his version was correct but Rodney disagreed, calling him a "quiblur." (Kline 2:1024.) Judge Bruin, who sat on the bench with Rodney and was a friend of Burr's, tried to help but ultimately decided that Rodney's version must guide the court. (Why is unclear.)[57] Rodney wrote in his diary that "Burr would not have departed if he had not been induced to believe he was clear . . . I was sure he would not purposefully commit his surities &c." (Id.) Why, then, insist on ruling against Burr?

Burr wrote Williams that he had decided "to withdraw for the present from public view" because of "the vindictive temper and unprincipled conduct of Judge Rodney" but "[I] nevertheless continue in the disposition, which has been uniformly manifested, of submitting to civil authority so long as I can be assured that it will be exercised toward me within the limits prescribed for other citizens." (AB to RW, [February 7?, 1807], Kline 2:1022.) Burr requested to be "informed of the cause or charge, if any, for which it is proposed to arrest me" and asked "further, you assurance that no attempt to send me out of the Territory shall be countenanced or permitted and that my person shall not be subjected to any military authority." (Id.)

---

56 See citation in following footnote. Poindexter also noted that "I do not think [Harding's account] was believed by one honest man in the Territory." Why ever not? (Poindexter's Testimony, Burr Trial, Annals of Congress, 10th Congress, 1st Sess., 1807-08 (October 7, 1807) 581-87.)a Poindexter understood that Burr's recognizance was "not reduced to writing until the departure of Colonel Burr from [Judge Rodney's] presence." (Id., 587.)

57 Unless declared a material witness, no man may be indefinitely bound to daily appear in court without an indictment or warrant against him. As HB put it in a separate event related to the expedition, he "could not suppose the government disposed to molest individuals not offending against any law and avowing a lawful object of their pursuits." (Fitch, *Breaking with Burr*, 204 [HB's Brief].) But according to Poindexter this "was in the usual form in which Judge Rodney took other recognizances; that the persons bound should attend from day to day, until discharged by the court. The recognizances of Blannerhassett and others, taken on the same occasion, were in the same form." (*Op. cit.,* footnote above.)

However, Governor Williams nonetheless issued a proclamation offering $2000 reward to any person "who will take the person of said Aaron Burr, and cause him to be delivered to me at this place or to the President of the United States." (Kline 2:1021, citing Miss. Archives, *3d Annual Report*, p. 73-74.)

It was not only Rodney's conduct that prompted Burr to withdraw. That was the last straw. He had learned of Jefferson's proclamation and Wilkinson's perfidy.[58] He knew that there were military men sent by JW to (unlawfully) arrest him in the area. (Kline 2:1018, citing Abernethy, 218-19, *see also* Poindexter's testimony, 585-87.) He told the Mississippi prosecutor, George Poindexter, that he feared assassination.[59] He knew of the arrival of John Graham, who had in late November carried a warning from Jefferson to Burr through Blennerhassett and who showed up in town on January 30. (Fitch, *Breaking with Burr*, 204-05 [HB's Brief]; *Editorial Note: Burr's Flight* [February 7?, 1807], *Kline* 2:1018.) Burr then heard that Gov. Williams intended to seize him "the moment he was discharged." (Kline 2:1020, citing *Blennerhassett Papers*, p. 205.) Although there is no evidence that Williams had reached such a decision, the day after Burr's discharge, Williams was visited by Judge Harry Toulmin, who determined to obtain further warrants against Burr and his associates. (*See* footnote 49 above.) Burr's anxieties were well warranted.

On the 12th, Burr again wrote Williams stating he had seen his proclamation: "It was unworthy of you to lend the sanction of your name to a falsehood." (AB to RW, February 12, 1807, Kline 2:1022.) Burr then explained, as noted above, that he was bound only "in case an indictment should be found against me, and not otherwise."

Williams then wrote Burr back, concluding that "without animadverting on the unusual style which you have permitted to yourself – I can only say that from the judicial proceeding in this Territory you cannot be considered in any other light than as a fugitive from the laws of your country." Williams continued:

[W]ith these [laws] you are too well acquainted not to know

---

[58]   According to Poindexter, Burr told him: ""As to any projects or plans which may have been formed between General Wilkinson and myself heretofore, they are now completely frustrated by the perfidious conduct of Wilkinson and the world must pronounce him a perfidious villain," adding: "If I am sacrificed, my portfolio will prove him to be a villain." (Id. 581-83)

[59]   *See* Statement of George Poindexter, quoted at length in Kline 2:1015, citing Poindexter's testimony at Burr's trial, *American State Papers: Misc.* 1:568. Burr was deterred from meeting with Governor Mead "by a belief that he would be assassinated." (Also in Annals of Congress, *op. cit.* previous footnotes.)

that it belongs to a department different from mine to determine as to the nature of your offense, and to decide as to the manner in which you are to be treated – Hence you must see it would be improper as it would be undignified in me to enter into any stipulations as to your surrender."

(RW to AB, February 13, 1807, Kline 2:1024.) Burr had been before 4 grand jury inquests and released, not charged with any offense. Indeed, the 4th grand jury had now not only released him but had censured the government for harassing him. How could he be a fugitive from justice? Instead of chastising Burr about his "unusual style" and assuming that Burr had committed an offense, Williams ought to have checked his facts and been more concerned with protecting the rights of a law-abiding citizen.

Williams took a superior tone that was hardly reassuring when he informed Burr that he "never use[d] the military, except in aid of the civil authority" and Burr could "be assured [the law] shall be exercised towards you within the limits prescribed for other citizens similarly situated." (Id.) How *was* he situated? The lawlessness to which Burr has already been subjected made this reassurance empty, at best.

Burr had done nothing wrong but now his disappearance – which he had done out of fear of being seized by Wilkinson's men and assassinated, feeling as he did that Judge Rodney had betrayed him too – had further alarmed and prejudiced officials. All the documents were forwarded to Jefferson, who ignored Burr's reassurances that he had no "designs unfriendly to the peace and welfare," that his "pursuits are not only justifiable but laudable, tending to the happiness and benefit of my countrymen and such as every good citizen and virtuous man ought to promote," and inviting his "fellow citizens to visit me at this place and to receive from me in person such further explanations as may be necessary." (AB to Cowles Mead, January 12, 1807, Kline 2:1008.) Instead, TJ wilfully interpreted as proof of treason Burr's "letter to the acting governor of Misipi, on holding up the prospect of civil war [and] his capitulation regularly signed with the aids of the governor, as between two independent & hostile commanders." (TJ to William B. Giles, April 20, 1807.) The letter to then acting governor Cowles Mead, contained no prospect of civil war except that which might occur if the *governor* "arm[ed] citizen against citizen." (AB to Cowles Mead, January 12, 1807, Kline 2:1009.)

Burr had written Mead: "It is hoped sir that you'll not suffer yourself to be made an instrument of arming citizen against citizen and of involving the country in the horrors of civil war, without some better foundation than the suggestions of rumor or the vile fabrications of a man notoriously the pensioner of a foreign government." Burr asked that the acting governor read his letter to the militia when assembled and hoped "from your candor that you will confirm the sincerity of the declaration by remarks derived from your personal knowledge of me, and to be inferred from the whole tenor of my conduct, as well in public as in private life." (Id.) Mead did forward Burr's letter to the militia commander but when he wrote to Dearborn, he told him that Burr's protestations would have "no influence on my conduct." (Kline 2:1010, citing to Miss. Archives, *3d Annual Report*, p. 51-52.)

Notwithstanding Burr's repeated requests to civil authorities for protection and a promise that he would not be put in the hands of the military, and notwithstanding repeated assurances by civil authorities that they would protect him, once Burr "fled" and was captured, as his note to Biddle shows, he was transported to Richmond by a military escort.

George Poindexter noted at Burr's trial that "[m]any of the young men arrested at Natchez declared that if Burr's designs were against the Government of the United States, they would be the first men to turn against him, and cut his throat. There are a number of them now remaining at the Territory; for he has supplied us with schoolmasters, singingmasters, dancingmasters, and doctors in abundance." (Poindexter's Testimony, *op. cit.*)

~

Jefferson's Mirror

Part One: Misdemeanor

Where did Jefferson get the misdemeanor charge from?

[Jefferson] thought a little spontaneous irruption of the inhabitants of Kentucky into New Orleans could advance matters.
Edmund Charles Genet, post 1793[60]

Jefferson "did not care what insurrections should be excited in Louisiana."
Jefferson, Memorandum, July 5, 1793[61]

[I]f they see their interest in separation, why should we take side with our Atlantic rather than our Mississippi descendants? It is the elder and the younger son differing.
Jefferson (in Paris) to Madison, January 30, 1787[62]

The so-called Burr Conspiracy was a mirror image of Jefferson's own intentions and pursuits, projected onto Burr. It was a fiction created by Thomas Jefferson to divert Americans, both contemporary and posthumous, from the real conspiracy: Jefferson's conspiracy. For TJ, the Burr expedition was a convenient red herring, an opportunity Jefferson seized and shaped to divert people's attention away from what he was doing. One goal was to divert; the other was to destroy Burr.

As is often the case with projections, the charges against Burr mirrored what Jefferson was doing himself. In other words, Jefferson projected onto Burr his own intentions and actions. Here I refer to the psychological mechanism, which the dictionary refers to as "the unconscious transfer of

---

[60] Kennedy, 127 (citing to Stanely Elkins & Eric McKitrick, *The Age of Federalism: The Early American Republic, 1788-1800* (Oxford University Press, 1993), 350.)
[61] Kennedy, 128 (citing to James Roger Sharp, *American Politics in the Early Republic* (Yale University Press, 1993), 107)
[62] Kennedy, 151-52 (citing to TJ's "*Writings,*" 882 – unclear which edition he means).

one's own desires or emotions to another person." (*New Oxford American Dictionary.*) Jefferson determined to throw blame on Burr but this does not mean he was conscious that he was projecting his own drives. Whether conscious or unconscious, the Burr Conspiracy was not a thing committed by Burr but was an invention of Jefferson's. In this chapter, I show the origins of Jefferson's misdemeanor charge.

The misdemeanor charge was a violation of the Neutrality Act of 1794, which provided, in pertinent part, that:

> If any person shall ... set on foot ... any military expedition or enterprize [sic], to be carried on from thence against the territories or dominions of any foreign prince or state with whom the United States are at peace, every person so offending shall, upon conviction, be adjudged guilty of a high misdemeanor, and shall suffer fine and imprisonment ... so as that such fine shall not exceed three thousand dollars nor the term of imprisonment be more than three years.

(Robertson, *Trial of AB*, 1:4.)

The first charge against Burr was:

> "**1st,** For a **high misdemeanor**, in setting on foot, within the United States, a military expedition against the dominions of the king of Spain, a foreign prince, with whom the United States, at the time of the offence [sic], were, and still are, at peace."

(Robertson, *Trial of AB*, 1:3-4).

Roger G. Kennedy writes: "Washington wished to stop the French-sponsored attacks upon British shipping that had been based in American ports and also to prevent French-sponsored filibustering against Spanish Florida and Louisiana." (Kennedy, 112.) "[T]hose provisions of Washington's law applicable to Burr in 1806 applied just as well to Hamilton in 1798 and to a series of filibusters sponsored by Jefferson and his successor, James Madison, from 1786 through 1812. Jefferson was willing to encourage filibusters when they were led by men he chose or approved." (Id.)

At the very time when Jefferson brought this charge against Burr, he was funding unlawful expeditions into the Spanish territories. Jefferson didn't dare to send what army he had to make war on Spain, although he repeatedly told the public about Spanish depredations and violations, and repeatedly threatened war.

Burr and his colleagues, like many Americans, were anticipating war with Spain. If war broke out, Burr would sign up recruits with the blank muster forms the Secretary of War had provided him, and would lead men to defend American territories and interests. Burr's maps (which were those from Wilkinson) show the land and sea routes into Mexico.

It is also clear that Jefferson knew exactly what Burr was planning. Not only did the Administration look on his plans with complacency, as Burr put it, and Dearborn encouraged him in Jefferson's name, but as we have seen, Jefferson primed and prepped Burr himself by removing all avenues in the East and pushing him westward. And we have HB's Brief showing the Administration's secret approbation of their "contingent plans against Spain." It is hard not to conclude that in at least one of Burr's last meetings with Jefferson, he discussed his project. This was, in fact, perhaps TJ's biggest secret, as we shall see later.

Wilkinson had been appointed civilian governor of Upper Louisiana.[63] This gave Wilkinson both military and civilian powers, for he was also commander of the military forces in both Upper and Lower Louisiana (then called the Orleans Territory). As the commander of the forces that were along the border, Wilkinson could provoke war if he wished to. If war was declared, he was to be prepared for it and he had pulled Burr into his dream of using war with Spain as the pretext for marching into Mexico for gold and glory. At least that was Wilkinson's purpose.

Burr was following the lead of others before him, including Jefferson's. Long before Jefferson accused Burr of separatist activities and unauthorized warfare against a foreign nation, Jefferson had been involved in exactly the same things, although Jefferson never had the courage to engage himself directly.

---

[63] This was one of the few Burr recommendations that TJ effected. The irony could not have been lost on Burr when Wilkinson turned against him.

When Jefferson was Governor of Virginia, he had sent George Rogers Clark, the brother of William Clark of the Lewis & Clark Expedition, northward against the instructions of President Washington, "to worry the British at Detroit and to cut off any movement westward of the forces of Pennsylvania, rather than to cooperate in joint maneuvers with Pennsylvanian commanders appointed by Washington." (Kennedy, 122-23.) His explanation to Washington was that Clark and the Pennsylvanian commander "cannot act together," but he "neglected to inform Washington that he had ordered Clark *not* to 'act together' with [the PA commander] or that he *had* ordered him to give assurances to the slaveholders of St. Louis, Cahokia, Kaskaskia, and Vincennes that they need not worry about their human property if Virginia were the occupying power." (Id.)[64]

After the war, Jefferson asked Clark "to set forth up the Missouri Valley, on a Virginian version of the exploration Jefferson [later] nationalized . . . as President." George declined what his brother William later undertook. (Id., 123.)

Then, in another set of events from which Burr borrowed and Jefferson projected onto Burr, George Rogers Clark, unhappy with the federal government's failures to protect his Kentucky home state or repay Clark's wartime expenses, finding "freshwater piracy against Spanish shipping" unfruitful, offered to work for the Spanish if they would commission him to defend Kentucky against the Indians. (Id., 123-24.) Rebuffed by Spain, Clark turned to France in the early 1790's to "take the whole of Louisiana" for them, if they would "be hearty and secret in the business." (Id., 124.)[65] He agreed to set up in Virginia's "trans-Appalachian territories an independent western state under French protection." (Id., 125.)

Having encouraged Clark to follow the path he made for him, Jefferson then later declared Burr was doing the same

---

[64] Kennedy quotes but does not cite to the original source of Jefferson's statement to Washington. He simply cites to a secondary work: Anthony Marc Lewis, "Jefferson and Virginia's Pioneers," *The Mississippi Valley Historical Review,* vol. 34, no. 4, p. 579 (March 1948).

[65] Again quoting Clark but not providing the primary source, Kennedy cites to James T. Flexner, *George Washington and the New Nation: 1783-1793* (Little, Brown, 1970), vol. 3, p. 290.

thing and called it a crime. The thing did not originate in Burr.

In another set of events, during the presidency of George Washington, when Jefferson was Secretary of State, the President had issued explicit instructions to his cabinet not to encourage filibusters or invasions of Spain of any other territories or nations with which the United States was at peace. But Jefferson directly disobeyed those instructions. He "failed to warn Washington of the French plots to which he had become privy and assisted [the Minister from France, Edmund-Charles] Genêt in dispatching their mutual friend the botanist André Michaux to the West." (Id., 125.) Along with Michaux went letters of introduction, Clark's French commission, and botanical instruments. Kennedy observes: "Research could be done along the way, so any qualms felt by the Secretary of State were, it seems, overwhelmed by the prospect of advancements in science," adding sardonically that "[i]t is one of Jefferson's virtues that he preferred to use as intelligence agents people who practiced good science as well." (Id., 407, n20.)

Genêt meantime outfitted his brig to attack New Orleans – another foreshadowing of the alleged Burr Conspiracy. It set sail against Washington's explicit instructions, assaulted British ships and returned into Delaware Bay. Washington ordered Genêt recalled but instead Genêt retired as minister to France, married New York Governor George Clinton's daughter, moved to Long Island, and became a potato farmer. (Id. 125-26.) As Kennedy writes: "The marvel is that before Thomas Jefferson turned to Wilkinson [in 1806] he managed to escape any opprobrium for his sponsorship of Clark" or his assistance to Genêt and Michaux. (Id., 126.)

Jefferson's connection to "French agents of sedition" and secessionist Kentuckians goes deeper, however, than mere sponsorship. Genêt recounted that Jefferson:

> gave me to understand that he thought a little spontaneous irruption of the inhabitants of Kentucky into New Orleans could advance matters; he put me in touch with several deputies [congressmen] of Kentucky, notably with Mr. Brown, who, convinced that his region would never flourish as long as the navigation of the

>   Mississippi were not free, adopted our plan with as
>   much enthusiasm as an American can manifest.

(Id., 127.)[66] Kennedy's conclusions are worth quoting at length:

>   Jefferson had take an oath of office to the United States
>   government led by a President who had made clear his
>   opposition to filibustering irruptions anywhere . . .
>   When Clark coupled separatism to filibustering against
>   Spain (Jefferson's charge against Burr in 1806),
>   Jefferson would only say that the risk of hangings in
>   Kentucky would diminish if Clark's men quietly packed
>   their weapons, moved stealthily down the Mississippi,
>   and assaulted New Orleans. If that filibuster were to get
>   underway, Jefferson indicated, he "did not care what
>   insurrections should be excited in Louisiana."

(Id., 128, quoting Jefferson's memorandum of July 5, 1793, from James Roger Sharp, *American Politics in the Early Republic* (Yale University Press, 1993), p. 107.) Kennedy continues:

>   Though in 1794 the Jeffersonians charged Hamilton
>   with an intention to organize a putsch against
>   democratic government, recycling that allegation
>   against Burr in 1806, neither of [those men] gave aid or
>   comfort to separatists, though the ambitions of both did,
>   in fact, include filibusters upon the Spanish
>   possessions. * * * [Jefferson and Madison's]
>   professions of dismay about Burr's threat to Spain are
>   unconvincing to those who recall their smug silence in
>   the face of the proclaimed purposes of Clark, Clarke,
>   Sevier, and Blount and Madison's support of Reuben
>   Kemper, John Joustoun McIntosh, George Mathews,
>   and Fulwar Skipwith once Burr was out of the way.

(Id., 128-29.)

In addition to sponsorship of filibusters, Kennedy reveals what he calls Jefferson's "system of sponsored colonization" in the Floridas and Texas, which he refers to as "amoebic imperialism":

---

[66]   Kennedy cites to Stanley Elkins & Eric McKitrick, *The Age of Federalism: The Early American Republic: 1788-1800* (Oxford University Press, 1993), p.350 for Genêt's quote.

[A]s Secretary of State he recommended, and as President set in motion, a system of sponsored colonization, by which the colonists accepted the invitation of the Spanish authorities, assembled critical mass, declared independence, and then united themselves to the sponsoring state [i.e., America].

(Id., 129.) Writes Kennedy, "This was the story of McIntosh's East Florida Republic, of Skipwith's West Florida Republic, of the Texas of the Austins and Houston, and of Frémont's California." (Id.) For Jefferson, Spain's invitation to "foreigners to go and settle in Florida . . . will be the means of delivering us peaceably, what may otherwise cost us a war." (Id., quoting TJ to Washington, from Rembert W. Patrick, *Florida Fiasco* (University of Georgia Press, 1954), p. 50.)

"Jefferson did not rebuke . . . Genêt, or Michaux" or any of the others he sponsored or supported, "but, in March 1794, Washington did." (Id., 130.) Washington issued a proclamation forbidding American citizens from "invading and plundering the territories of a nation at peace with the United States," which Congress passed into law as the Neutrality Act of 1794. (Id., citing to Sharp, cited above, p. 107.)

Thus, the Neutrality Act, which Jefferson charged Burr with violating, had ironically been enacted as a result of filibusters which Jefferson had himself encouraged and sponsored.

*

According to Milton Lomask, "nobody was much exercised about" the misdemeanor charges against Burr. "Many Virginians saw the interests of the West as identical with their own, and in that part of the country, efforts to smash the power of the hated Spanish, legal or otherwise, were regarded with complacency." (Lomask, 2:283.)

Again illustrating not just Jefferson's antipathy for Burr but a wish to interfere with the prosecution and with the judiciary's work, he wrote to Hay: "If [Burr] is convicted of the misdemeanor, the Judge must in decency give us a respite by some short confinement of him; but we must expect it to be very short." (TJ to George Hay, Sept. 4, 1807, Lipscomb, *Writings of TJ,* 11:360.)

The prosecutor ultimately withdrew the misdemeanor charge (Lomask, 2:287), and Jefferson did not pursue it further, until after the treason charge was dismissed. It is clear that his wish was not merely to imprison Burr but to make him, as he later told Hay, "become absolutely invisible."[67]

~

---

[67]   TJ to George Hay, February 16, 1808 (https://archive.org).

Jefferson's Mirror

Part Two: Treason & Other Hanging Offenses

Where did Jefferson get the treason charge from?

When in the Course of human events, it becomes necessary for one people to dissolve the political bands which have connected them with another, and to assume among the powers of the earth, the separate and equal station to which the Laws of Nature and of Nature's God entitle them, a decent respect to the opinions of mankind requires that they should declare the causes which impel them to the separation. **Declaration of Independence, Preamble, 1776**

No one pretended then that the perpetrator of crimes who could successfully resist the officers of justice, should be protected in the continuance of them by the privileges of his citizenship, and that baffling ordinary process, nothing extraordinary could be rightfully adopted to protect the citizens against him.
Thomas Jefferson to L.H. Girardin, March 12, 1815
Lipscomb, *Writings of TJ*, XIV, 271-78**.**

The second charge against Burr, that of **treason**, claimed a constitutional crime – the only crime specifically addressed in (and limited by) the Constitution, which states:

"Treason against the United States shall consist only in levying war against them, or in adhering to their enemies, giving them aid and comfort. No person shall be convicted of treason unless on the testimony of two witnesses to the same overt act, or on confession in open court." (*United States Constitution*, Sec. 3 [1].)

What was the evidence of treason? Burr was not accused of adhering to the enemies of the U.S., or of giving them aid or comfort. He was accused of "assembling an armed force, with a design to seize the city of New-Orleans, to revolutionize the territory attached to it, and to separate the western from the Atlantic states" – or as the prosecution later framed it: to levy war against the U.S.

Jefferson was waiting for Burr to commit "an overt act" so he could charge him with something. The alleged "warlike" assemblage on Blennerhassett Island was to be the overt act.

There had to be two witnesses to this overt act of levying war against the U.S. How do you prove that a group of men gathering on an island, preparing to go downstream through Indian territory are assembling for the purpose of levying war against the U.S.? Jefferson wrote:

> I do suppose the following overt acts will be proved 1. the enlistment of men, in a regular way. 2. the regular mounting of guard round Blannerhasset's island when they expected Govr. Tiffin's men to be on them, *modo guerrino arraiati*. 3. the rendezvous of Burr with his men at the mouth of Cumberland. 4. his letter to the acting governor of Misipi, on holding up the prospect of civil war. 5. his capitulation regularly signed with the aids–of the governor, as between two independant & hostile commanders.

(TJ to William B. Giles, April 20, 1807.) None of these, either alone or together, is or are proof or even evidence suggestive of treason. Even strung together, they do not provide a chain of circumstantial evidence that indicates an intent to levy war against the U.S. – or even to assemble an armed force to do so. Or to seize New Orleans. Or to "revolutionize" the territory or separate the states.

What is a warlike array (*modo guerrino arraiati*)? Men in the wilderness carried rifles.[68] If Burr enlisted men "in a regular way," what does that prove? He did so with Dearborn's permission and because he expected the U.S. to go to war with Spain. The men at HB's Island mounted guard when they expected to be invaded by a hostile and unlawful military force.[69] Their departure from there and rendezvous with Burr at the mouth of Cumberland was an effort to get on their way

---

[68] TJ, had he known of it, would have made much of Blennerhassett's revelation in his private journal that Burr "*hid* and sunk in the river" all their arms, but Burr understood by that point what was going to be charged against him and his followers. The presence of arms does not prove treason but TJ would have claimed it did. (Fitch, *Breaking with Burr,* 113.) (*See* Lomask 2:265-69 for summaries of trial testimony relating to arms, assemblage, and levying war.) (*See also* Abernethy, *Burr Conspiracy,* 210: Burr "suspend[ed] under water about 40 muskets with bayonets.")

[69] *See* Lomask 2:268, testimony of William Love: "the men were in a state of preparation to defend themselves because they expected people [the Wood County militia] to attack Blannerhassett and the island ... they did not mean to be killed, without some return of the shot ..."

southward. Burr's letter to Governor Mead claimed his views were "grossly misrepresented."[70] He never held up the prospect of civil war or "capitulated . . . as between two independent and hostile commanders." He refused to "surrender" to a military despot. These are simply no proofs.[71]

The Declaration of Independence cited one of the crimes of a tyrant as "He has affected to render the military independent of and superior to the civil power." Yet Jefferson supported Wilkinson's military despotism.

The concept of treason was not new to Jefferson, of course. Jefferson wrote the the Virginia treason statute of 1776, which mirrors closely the clause included 11 years later in the U.S. Constitution. It defined the crime as levying war against the commonwealth, adhering to its enemies and giving them aid and comfort, attested to by two voluntary witnesses to prove the "open deed." (Levy, *TJ and Civil Liberties,* 28, citing to *The Statutes at Large, Being a Collection of All the Laws of Virginia: 1619-1792* (William W. Hening, ed.) (Richmond, 1809-23, 13 vols.) IX, 168 (Oct. 1776 sess., ch. V.)

Levy points out that the act against crimes *less than* treason was "a loosely drawn interdict against freedom of political expression" (id., 28-29) and that while Governor of wartime Virginia, Jefferson ordered the imprisonment of all persons against whom "legal evidence cannot be obtained [despite] [s]uspicion that they have been guilty of offences of treason or Misprision of Treason, or . . . are disaffected to . . . the [U.S.]" and might aid the enemy. (Id., 30, quoting TJ to James Innes, May 2, 1781, Boyd, Julian P. et al., eds. *Papers of TJ* (Princeton, 1950--, 16 vols.), V, 593.) Imprisonment for those against whom there was no evidence but only a suspicion

---

[70] AB to Cowles Mead, January 12, 1807, Kline 2:1008-09. Mead, however, wrote Dearborn that Burr "hints at resistance to any attempt to coerce him and deprecates a civil war." (CM to HD, January 13, 1807, quoted in Kline 2:1009.)

[71] At trial, Burr said "Our president is a lawyer and a great one, too." (Robertson, *Trial of AB*, 1:78.) But if TJ believed his list contained proof of overt acts, he was either a poor lawyer, deluded, or lying. As Blennerhassett (a lawyer himself) observed at trial about TJ's mentor, William Wirt, who was co-counsel on Burr's prosecution: "Wirt spoke very much to engage the fancy of his hearers to day without affecting their understanding. For he cannot reason upon the facts before him, and can no more conduct law argument than I could raise a mountain." (Fitch, *Breaking with Burr*, 133.)

that they were disaffected or aided the enemy. This was, of course, during a time of war.

Jefferson further enforced a loyalty oath that punished persons who, according to Jefferson, were "traitor[s] in thought, but not in deed." (Id., citing Jefferson's *Notes on the State of Virginia* [Peden, *Query XVI*, p. 155].) Levy points out that both Jefferson and Washington agreed that those who refused to swear an oath of loyalty were "secret enemies." (Levy, id., citing to Harold M. Hyman, *To Try Men's Souls: Loyalty Tests in American History* (1959), 85.) (Levy notes that Hyman provided him with a true copy of an undated and unpublished manuscript fragment from the Jefferson papers, which included TJ's remark: "General Washington's work against Tories best. Uses oaths well." Levy, 191, n17.)

Levy continues that "Jefferson also supported a statute which legalized the . . . rudimentary precursor of modern internment camps for political suspects." (Id., 31.) "[F]earing that the executive had acted unconstitutionally," the assembly subsequently "passed a special act of immunity" framed by a committee of which, Levy notes, "Jefferson was a member, which 'indemnified' and 'exonerated' the government and . . . his council from any suits brought by or on behalf of any persons who had been evacuated and interned." (Id., 32, citing *The Statutes at Large, Being a Collection of All the Laws of Virginia: 1619-1792* (William W. Hening, ed.) (Richmond, 1809-23, 13 vols.) IX, 373-74 (Oct. 1777 sess., ch. VI).)

"Jefferson thus participated in retroactively constitutionalizing the executive act by which political suspects and nonjurors" – those who had not taken the loyalty oath – "were interned because they *might* commit a crime at some future time." (Levy, 32.)

Again, this was during wartime. But recall that Jefferson declared Burr's expedition a war and claimed that during time of war, the law is silent, and that he, as President, was therefore authorized to shut down the courts, suspend habeas corpus, arrest and detain suspects, and, of course, declare the principal guilty before trial.

Levy concludes that in the statutes Jefferson participated in enacting, "the most striking departure from standards of due process of law was undoubtedly the bill of attainder and outlawry" which Jefferson drafted against a certain Josiah Philips and "unnamed members of his gang of robbers." (Id., 33.) Bills of Attainder had been outlawed by the Magna Carta in 1215, which provided that "No freeman shall be taken or imprisoned or disseised, or outlawed, or exiled, or anyways destroyed . . . unless by the lawful judgment of his peers, or by the law of the land." ((Id., 33-34, quoting Magna Carta, chp. 39.) Levy remarks: "One could still be declared outside the protection of the law and be treated as a wild beast whom any man might slay with impunity; but an elaborate common-law procedure, involving the courts and county coroners, insured some standard of fairness in the declaration of outlawry." (Id., 34.)

Jefferson wrote the bill of attainder against Philips "for having levied war against the commonwealth, committed murder, burned houses, and wasted farms" (Levy, 35), alleging that "the usual forms and procedures of the courts of law" would leave the people exposed to further crimes, and provided that if Philips did not surrender he "shall stand and be convicted and attainted of high treason, and shall suffer the pains of death" etc. (Id., citing *Statutes of VA* (Hening), IX, 463-64 (May 1778).) So, if he did not surrender, he was deemed guilty, and of course if he did surrender, he would be tried and probably convicted anyway, since they had already declared him guilty. Very similar to Jefferson's anticipatory declaration of Burr's guilt before he was charged with anything, before (as Jefferson himself told others) he had even committed any overt illegal act of any kind.

Levy notes that "the most sinister aspect of the bill was its declaration of an open hunting season on the unnamed men [Philips' cohorts] whose guilt for treason and murder was legislatively assumed." (Id.) Again reminiscent of Jefferson's orders to hunt Burr down and kill him on the basis of Jefferson's assumption of his guilt.

Levy elaborates that the Philips gang members were later caught and tried, not for high treason "not even [for] murder or arson" but only for robbery, which in any event was still a capital offense.[72] Levy speculates that the fact "[t]hat only a charge of robbery was pressed suggested that the evidence of treason and murder would not stand up in court, making the legislature's assumption of his guilt rather arbitrary, as well as grossly violative of" his rights under the Virginia Declaration of Rights, adopted only two years before. (Id., 36.)

Edmund Randolph, who had been the prosecutor in the Philips case and later became one of Burr's defense attorneys, told the Virginia Convention to ratify the U.S. Constitution in 1788 that ". . . [Philips] was attainted very speedily and precipitately, without any proof better than vague reports" and "[w]ithout being confronted with his accusers and witnesses, without the privilege of calling for evidence in his behalf, he was sentenced to death, and was afterwards actually executed." (Id., 37, citing to Jonathan Elliot, ed., *The Debates in the Several State Conventions on the Adoption of the Federal Constitution* (Philadelphia, 1941, 5 vols.) III, 66-67.) Randolph declared that this was "an example so horrid that if I conceived my country would passively permit a repetition of it . . . I would seek means of expatriating myself from it." (Id.)

But Patrick Henry, whom at another time Madison and Jefferson had devoutly wished dead (TJ to Madison, December 8, 1784, in Burstein & Isenberg, 112), then rose to speak words that were almost identical to those Jefferson himself later used to declare Burr outside the law. Philips was no Socrates, said Henry:

> He was a fugitive murderer and an outlaw . . . Those who declare war against the human race may be struck out of existence as soon as they are apprehended. He was not executed according to those beautiful legal ceremonies which are pointed out by the laws in criminal cases. The enormity of his crimes did not entitle him to it.

(Id., 38, citing to Elliot, *Debates*, III, 140.) Interestingly, John Marshall, a Federalist, who later sat as Burr's judge at his

---

[72] The bill of attainder and outlawry is in Hening, *Statutes*, IX, 463-63 (May 1778 sess.) and copies of the indictment, trial minutes, sentence, and notice of the execution are in William Wirt, *Sketches of the Life and Character of Patrick Henry* (NY, 1832, 2 vols.) vol. II, app. Note C., pp. 17-19.

treason trial and whom Jefferson, after the trial, wanted to impeach for failing to obtain Burr's conviction, responded to Henry's philippic with a rousing libertarian speech:

> Can we pretend to the enjoyment of political freedom or security, when we are told that a man has been, by an act of Assembly, struck out of existence without a trial by jury, without examination, without being confronted with his accusers and witnesses, without the benefits of the law of the land? Where is our safety, when we are told that this act was justifiable because the person was not a Socrates?

(Id., citing to Elliot, *Debates*, III, 223.)

Levy remarks that 37 years later, Jefferson still upheld his opinion of the rectitude of the Philips attainder. (Levy, 38, citing TJ to L.H. Girardin, March 12, 1815 in Lipscomb, XIV, 271-78.) This was where he recorded that "[n]o one doubted that society had the right to erase from the roll of its members any one who rendered his own existence inconsistent with theirs, and to remove him from among them by exile, or even by death if necessary."

That is just what Jefferson told James Brown about Burr in 1808:

> I did wish to see these people [Burr and his followers] get what they deserved; and under the maxim of the law itself, that *inter arma silent leges*, that in an encampment expecting daily attack from a powerful enemy [i.e. Burr's 60-100 men], self-preservation is paramount to all law, I expected that instead of invoking the forms of law to cover traitors, all good citizens would have concurred in securing them. Should we have ever gained our Revolution, if we had bound our hands by manacles of the law, not only in the beginning, but in any part of the revolutionary conflict? There are extreme cases where the laws become inadequate even in their own preservation, and where the universal resource is a dictator, or martial law.

(TJ to James Brown, October 27, 1808, Founders Online.) But had the court or jury decided that Burr was a traitor? No, of course not.

It is moreover absurd to posit that Americans were not bound by the manacles of the law when the basis of the Revolutionary War was that King George had committed a "long train of abuses and usurpations."

Jefferson's philosophical approach in the Declaration of Independence "took the whole controversy out of the realm of petty and selfish squabbling by setting it on a high background of philosophy." (Malone, *Jefferson the Virginian,* 224.) This is another way of saying that for Jefferson, it was all abstract – but then that is also what was powerful about the Declaration: that it stood above the fray and commented.

Malone points out that Jefferson's "personification of grievances [in the Declaration] was unwarranted on strict historical grounds," which "historians of a later generation, who have been in a position to study . . . calmly, assign . . . to official stupidity or to helplessness in the face of the larger imperial problem, rather than to a deliberate design to reduce the colonies 'under absolute despotism.'" (Id., 224-25.) But Jefferson "carried this oversimplification of grievances even further in another paper," writes Malone, "which was written five years later and has remained obscure." (Id., 225.) Jefferson described the causes of the Revolution to an Indian chief:

> . . . You find us, brother, engaged in war with a powerful nation. Our forefathers were Englishmen, inhabitants of a little island beyond the great water, and, being distressed for land, they came and settled here. As long as we were young and weak, the English whom we had left behind, made us carry all our wealth to their country, to enrich them; and, not satisfied with this, they at length began to say we were their slaves, and should do whatever they ordered us. We were now grown up and felt ourselves strong; we knew we were free as they were, that we came here of our own accord and not at their biddance, and were determined to be free as long as we should exist. For this reason, they made war on us.

(Malone, 225, quoting from TJ's address to John Baptist de Coigne, June 1781.) And as Malone summarizes Jefferson's view: "To his mind the fundamental issue was simple: British policy constituted a perilous threat to liberties that were dearer to him than life itself." (Id., 226.) Malone notes that to Jefferson, King George "was not merely a symbol but a powerful personal obstacle to the sort of self-government he and his fellows were claiming as a nature human right." (Id.) In other words, it was not simply "liberty" that mattered, but freedom from tyranny.

For Americans, this liberation could mean death – and thus the famous phrase attributed to Patrick Henry: "Give me liberty or give me death!" This was the origin of the idea that one could be put to death simply for maintaining one's independence. It wasn't just an idea, of course. It was the truth.

In archetypal terms, the mental juxtaposition of liberty, independence, and death had to have existed even prior to the Declaration of Independence, both in Jefferson's mind and in the minds of the others declaring their independence. The idea did not appear magically out of nothing. It came, as Jefferson explained to Coigne, as a consequence of *growing up and feeling oneself strong*, and feeling that one's strength was being sapped by those who wished to enslave us and enrich themselves off the wealth we generated.

So, it was the moment of a man's attainment to his full powers and strength that was the moment of greatest threat. This was the message embedded in the cause of the revolutionary war, as Jefferson saw it. The threat to the fatherland came from that attainment of the child-colonist coming into manhood and this was also the moment of greatest danger to that emerging man.

This is the second of Jefferson's mirrors. Burr – the man whom the Virginia Republicans had declined to nominate for VP in 1792 on account of his youth – had attained strength and power sufficient to challenge the older man – the one now in power. That Jefferson's father died just as the son was reaching manhood affirms that this template was in Jefferson's subconscious. The father died as the son attained manhood. Did Jefferson's manhood kill his father?

Jefferson could not let Burr, the son, reach that point of ability. He had to disempower him. It was not enough to merely remove him. In the Oedipal conflict, as in the

Revolutionary War, either the father or the son must die. Great Britain fought to retain its power and was willing to kill American rebels, who in turn risked their lives to stamp out British power forever. Burr had been one of those to risk his life. Perhaps he would do so again, now that Jefferson had become the man in power, the king.

Turning back to the misdemeanor charge, we find that within that drama may be found another dance of treason, for Jefferson, as Virginia's Governor and as Washington's Secretary of State, repeatedly undermined and betrayed the President and the laws. Both Jefferson and Hamilton – if anyone had cared to look – could have been found guilty of treason in those years. (Hamilton plotting to undermine Washington with British agent Major Beckwith.) Perhaps having stepped outside the borders of patriotism and integrity himself, Jefferson imagined it in Burr or wanted to paint onto his VP the image he feared would be painted on him otherwise.

In any event, we know these templates all existed within Jefferson himself. Burr became Jefferson's looking glass.

~

Jefferson could not back down.

"Exhilarated by the experience of putting an idea in motion and backing it by force, [Jefferson] could not back down or admit that he had been wrong. What counted most was the attainment of his objective, the validity of his conviction, not its impact on those who, failing to appreciate his idealism or personal stake, hollered long and loud. He reacted not by relieving their hollering but by a stretch of the rack that increased their protests and his own power to override them."
Leonard Levy, "Civil Liberties," in *Thomas Jefferson: A Reference Biography* (Merrill D. Petersen, ed.) (Charles Scribner's Sons, 1986), 343.

"The unfamiliar Jefferson at one time or another supported loyalty oaths; countenanced internment camps for political suspects; drafted a bill of attainder; urged prosecutions for seditious libel; trampled on the Fourth Amendment's protection against unreasonable searches and seizures; condoned military despotism; used the army to enforce laws in time of peace; censored reading; chose professors for their political opinions; and endorsed the doctrine that the means, however odious, were justified by the ends." (Id., 334.)

Of Hatred & Murder

[There was] a grievous weakness in [Jefferson's] character – that his great mind could harbor hatreds malignant enough to poison his love for justice. For did he not instruct Hay to pardon all the accused provided the principal might be convicted?
McCaleb, 250.

[Burr] said, that an order had been issued to kill him, as he was descending the Mississippi, and seize his property. And yet, they could only have killed his person, if he had been formally condemned for treason.
Aaron Burr at trial, May 25, 1807
Robertson 1:77-78.

I have seen the order of the navy in print and one of the officers of the navy had assured me that this transcript was correct. The instructions in this order were to destroy my person and my property in descending the Mississippi.
Aaron Burr at trial, June 9, 1807
Robertson, *Trial of AB*, 1:113-14

[The President] has let slip the dogs of war, the hell-hounds of persecution, to hunt down my friend.
Luther Martin (Burr's defense counsel), June 10, 1807
Robertson, 1:128

I affirm, with the power of proof to support me, that such orders never were given; though if it be true that Aaron Burr had placed himself in a state of war with his country, was aiming a blow at the vitals of our gov't and liberty, and that blow could be averted no other way, I hold that his destruction would have been a virtue, a great and glorious virtue.
William Wirt, for the prosecution, June 10, 1807
Robertson, 1:139

I did wish to see these people [Burr and his followers] get what they deserved; and under the maxim of the law itself, that inter arma silent leges, *that in an encampment expecting daily attack from a powerful enemy [i.e. Burr's 60 men], self-preservation is paramount to all law, I expected that instead of invoking the forms of law to cover traitors, all good citizens would have concurred in securing them.*
TJ to James Brown, October 27, 1808, Founders Online
(quoted in Levy, *"Civil Liberties,"* Peterson, 334)

I detailed the whole project of Mr. Burr to certain members of Congress. They believed Colonel Burr capable of anything, and agreed that the fellow ought to be hanged . . .
Deposition of William Eaton, January 26, 1807
(quoted in Henry Adams, *TJ Administrations,* 771)

PART TWO:

JEFFERSON –

FROM MISTRUST

TO MALICE

I had never seen Colo. B till he came as a member of Senate. His conduct very soon inspired me with distrust. I habitually cautioned Mr. Madison against trusting him too much.
Thomas Jefferson, Memorandum, January 26, [1804]
Kline 2:822

Against Burr personally I never had one hostile sentiment. I never indeed thought him an honest frank dealing man, but considered him as a crooked gun or other perverted machine whose aim or stroke you could never be sure of. Still, while he possessed the confidence of the nation, I thought it my duty to respect in him their confidence, & to treat him as if he deserved it.
Thomas Jefferson to William Branch Giles,
April 20, 1807
National Archives

Character & Circumstance

As a conspirator – or as a politician – [Burr] has a fault – he is too cunning – too secret – even in business where frankness & openness would not injure him. The reputation of being a cunning *man, is enough to blast any man's popularity – It at once renders him an object of suspicion. Burr's lawful business always appears enveloped in mystery. This trait in his character is strong & marks all his conduct.*
William Plumer, December 24, 1806,
Memorandum of Senate Proceeding, 540.

Jefferson cannot be measured except sympathetically and uncritically.
Julian P. Boyd to Leonard W. Levy, circa 1963
(paraphrased in Levy, *Jefferson & Civil Liberties*, xii)

It matters what your underlying premises are. Even if Burr was secretive (even if Plumer was right that Burr's behavior made others suspicious), that does not mean he was cunning. Or that he was a conspirator. And the belief that the only way to assess TJ is sympathetically and uncritically, while Burr is crucified, is grossly unfair to Burr and in my view completely undermines any assessments made by Boyd. Similarly, Malone's view that the very concept of Levy's book was objectionable – that, in other words, looking at TJ's civil liberties record is itself unacceptable – undermines the credibility of Malone's conclusions. Such erroneous premises must be avoided. Here, I propose another foundation.

The watershed event in the story of Thomas Jefferson and Aaron Burr is the prosecution brought against Burr by President Jefferson. All things in the lives of both men may be counted forwards and backwards from that event, for the trial was the end of Burr's public life and aspirations, and it was the first and last time Jefferson publicly showed the deepest layer of his character – the aspect of Jefferson that has most mystified scholars and the one that holds the key to understanding him.

Jefferson's dislike of Burr has often been identified as having arisen from Burr's betrayal during the 1800-01 electoral tie, although, as Jefferson himself recorded in his memoirs, it began a decade earlier. Jefferson claimed that he "had never seen Colo. B. till he came as a member of Senate [1791]" and his conduct as U.S. Senator "very soon inspired me with distrust," and that he had "habitually cautioned Mr. Madison against trusting him too much," adding that Burr "was always at market." (*Thomas Jefferson: Memorandum of a Conversation with Burr,* January 26, [1804], Kline 2:822.) Whether Jefferson formed his distrust very soon after Burr entered Congress in late 1791 or four months before, as Federalist Robert Troup claimed, or even earlier, it was long before either the 1801 election or the 1806 Burr expedition.[73]

Long before the election, long before Burr's expedition, Jefferson was, by his own admission, so biased against Burr that his opinions about him could not be trusted, so that by the time of Burr's apparent vacillations about whether or not he would resign if elected President, Jefferson had already determined to construe Burr's conduct in the worst light.

Scholars have failed to notice that Jefferson's remark is what is called an "admission against interest." If Jefferson didn't like Burr from the start, for whatever reasons, all his subsequent words and actions towards or in relation to Burr were colored by his prejudice. Not Burr's words or actions, but *Jefferson's* cannot be trusted.

Jefferson's admission also provides the foundation for the likelihood that his dislike evolved into malice, which is an element of premeditation ("malice aforethought").

Burr's own peculiarities surely contributed to Jefferson's dislike. His secrecy, his need to be mysterious and different, to ignore social or political opinion and do what his judgment told him was right (not really a fault, though potentially unwise socially and politically), his need for independence (not so unusual in that era) – these were provocative to many, especially Jefferson.

But these alone do not explain Jefferson's malice. For 10 years it seems that Jefferson quietly waited for a chance to remove Burr, and from 1801 onward consciously pressed Burr

---

[73] On June 15th, 1791, Robert Troup reported to Hamilton that there was "every appearance of a passionate courtship between the Chancellor [Livingston], Burr, Jefferson & Madison when the two latter were in town." (RT to AH, 06-15-1791, quoted in Lomask 1:151.) . It is also possible they first met the year before when Jefferson was in New York (TJ arrived in NYC 3-24-1790, Bowers, *Jefferson and Hamilton,* 64.)

towards his own destruction. By his admission, he had "legal malice" towards Burr from the start. Not that Jefferson consciously *felt* malice. In the legal context, malice means ill will.

I distinguish between distrust and malice but the dividing line between them is not a bright line. In Jefferson, the two were much closer together than in most people. If he distrusted you, you were disenfranchised, excluded, privately defamed and maligned. It was not hard to earn his distrust.

Jefferson certainly felt that his ire towards Burr was justified. So, for years he contemplated how he could rid the world of Burr, and over the course of the five years leading up to the co-called Burr Conspiracy, Jefferson gradually took everything away from Burr, pushing him into the hands of his enemies and forcing him into an ever narrowing set of choices until finally Jefferson had him right where he wanted him and sprang his trap, blaming it all on Burr. To use another legal term, it was entrapment. As smart as Burr was, he tended to be trusting of confederates. He never anticipated Jefferson's trap.

Beyond simply stacking the cards against Burr, Jefferson not only prejudged (and misjudged) Burr himself but actively sought to influence others to adopt his prejudicial views against Burr. He specifically told Madison (who had received kindnesses from Burr) not to trust him. Once he had announced Burr's guilt, he continued to frame Burr's actions in prejudicial ways to anyone he spoke or wrote to.[74]

This caused irreparable damage to Burr and prevented him from doing the good he intended with his expedition (or with anything else on a public scale). Jefferson further prevented others from fairly assessing Burr on his own merits, creating a climate of prejudice in which Burr had to navigate. He planted the negative idea of Burr in the minds of the public so that everything Burr did thereafter was viewed through that dark lens.

There were, of course, other causes for Burr's diminishing popularity. Alexander Hamilton was one, but it is notable that the duel with Hamilton occurred at the end of

---

[74] One example is Plumer 543-44, 561-63 ("The President assured me he had no doubt of Burr's traitorous designs...")

Burr's term as VP, after four years of laboring under Jefferson's repudiation and plotting.

Of course, the reasons for Jefferson's alleged mistrust (if it really existed)[75] are important. He provides no examples of Burr's Senate "conduct" that "inspired" his mistrust other than that when any military post opened, Burr sought a command.

Although Jefferson later remarked that he had nothing to fear from Burr, his need to make that remark suggests otherwise. Jefferson kept slinging arrows at Burr. In fact, we know that Jefferson had many reasons to fear, few of which had to do directly with Burr. Those reasons began with his rebellion against King George and did not end with his relations with his slave, Sally Hemings. Indeed, nearly all of *Jefferson's* actions discussed in this book should have given Jefferson good reason to fear.

Jefferson's efforts against Burr were intended to prevent people from listening to him. I suggest that this was a core underlying cause of Jefferson's actions. What Clark says about Wilkinson applies to Jefferson here: "Instead of defending his own character, he attacked that of his accusers, and flattered himself that the public attention was withdrawn from his infamy . . ." (Clark, *Proofs of the Corruption of JW*, 29.) Here, however, Jefferson attacked Burr pre-emptively, before Burr could do or say what he might do or say to destroy Jefferson.[76]

Plumer records that Jefferson told Senator Gilman the same thing he had recorded in his memoirs, that Burr had told him "last winter . . . that [Jefferson] would find [Burr] had it in his power to do Mr. Jefferson much injury." (Plumer, 575 - July 15, 1807 entry; *see* Kline 2:962.) But interestingly, the fear Jefferson showed of the destruction he imagined was in Burr's power foreshadowed the humiliating destruction of nearly all Jefferson's fondest and most sincerely and closely-held policies and the loss of his tremendous popularity within the party he had worked so hard to build, and in the public at large.

---

[75] Jefferson told William B. Giles that he " never had one hostile sentiment." (TJ to WBG, April 20, 1807, National Archives.)

[76] Levy writes "Jefferson lived in a time of danger . . . At such a time, Jefferson, the idealist come to power, did unto his enemies before they did unto him." (Levy, viii.)

In his persecution of Burr, Jefferson gave the world a glimpse of his own deeper nature. Even his friends were perplexed at Jefferson's behavior and attributed the apparent change in his character to the suspected evil deeds of Burr. But to Jefferson, Burr was a witness that had to be eliminated, a man who stole precious light away from him, and whose deeds showed his own deeds as empty. Burr put into practice much that Jefferson only talked about.

Burr got the dark side of Jefferson projected onto him in part because Burr was looking for it. Burr saw into people. Burr was able to see both the good and bad parts of Jefferson and still admire and love him. (Madison was able to do this with Jefferson as well but he re-channeled the unworthy parts into worthy pursuits. He was also wise enough to coddle and reassure Jefferson that he would do nothing to harm him. Burr, on the other hand, expected Jefferson to man up.)

TJ's projected dark image did not emanate from Burr. Others mistook Burr's ability to accept another's dark side as being his own. Where the natural thing, according to others, would have been for Burr to respond with shock and alarm at what he claimed he saw in Jefferson, to do what others did who encountered this part of Jefferson: scream out, cry foul, point fingers, up and leave -- Burr's stillness, his apparent complacency and acceptance suggested he was the one covering something up. That is, Burr's complacent response suggested to others that he accepted the alarming specter because *he* had caused it, endorsed it, or possessed it himself.

Burr saw Jefferson's authentic self, the wellspring of both the remarkable man and the monster. But because Burr did not feel hatred, he did not sense the depths of Jefferson's hatred for him or anticipate the consequences.

Differences in Ideals

There were a number of ways in which Burr and Jefferson's political and practical ideas and ideals differed. As a military man, Burr did not fear the establishment of a standing army under a strong executive or its use to protect American borders. Jefferson was against using the military, at least until he let JW use it against Burr. He was also theoretically against a strong executive and he deeply feared the violence of war.

Jefferson preferred to use economic sanctions than go to war. Burr found Jefferson's economic sanctions weak, ineffective and destructive to internal commerce, a view shared by many northerners that events bore out. Jefferson saw and dealt with the great foreign powers (England, Spain, and France) quite differently than Burr did or would have. If Burr had become president, he would most likely have immediately strengthened military and naval forces. His later preparations to invade Mexico in case of war show something of his military strategic thinking, where he planned to use both naval and ground forces in concert. His response to Native American aggression shows his efforts to find common ground and establish peace, but also a willingness to increase American military presence to protect western settlers. Jefferson had no such military expertise to draw from. He felt himself at the mercy of warmongers and violent men.

Burr's manner of dealing with miscreants, even powerful ones, was to publicly embarrass and humiliate them. It is what he did with Justice Chase (and with discourteous senators) during the impeachment trial in the Senate. It's what he did with Alexander Hamilton that caused AH to hate and fear Burr so. It's what he was doing with the Spanish and British ministers in 1805-06, though they didn't know it yet. He even used this tactic as a teenager with one of his Princeton professors, berating him for arriving late to a debating society meeting. This is how he would have dealt with the great foreign powers if he were the executive. Jefferson preferred conciliation, evasion, subterfuge. Burr's style was collaborative as long as others were. But if they abused power or bullied, he found a way to out-move them strategically, causing damage or even taking them out of the game. Most men simply could not win against him. He was a superb strategist. Jefferson's style was to evade, hide his intentions, move sideways, wait.

Jefferson felt strongly (at least until he was in office) that each state had the right to decide for itself what federal laws it would accept and what laws it would "nullify." (He was the instigator of the Republican campaign in 1799 to nullify the Alien and Sedition Acts via the KY and VA Resolutions, which were sent to every state legislature for consideration.) As an elected independent democrat in the New York Assembly, Burr attempted to find common ground between the Democrat/Republicans and Federalists on the adoption or rejection of these Resolutions by moving to add language that "the citizens of [each] state and their representatives … have a right either individually or collectively to express their opinions respecting any act of the Congress." (Burr's *Amendment to a Motion on the Virginia and Kentucky Resolutions*, NY Assembly [16 February 1799], Kline 1:393.) This was language that everyone could endorse. But as a lawyer and former Revolutionary officer, Burr would have understood that, strictly applied, Jefferson's nullification doctrine was highly risky and could tear the states asunder. (Sixty years later, in fact, it was the doctrinal basis for the secession of the South that began the Civil War.)

Jefferson desired America to be founded on agrarianism and was suspicious of land jobbers and speculators, mechanics, and city life. As a New Yorker, Burr had no such prejudices. He supported widening suffrage to include smaller land owners, and himself engaged in land speculation. TJ was a slaveowner; Burr worked to abolish slavery.   ~

Events: 1791-1801

There was "every appearance of a passionate courtship between the Chancellor [Livingston], Burr, Jefferson & Madison when the two latter were in town."
Robert Troup to Alexander Hamilton, June 15, 1791
Lomask 1:151.

Mr. Burr however appeared averse to be the Candidate. He seemed to think that no arrangement could be made which would be observed to the southward, alluding as I understood to the last election, in which he was certainly ill-used by Virginia & North Carolina.
James Nicholson to Albert Gallatin, May 7, 1800
Kline 1:433

First Meeting

Their first known meeting (or what we think was their first meeting) took place in June 1791 in New York City.

Robert Troup claimed they met but we know nothing about the meeting itself. What we do know is that Jefferson and Madison were on the last leg of their six-week-long botanical trip through New England. Although the two men genuinely wanted to visit the region and see the flora, it also seems to have been a political trip. The trip generated several crucial things: it cemented the friendship and political collaboration between the two men (Madison and Jefferson) and probably helped to create the practical beginnings of the Republican party.

The two men also apparently met with local political leaders in Albany and New York, if not elsewhere, and began to build a political base, suggesting ways to organize for their followers and cohorts. There is little doubt that they discussed such matters with Burr. (*See generally,* Bowers.)

In Jefferson and Madison's eyes, they were the originators of the movement and local leaders were the lieutenants. (See Bowers, *Jefferson and Hamilton,* Chapter VII, "Jefferson Mobilizes.") As leaders, TJ and JM were not the ones who got down in the trenches and campaigned directly. The local leaders and their cronies were to do that, which is exactly what Burr did.[77] In the Jefferson-Madison scheme, Burr, then, inhabited a lower rung. Although Madison was younger than Burr and had hardly contributed to the fighting during the Revolution, Madison had attended the Constitutional Convention and was instrumental in the passage of the Constitution. He was thus viewed as a national leader.

In the Spring of 1791, Burr had just been elected to the U.S. Senate and would be entering national politics in the next session, but at the time of his meeting with TJ and JM, Burr was just finishing what he thought was his last session as New York Attorney General, the state prosecutor, the duties for which were incredibly onerous and the last court term for which he declared "has been unusually laborious to me" (AB to Theodore Sedgwick, February 3, 1791, Kline 1:67.)[78]

---

[77] *See* Lomask 1:238-47.

[78] According to Milton Lomask, "When on 24 October 1791 the second Congress came to order, Burr was still attorney general of New York. He would remain so until the eighth of the following month." (1:153.) Nathaniel Hazard wrote to Alexander Hamilton that "[Governor] Clinton is staggered, he is afraid to turn

As attorney general, Burr was *ex officio* member of the NY Land Office Commission and was involved in the disposal of public lands and contracting of roads, bridges, and canals. His time with this office involved Burr in what some have viewed as shady dealings. Jefferson may have been aware of these events and the charges against the commissioners.

The NY Land Office Commission

Mary-Jo Kline, the editor of the only scholarly volume of Burr's public and political papers, includes an excellent, detailed, and thorough editorial note on the NY Land Office Commission and Burr's involvement in it. But like so many before her, in the guise of scholarly disinterestedness, Kline finds opportunities to denigrate Burr's activities where alternative, more favorable readings are possible and even probable. Kline's main complaint is that the commissioners "overstepped their authority." (*Editorial Note: The New York Land Office Commission* (28 March 1791); Kline 1:80.) And with respect to Burr: "Not only was [the meeting at which this overstepping occurred] favored by Burr's presence, but … it was also influenced by the interests of more than one of his kinsmen and personal friends." (Id. at 80.)

Yet Kline herself points out that the commission was given "broad powers" and, quoting from the legislation, notes that the commission "received a veritable carte blanche 'to sell and dispose of any of the waste and unappropriated lands in this State, in such parcels, on such terms, and in such manner as they shall judge most conducive to the interest of this State.'" (Id. at 78.) How could this broad mandate be overstepped?

Moreover, in other places, Kline notes that such mixing of personal and public interests was not at all uncommon. For example, "… in New York, as in neighboring states, it seems to have been commonplace to maintain a private legal practice while holding the office of attorney general …" (*Editorial Note: The New York Attorney Generalship* [14 November 1789], Kline 1:47.)

Finally, Kline comments: "That the commission's liberal interpretation of its mandate seems to have escaped

---

Burr out, and Burr won't resign … if he can avoid it." (Lomask 1: 152.)

contemporary criticism may be ascribed not so much to public indifference as to recognition that a public need had been met." This is as if to say that criticism was deserved but the commission "escaped" it because by chance their actions had met a public need. (Id. at 79.) But in the very first letter Kline includes following the editorial note, Burr's uncle, Timothy Edwards, asks Burr rhetorically "... where shall [the road] be laid out to the best advantage of the public?" (TE to AB, March 28, 1791, Kline 1:80.) The public need was met because the commission, the contractors, and Burr himself, had acted for the purpose of meeting that need.

Finally, Kline concedes that the "network of roads and bridges created in the region by the Land Office Commission in 1791 was indispensable to ensuring that the settlers of western New York contributed to their state's economy and not to that of its neighbors" yet nonetheless concludes that Burr's actions were improper. (Kline at 80.)

One might ask why Burr's activities which so greatly benefitted upstate New York, creating the crucial transportation networks needed to develop those regions, are delegitimized as corrupt because Burr sought the opinions and expertise of some of his upstate friends and kinsmen, and compensated them for their work, while Jefferson's spoils system of political appointees was acceptable.

The mixing of public and private interests, which today is more strictly prohibited (but nonetheless still frequently violated by public officers), does not automatically indicate legal or moral wrong. Where your job is to benefit people in a particular region, seeking the opinions, using the expertise, and compensating the work of those in the region whom you personally know and trust is a sensible and ethical approach.

But if Jefferson knew about the controversy and Burr's role in it, that probably gave Jefferson an excuse to mistrust him. Burr may have operated too visibly close to the ethical line for Jefferson and he had an extreme dislike of those involved in land jobbing.

In the Senate:
Denial of Access to Correspondence of Foreign Ministers
The first written record of Jefferson taking official

action with respect to Burr was a 1793 letter that Jefferson as George Washington's Secretary of State wrote Senator Burr denying him access to records of foreign ministers: "Th[omas] Jefferson presents his respectful compliments to Colo. Burr and is sorry to inform him it has been concluded to be improper to communicate the correspondence of existing ministers. [H]e hopes this will, with Colo. Burr, be his sufficient apology." (TJ to AB, 01-20-1793, Kline 1:145.) Jefferson's use of the passive voice was intended to imply that it was President George Washington – or the Cabinet, the royal We – who concluded to prohibit access to Burr. But the decision was well within the provenance of the Secretary of State. It closely resembles the letter Jefferson sent Burr about patronage appointments eight years later. (TJ to AB, November 18, 1801, *TJ Papers,* Library of Congress, quoted in Lomask 1:302.) (See "Moving Against Burr" chapter below.)

Perhaps in Washington and Jefferson's eyes, Burr appeared to be meddling in affairs above his station, doing what he ought not, but as a U.S. Senator, it was his right to view correspondence from foreign ministers and to view them contemporaneously. Congress needs to be informed about matters within its purview if it is to make appropriate decisions. Executive secrecy, then, keeping things from the eyes of congressmen, did not start with Nixon or Roosevelt.

The 1790's

Twice during that decade, in the 1792 and 1796 presidential campaigns, Burr was asked by Virginia Republicans to be the Democratic/Republican candidate for Vice President. Both times the southerners "trifled with" Burr's good name (Burr's words)[79], politically embarrassing and undermining him, by dropping their votes for him at the last minute, despite promises to support his candidacy. This public political betrayal was considered perfectly acceptable by them, by Jefferson, and by most others (and has in fact been blamed on Burr's character since; *see e.g.,* Adams, *TJ Admins*, 155)

---

[79]   AB to John Taylor of "Caroline," October 23, 1800, id. at 451 ("As to myself, after what happened at the last election (*et tu Brute!*) I was really averse to have my Name in question. Yet so it has happened – how, is not now material; but being so, it is most obvious that I should not choose to be trifled with – " (See "Conspiracy Overview" chapter, footnote 29, for other examples.)

though it was damaging to Burr's image and was a betrayal of a political friendship.

During those years, Burr was elected to the U.S. Senate (1791), he declined an offer for a position as puisne justice of the NY Supreme Court of Judicature (1792), twice ran for governor (1792 & 95), was nominated (by James Monroe) for the ambassador post to France (1794, Monroe was chosen instead), and finally was chosen to be Jefferson's running mate for the 1800 election, which meant Burr spent most of 1799 and 1800 campaigned statewide and then throughout New England, built a campaign organization in NYC, worked to "revolutionize the state" (Robert Troup's words)[80], and finally succeeded in having the Federalists voted out of the NY government, which assured success for the Republicans in the national election. What Jefferson later called the Revolution of 1800 was brought about to large degree by the "extraordinary exertions and successes" (*TJ: Memorandum,* January 26, 1804, Kline 2:822) of Aaron Burr in New York, from which Jefferson benefitted. Burr ultimately received neither benefit nor credit nor reward.

During those years, Jefferson served as Washington's Secretary of State opposite Hamilton as Secretary of Treasury (until both resigned), he ran for President against John Adams (1796) and came in second, thus acquiring the vice presidency under the original constitutional regime (amended in 1804 after the 1801 tie with Burr). Whatever had caused Jefferson's suspicions of Burr did not stop him from agreeing to run three times with Burr as his second.

Burr's Attempt to Make Peace and
Prevent the Decimation of Native Americans

Burr's activities in 1791-92 in relation to hostilities between western Indians and white settlers didn't directly relate to the development of Burr and Jefferson relationship (as far as is known) but is revealing about Burr's activities, intentions, and *modi operandi.* If Jefferson knew of the different aspects of Burr's involvement, he would very likely have disapproved of Burr's meddling. But once again, Burr's actions may also be

---

[80]   Robert Troup to Rufus King, May 6, 1799, quoted in Editorial Note: *The New York Elections of 1800* [May 3, 1800], Kline 1: 420.

viewed in a more favorable way that throws a different light on his character.

In May 1791, only a month before his first meeting in New York with Jefferson and Madison and five months before he entered the U.S. Senate, Burr planned to go with John Tayler (1742-1829) a New York politician and former Indian trader, to Fort Schuyler, apparently to meet with Joseph Brant (1742-1807), the half white Mohawk leader (distantly related to Burr through Brandt's marriage to the daughter of Burr's wife's sister's legator, George Croghan), possibly to suggest to Brandt a plan Burr had to bring peace between the hostile western Native Americans and the former colonialists (i.e., "Americans"), using Brandt as an intermediary. (AB to John Tayler, May 22, 1791; Kline 1:82.)

Burr's views on this subject are clarified in a letter he wrote ten months later to Secretary of State Jefferson offering his assistance in making peace with hostile western Native Americans. He offered to "point out characters who are known" to friendly Indians, "who possess their confidence and in whom they confide," to "assist in bearing" messages to hostile Indians. Burr specifically proposed using someone from the Six Nations of the Iroquois (which included the Mohawks) or from the Stockbridge Indians (with whom he had a connection through his maternal grandfather). He stated "[a]n Opinion has for sometime prevailed that peace with the Indians is attainable," that the war had "arisen from a belief that this Government seek[s] to dispossess them of their Lands" and that "since the commencement of hostilities [no U.S. agent had] conveyed to them any direct assurances of our Wishes and designs towards them." He added that "The late attempt to negociate thro' Col. Proctor at the very time hostile expeditions were Authorized by Government and actually executed by the Kentucky Militia, could not have tended to conciliate or undeceive." (AB to [TJ?], March 13, 1792; Kline 1:101.)

No response exists to Burr's letter but Kline writes that "Jefferson and Hamilton conferred on the implications of the [Iroquois] delegation's visit and agreed that the Iroquois should not be used as intermediaries with hostile tribes in the west." (Kline 1:102.) It is likely that Jefferson would have seen Burr's offer of assistance as meddling in affairs above his pay grade and self-centeredly putting himself forward as the go-to man. That Burr might actually have had special knowledge and a humanitarian purpose in mind does not seem to have occurred to him.

Due to "some unexpected public business," Burr was unable to go on the trip with Tayler to Fort Schuyler. (AB to JT, Kline 1:82.) He asked Tayler to convey to Brandt his intentions and tell him that he would meet and accompany Brandt on his way back to New York from Fort Schuyler in late May. Interestingly, Burr charged Tayler to "say Nothing ... to any other person" of this. (Id.) By this, he likely meant New York Governor Clinton, President George Washington, and Secretary of State Thomas Jefferson. Why? Probably because Burr's avenue was not official. In effect, Burr was saying not to credit him with the suggestion.

Instead of using Burr as an avenue, in April, Secretary of War Henry Knox wrote to Burr's rival Governor George Clinton "asking him to use his influence with Joseph Brant." (Kline 1:82, n1, quoting from HK to GC, April 12, 1791.) Knox suggested Marinus Willet, a merchant and former Revolutionary War supplier (actually a revolutionary comrade of Burr's and a sometime Burr supporter), to meet with Brant, though Clinton, despite saying he wouldn't intervene, apparently chose Tayler instead. Knox also told Clinton that "Brandt's attachment may be doubted, and his views may be dangerous." (Id., quoting from HK to GC, May 11, 1791.)

Fifty sachems of the Five Nations, along with the Stockbridge Indians, agreed to conduct a peace mission to the western Indians but were delayed. (Kline 1:103, n4.) The outcome of the Five Nations' peace mission was not favorable. According to Kline, the "fruitless mission" of Major Thomas Proctor, who was commissioned to treat with the Miami and Wabash Indians in March 1791, "and the abortive attempt to enlist Joseph Brant's good offices as peacemaker coincided with the administration's preparations for a military campaign against the western tribes." (Kline 1:102, n1.)

General Charles Scott and Lt. Col. James Wilkinson both made raids to "carry terror and desolation" to the hostile western tribes. (Scott to Knox, June 28, 1791, quoted in Kline 1:102n1.) Wilkinson's account is worth quoting here, as a foreshadowing of his character and role in Burr's political demise. Although the raid fell short of his expectations, he said, "I have destroyed the chief town of the Ouiatanon nation and made prisoners of the sons and sisters of the king. I have burnt a respectable Kickapoo village, and cut down at least 430 acres of corn, chiefly in the milk. The Ouiatonons, left without houses, home, or provision, must cease to war, and will find active employ to subsist their squaws and children during the impending winter." (JW to Knox, August 24, 1791; Kline 1:102-03, n1).

Interestingly, given Burr's clear attempts to assist the administration to make peace with the Indians, in mid-February 1792, according to Kline, Burr and Rufus King (the two Senators from NY) "returned to the Senate after an absence of several days to add their votes to passage of the administration's bill that authorized raising five new regiments of the regular army for duty on the western frontier. This vote, which raised the specter of a standing army before the eyes of horrified republicans, was a controversial one for AB." (Kline 1:103, n1.) In other words, Burr was again blamed for being anti-republican when in fact he was the only one to attempt any peacemaking.

Burr wrote his wife: "You may expect a host of such falsehoods as that about the Indian war. I have not been offered any command. When the part I take in the bill on that subject shall be fully known, I am sure it will give entire satisfaction to my friends." (Id., quoting AB to TPB, February 19, 1792, from Davis, *Memoirs of AB*, 1:315.)

As noted above, Jefferson's likely view of Burr would be the negative view, the least favorable, the most critical. What the great Washington and great Jefferson did not like was Burr's meddling but Burr was sincere and had good and well-founded reasons. Burr's maternal grandfather, Jonathan Edwards, who loomed large in his life (although he and his wife both died not long after Burr's parents in Burr's early childhood), had lived with the Stockbridge Indians for a time and had published the only written grammar of their language.

Burr had travelled to Stockbridge, Massachusetts with his mother as a baby to visit Edwards and the boy and his sister, Sally, lived there for a time with their uncle, Timothy Edwards, after their parents and grandparents passed away. (Kline 1:lvi-lvii.) Many years later while in Europe, Burr dubbed his misfortunes "The Adventures of Gil Blas Moheagungk de Manhattan." (Davis, PJAB 1:123, 167.) In the 1792 letter to Jefferson, Burr refers to the Stockbridge Indians as "remnant of a Moheagungk [Mohican] Tribe." (Kline 101.) (Gil Blas was the title character of a French comedic adventure novel.) That Brandt also was a distant relative adds weight to the interpretation that Burr identified with the Indians, sincerely wanted to help the tribes find peace with the white settlers, and felt he had a unique understanding to offer.

When Burr voted with Federalist Rufus King to authorize the creation of five new regiments to serve on the western frontier, it was probably viewed by Jefferson and other Republicans as insincere, vacillating, or duplicitous. Again, as a military man, Burr understood the need for military strength to protect Americans, and that is also precisely how he viewed the military: as a protector, as an organ made up of brave men who were trained to fight for their nation.[81] Burr wanted peace and he tried to aid in bringing it, pointing out the hypocrisy and stupidity of attempting to negotiate peace at the same time as engaging in hostile expeditions. But if peace was impossible, he knew we needed to authorize military force.

It appears that Burr might not have known the real American policy towards the Indians: to dispossess them of their lands and drive them out utterly, for Burr seemed to think that an American agent should convey to them "direct assurances of our Wishes and designs towards them." That Burr naively thought peace was attainable shows his good intentions, as it shows the hostile intentions of the American government. That Burr also believed that the two *could* have peace, even though as Burr well knew, the western Indians

---

[81] See Biddle, *Autobiography*, 314. (Burr told Biddle that if he had not been stopped on his western expedition, he "would have collected a number of military men round him near the [western frontier] lines, formed a barrier between us and the Spaniards which would have prevented them from disturbing us.")

were attacking Americans on the frontier, shows something else important about him: he could see the two were not mutually exclusive. He could see ways in which both sides could have what they wanted and had rights to. This illustrates Burr's superb ability to mediate, to find common ground, build coalitions, make peace, which history shows repeatedly throughout his adult life in a variety of circumstances, both personal and professional.

But for Jefferson, if he observed these traits in Burr at all, he probably felt confirmed his opinion of Burr's crookedness. Jefferson was so busy forming this negative image of Burr in his mind that he never really got to know Burr's character, never utilized his talents, instead actively prevented the nation from having the benefit of them. Indeed, he never cared to know Burr, for what mattered to Jefferson was not how wonderful or useful Burr was or what Burr could do for the nation but what *Jefferson* could do and how much *he* was loved for being the greatest civil libertarian in history. Jefferson's jealousy of Burr and his final determination to destroy him may in part be explained by this, not by any invention of Burr's crookedness, ambition, or treason. It would take a long and sustained effort to turn the well-known great qualities Burr possessed, his generosity and humanity, into something crooked and despicable.

The 1801 Electoral Tie

The 1801 electoral tie caused a genuine constitutional crisis, which could have resulted in the dissolution of the union, and the convoluted events – who said and did what -- are difficult to unravel. Burr's apparent shifts have garnered much attention and criticism.

In my opinion, apart from the general human belief that anyone different is bad, there were two things that led others to suspect Burr of ill intentions. First, he made distinctions that others simply could not discern. Second, partly because of those distinctions and partly based on advice from his advisor-friends, he went through a series of apparent vacillations: (a) reassured Jefferson of his support, then (b) declined to resign if elected, then (c) refused to come to an understanding with the Federalists, and finally (d) publicly relinquished all pretensions for the first office.

Jefferson's actions were less confusing but, as usual, darker, more obscure, and deniable, but it was Jefferson who came to an understanding with the Federalists. (Jefferson denied doing so, of course, but he permitted several others to believe he was agreeing to terms.)[82]

Burr's apparent vacillations were construed in a variety of ways unfavorable to him. Remarkably, no one (at least no one we know of) at the time seems to have discerned the consistent moral and constitutional grounding for his actions.

Burr made a distinction between, on the one hand, serving if elected president by the House (which, in his view, was a moral and constitutional obligation) and, on the other, taking action against Jefferson to obtain the office (which would have been improper and immoral).

Some insight into Burr's thinking may be derived from a letter he wrote to Oliver Phelps in February 1801, not on the subject of the tie. He wrote Phelps, urging him to consider running as Lt. Governor of NY under Governor George Clinton: "I hope to receive a line from you, saying that you submit to be disposed of as your friends may judge to be most for the general interest." (AB to OP, 02-10-1801, Kline 1:498.)

Thus, a man had an obligation to "be disposed of" as his friends (that is, other men of honor) judged "most for the general interest." Burr's syntax shows that in his mind, one had an obligation to serve the public interest, which meant submitting to the judgment of one's advisor-friends.[83] That following the advice of one's advisor-friends did not in Burr's mind require suspending one's own better judgment is illustrated by a passage in a 1792 letter he wrote during another election controversy. Burr said: "I was obliged to give an

---

82 *See* Van Bergen, *Aaron Burr and the Electoral Tie of 1801.*

83 Burr's reliance on advisor-friends is reflected in Theodore Sedgwick's remark to his son that in AB's supposed final determination to "resign[] his pretensions" Burr had been "instructed by those whom he deemed his friends here." (TS to TS Jr., 02-16-1801, quoted in *Editorial Note: The Electoral Tie of 1801* (01-11-1801); Kline 2:486.) Burr also referred to having followed the advice of his advisors: in his 12-29 letter to Smith, that "as at present advised, I should not" engage to resign if elected President." (Kline 1:479.) He refers to "my friends" in his 02-12-1801 letter to Jefferson, describing them as "more irritable and more credulous" than him. (Kline 1:501.)

opinion, & I have not yet learned to give any other than that which my judgment directs." (AB to Jacob Delameter, 06-15-1792, Kline 1:126.)[84]

The subtlety of Burr's distinctions and duality of his thinking surely confused many people. To Burr, these distinctions were obvious. They did not to his mind require high intelligence or special learning to grasp. To him, a man's highest obligation was to the principles of the Revolution and to the law and Constitution. He lived in accordance with these beliefs and his actions were consistent with them.[85]

Jefferson, on the other hand – the strict former constructionist – seemed to have had no qualms about deciding which parts of the Constitution to follow and which to ignore. As he had planned to offer to John Adams in 1796, when they had tied, he expected Burr to agree to step down if elected.

Burr viewed this situation as a legal/constitutional issue and never believed usurpation was a real possibility. Jefferson didn't see the House as a legitimate body but felt the "highflying federalists" were determined to "prevent a choice by the H. of R (which they are strong enough to do) and let the government devolve on a President of the Senate," so it was, to Jefferson's mind, perfectly legitimate for him to make a deal with the enemy to effect what he saw as good ends. (TJ to AB, 12-15-1800; Kline 1:469.)

Albert Gallatin, Jefferson's soon-to-be Secretary of

---

[84] But see where Burr says he was made a candidate against his advice and against his judgment. AB to SS, 12-29-1801, Kline 1:479.

[85] Lomask, quotes historian Richard Buel: "[A]lthough the architects of the first political parties were avid for posthumous fame, they tended to regard as 'counterproductive' any pursuit of fame that was not subordinated 'to the larger end of fulfilling the promise of the Revolution.'" (Lomask, 1:295, citing Richard Buel Jr., *Securing the Revoluion: Ideology in American Politics, 1789-1815* (1972).) According to Thomas Fleming, "fame was inextricably linked with honor and a special kind of achievement." Following the precepts of Sir Francis Bacon, "[w]inning fame … meant winning the praise of persons of judgment and quality." (Fleming, *Duel,* 19.) Burr wrote an interesting statement about fame to William Eustis: "[I]t was quite necessary that you should have the kind of celebrity which is produced by that sort of collision – It was necessary that you should be vilified – much more so than that you should be defended . . . To your fame it suffices that you be a topic of conversation & inquiry . . . the more enquiry, the more honor. – The mental spasms, unassisted by self reproach are transient and leave no sting behind, not even the sense of injury or desire of revenge." (AB to WE, October 10 [ie. November 9], 1800, Kline 2:454-55.)

Treasury, wrote his wife in January 1801 (perhaps after listening to Jefferson's alarums), speculating about what the Federalists might do. In the case of a deadlock, "what will be the plans of the Federalists, having, as they have, a majority of both houses? Will they usurp the Presidential powers? . . . Will they only pass a law providing for a new election?" If that happened, would certain state legislatures refuse to act, preventing the choice of electors in those states, robbing the Republicans of their votes? (Kline 1:485.) A week later, Gallatin subdued his alarm and told his wife that after all he didn't think Federalists wanted "[a]bsolute usurpation & the overthrow of our Constitution." (Id.)

As the electoral tie moved into the House in February 1801, Jefferson wrote Burr about a letter that was circulating that looked to be in Jefferson's hand but was forged and which contained "sentiments highly injurious to you." Jefferson assured Burr that "if it contains a sentiment unfriendly or disrespectful to you I affirm it solemnly to be a forgery." (TJ to AB, 02-01-1801, Kline 1:494.) This is the only time Jefferson showed the least concern for Burr's opinion of him. At that point, both men were aware of the tie. Given Jefferson's pre-existing distrust, the rumors circulating, and the ambiguity of Burr's several statements, Jefferson likely believed that Burr would try to steal the presidency away from him, if he could. It was in Jefferson's best interest to deny any "unfriendly or disrespectful" sentiments, even while we know he held and nurtured them in his breast.

Later, Jefferson was able to capitalize on nuances in Burr's explanations, fine distinctions that Burr was making that Jefferson was perfectly capable of understanding but which allowed the remarks to be construed as evidence of bad faith. Jefferson had no problem allowing other Republicans to defame Burr by falsely claiming Burr had schemed to steal the presidency, all along knowing that he, Jefferson, himself had made a deal with the Federalists in order to break the deadlock. In Jefferson's mind, Burr's refusal to resign if elected meant he wanted the steal the presidency.

Matthew L. Davis
The episode of Jefferson's handling in early 1801 of VP

Burr's recommendation of his political associate (and posthumous editor of his papers and biographer), Matthew L. Davis, for naval officer of NY marked Jefferson's first overt action to shut Burr out of power. Given Jefferson's prior ill will towards Burr, this event should not be viewed as having been caused by Burr's alleged treachery (which we know to be untrue anyway) during the 1801 tie. Jefferson, now in the seat of power, had gotten what he wanted and could afford to get rid of Burr. Burr's unwillingness to explain himself publicly, his need for mystery and independence, his fine distinctions and the inability of many people to grasp his reasoning gave Jefferson the opportunity to begin defaming and disempowering him.

While Jefferson may not have delayed his decision on Burr's nomination of Davis out of conscious malice, I believe this event was the turning point in the emergence of Jefferson's malevolent conduct towards Burr. In May 1801, Jefferson went behind his Vice-President's back and wrote to New York Governor George Clinton for his opinion about Davis' appointment. Clinton was Burr's enemy and rival. This contact opened the door to the joining of Jefferson's forces with those of Burr's arch-rivals.

Five weeks later, Burr wrote Gallatin: "Strange reports are here in circulation respecting secret machinations against Davis ..." (AB to AG, 06-28-1801, Adams, *TJ Administrations*, 157; Kline 2:602.) When Gallatin inquired, Jefferson told him: "Mr. Davis is now with me. He has not opened himself. When he does, I shall inform him that nothing is decided, nor can be till we get together at Washington." (TJ to AG, [n.d.], Adams, 158.) Henry Adams notes that "While Jefferson withheld from Burr all sign of support, De Witt Clinton and Ambrosee Spencer, acting in unison with the President ... divided [the state and city offices] between the Clintons and Livingstons, until the Livingstons were gorged; while Burr was left to beg from Jefferson the share of national patronage which De Witt Clinton had months before taken measures to prevent his obtaining." (Adams, 158.)

~

The 1804 Visit

Colo. Burr must have thot I could swallow strong things in my own favor, when he founded his acquiescence in the nomin[atio]n as V.P. to his desire of promoting my honor, the being with me whose company and convers[atio]n had always been fascinating to him &c.
TJ Memorandum, January 26, 1804
Kline 2:822 (original spelling)

Before moving into Part Three of this book, in which we discuss the conspirators, we shall discuss two visits from Burr that Jefferson recorded in his memoirs. His version of these visits is quite prejudicial and once again, no defense or explanation exists from or for Burr. The subject of the memo for the 1804 visit is largely about the public loss of faith in Burr. This where Jefferson says he distrusted Burr.

Both of these visits preceded Burr's expedition and Jefferson's decision to prosecute him for treason. It is significant that Jefferson chose to record his prejudicial version of these two events, almost in pre-emptive defense of his future decision to take Burr down.

In the 1804 memorandum, Jefferson notes that Burr said that the Livingstons and Clintons "solicited his aid with the people [and] he lent it without any views of promotion, that his being named as a candidate for V.P. was unexpected by him. [H]e acceded to it with a view to promote [Jefferson's] fame & advancement and from a desire to be with [Jefferson], whose company & conversation had always been fascinating to him." (*Thomas Jefferson: Memorandum of a Conversation with Burr*, January 26, 1804; Kline 2:820.) Jefferson remarked that "Colo. Burr must have thot I could swallow strong things in my own favor, when he founded his acquiescence in the nomin[atio]n as V.P. to his desire of promoting my honor, the being with me whose company and convers[atio]n had always been fascinating to him &c." (Id. at 822.)

It was mean-spirited for Jefferson, who craved adulation, to criticize Burr for saying nice things to him. Jefferson, after all, was in the position of power. Why harbor such resentment that you must write a spiteful note, later to be published in your memoirs? Jefferson was also calling Burr a liar, opening the door to base speculation about Burr's intentions.

But if we assume that Burr did in fact compliment Jefferson like this, why was that so terrible? Must we assume he did not mean it? However, it was too late for Burr to be complimenting Jefferson, even if Burr did find Jefferson's "company and conversation ... fascinating." Because it was flattering to Jefferson and TJ could deny the flattery, there is good reason to believe that he did record accurately what Burr said. Jefferson loved flattery, loved to be adored. Perhaps Burr knew this and, knowing too that he had fallen out of favor and was slowly being backed into a corner by Jefferson and Clinton, thought he could mends things with Jefferson this way.

Jefferson knew the moment was a signpost on the way to Burr's ultimate political demise and wished to make the most of it, giving nothing to Burr and relishing the opportunity to give the world proofs of Burr's corruptness, which was actually the result of Jefferson's own mean-spirited pressure and plotting.

As noted, this plotting began right after he was elected, when he "began undermining Burr's New York City political base – the keystone of Jefferson's own election victory – by cutting Burr off from political patronage." (Wheelan, *Jefferson's Vendetta,* 78.) The plotting continued as "Treasury Secretary Albert Gallatin hit upon the idea of a Constitutional amendment: requiring presidential and vice-presidential candidates to run on a party ticket, for which electors then would cast one vote. Should all of his other countermeasures against Burr fail, Jefferson could always select another running mate and keep Burr off the ticket altogether." (Id. at 79-80.) This is exactly what Jefferson did in 1804, replacing Burr with George Clinton as VP.

The plot was furthered when James Cheetham published "A Narrative of the Suppression by Col. Burr, of the Hist. Of the Administration of John Adams," claiming that Burr had suppressed the publication of this pamphlet in order to win favor with Federalists. According to Joseph Wheelan: "Several months before [Cheetham's newspaper] campaign against Burr began in the *American Citizen*, Jefferson, at Cheetham's request, inspected his plan of attack, and read a draft of Wood's *History* pamphlet." (Id. at 80.) Jefferson wrote Cheetham "I shall be glad hereafter to receive your daily paper by post as usual" and asked that their collaboration be kept a secret. (Id., *see* further discussion in the section on Cheetham in "The Knot of Knaves" chapter below.)

Mary-Jo Kline, after noting that it was Burr himself who helped Cheetham to obtain his position as editor, states that "Cheetham prepared for Jefferson an 'account of the plans and views of aggrandizement of a faction in the City of New York,'" in which Cheetham claimed that Burr's goal was "to bring the present administration into disrepute and thereby to place Mr. Burr in the Presidential Chair." (Kline 2:645.)

But in his memorandum, Jefferson said he disingenuously told Burr that "as to the attack excited against him in the newspapers, I had noticed it but as the passing wind; that I had seen complaints that Cheetham, employed in publishing the laws, should be permitted to eat the publick bread & abuse it's second officer" but the Secretary of State "appointed" the publishers of the laws "with[ou]t any reference to me." (Kline 2:821.)

Jefferson had to know that his evasions and lies were obvious to Burr. It was not enough for Jefferson to plot behind Burr's back, to obstruct him, make life as difficult as possible for him, and completely disable him. Jefferson felt compelled to make Burr feel his unquenchable, undying hatred, to make him suffer. He wanted Burr to know what TJ was doing and know that he, Burr, had no power to stop it. Seeing Burr grovel and squirm, pleading for any drop of favor, seems to have given Jefferson great pleasure – for, by his own description, he did not relent -- while he pricked Burr repeatedly and turned the screw in him, all the while insisting on his own rectitude.

While Burr's ill-timed flattery was certainly a big mistake on his part, the meeting as certainly marks the point by which Jefferson was already in mid-flow of acting on his malice towards Burr. By this point, Jefferson clearly had decided that Burr was working with the rabid Federalists and trying to bring his administration down. What Burr wrote to Samuel Smith in February 1801 could be said of Jefferson with respect to Burr: "You seem to believe every lie you hear." (AB to SS, February 10, 1801, Kline 1:498.)

Burr asked Jefferson for some mark of favor, which of course Jefferson declined to give.

~

Burr's Social Cluelessness

Jefferson probably did not believe Burr was so dimwitted as to think Jefferson "could swallow [such] strong things in my own favor." It never seems to have occurred to Jefferson that Burr might have been genuinely socially clueless. After all, Burr was widely considered brilliant and very charming. But Burr's charm was in his ability to see and appreciate the deep essence of each person, not in social astuteness.

The combination of Burr's social cluelessness with his high intellectual awareness and verbal ability is illustrated by an event he himself recounted to his daughter about his ill-fated courtship with a woman he dubbed "Celeste." Burr was aware that the "habits of life and singular education" of a woman like Celeste "forbid every thing like advance [on her part]; and that a lady may always presume that her lover, if sincere, will seize the slightest ground for hope; and that, in the logic of love, an equivocal refusal is assent," (June 11, Davis, 231) but Burr was still completely confounded by her behavior. She said an unequivocal no to his marriage proposal but then kept calling him back on various pretexts. To Theodosia, his daughter, he wrote that "there is reason to hope that there will be no hanging or drowning" (June 8), then appealing to her: "You could unravel this thing in five minutes. Would to God you were here[!]" (See, letters from AB to TBA, June 5, 6, 7, 8, 10, 11, 12, 1803 Davis, *Memoirs of AB,* 2:222-32.)

Writing back, Theodosia found it simple: "Voila mon opinion. [Celeste] meant, from the beginning, to say that awful word – yes; but not choosing to say it immediately, she told you that *you* had furnished her with arguments against matrimony, which in French means, Please, sir, to persuade me out of them again. But you took it as a plump refusal, and walked off. She called you back. What more could she do?" (TBA to AB, June 14, 1803, Davis, *Memoirs of AB*, 2:232.)

Burr recounted how he "was taken by surprise and remained dumb, with a kind of half grin" when she called him back one time, while she "was profoundly occupied in tearing up some roses which she held in her hand and [he] was equally industrious in twirling his hat and pinching some new corners and angles in the brim." (See especially Burr's "Continuation of the Story of the Loves of Reubon and Celeste," June 11, 1803, Davis, *Memoirs of AB,* 2:228-31.)

Here, thus, is this highly intelligent and accomplished military man and attorney, a man supposedly renowned as a charmer and womanizer – standing before this "Celeste," dumb and grinning, not knowing what to say or do in what was a rather straightforward (although highly charged) social situation. And it was not like Burr had not already gone through courtships or marriage before! He was 47 years old and this was his grown daughter from whom he was seeking advice! Even if Burr was making fun of himself, the result shows that he genuinely did not know how to handle the event.

In quite another context, Burr wrote Jeremy Bentham from Edinburgh, Scotland in 1809 (when Burr was in exile): "I have got on pretty well here, and with rather more discretion than usually falls to my lot, not having said or done, publicly, more than twenty outrageously silly things. Avoiding all ugly, naughty topics." (AB to JB, 01-23-1809 (01-31 entry), Davis, *Private Journal of AB,* 1:169.)

Clearly, Burr was aware of his social cluelessness and also of how others could interpret them (outrageously silly, ugly, naughty).

Three years later, in yet another context, Burr wrote a much more formal letter to Bentham about General Miranda: "There is not, to my knowledge, any hostility, nor any cause of hostility between us; nor is it easy to conceive how or why there should be." He and Miranda, he said, had met only once and "Nothing unpleasant passed at that interview; on the contrary, I was greatly pleased with his social talents and colloquial eloquence. It is true, however, that I did, from private considerations, studiously avoid anything which might afford him occasion to disclose his views. The bare suspicion of any connexion between him and me would have been injurious to my project and fatal to his; a circumstance of which he must have been ignorant. He afterward complained to his friend of my coldness and reserve, and he had reason; but I did not dare explain, not having sufficient assurance of his discretion." Burr said he had not "suppose[d] that any sentiment approaching enmity existed on his part; none certainly on mine." (AB to JB, October(?)16, 1811, Davis, *Private Journal of AB;* 2:254-55; Kline 2:1134.) (Kline states that in the William Bixby version of PJAB, Burr noted that he wrote JB on December 29, 1811. Kline, source note, 2:1135.)

These three examples show Burr's intellectual awareness combined with his virtual social cluelessness. Having been a married man and father, and intellectually knowing the social circumstances of Celeste, he still could not actually read her social cues (and asked his daughter for help). In Edinburgh, his description of his usual lot was saying and doing outrageously silly things and talking about forbidden topics. In both letters, while his written language is intellectually superior (probably far above the norm for most adults of the period and even superior to most well-educated men, and in his Reubon story, literary), he describes himself like a boy or teenager (half grin, twirling his hat; avoiding all ugly, naughty topics).

In the thoughtful letter about Miranda, Burr shows a sophisticated intellectual awareness of why Miranda had reason to complain about Burr. Nonetheless, Burr still was completely socially unaware of any sentiment of enmity on Miranda's part.

Burr may have had mild, high-functioning autism or Asperger's Syndrome, of which these may be examples. In any case, it is perhaps not that surprising that Jefferson would have wondered at or misconstrued Burr's actions, or even disbelieved he could be so socially naïve.

Nonetheless, it took something more, a predisposition

in Jefferson to develop such interpretations into something sufficient to create the vindictiveness he later exhibited. Jefferson believed every lie he heard because he wanted to, not because he had to. He believe ill of others because he was predisposed to. He was a lawyer, who surely knew the difference between supposition and fact, between rumor (hearsay) and proof. He constructed an image of Burr in his mind by selecting from the various rumors those that best served his purpose. That purpose may well not have been a conscious one. It was nonetheless one that Burr could not escape.

The Last Meeting

The last significant meeting between Burr and Jefferson was probably March 1806. To put this in context, within a few months after this meeting, Burr departed westward, spending the fall in Ohio, Tennessee, and Kentucky. In November, the U.S. Attorney for the district, Daviess, began attempting to have him brought to trial on treason charges in Kentucky. Burr was on the Mississippi River January 1st when he learned of TJ's proclamation and JW's betrayal and arrests of his friends in New Orleans.

So, this last meeting took place as the wave of Jefferson's slow-rising ire was just reaching its crest, before the take-down. On April 15, Jefferson wrote a memorandum about the meeting. (*TJ: Memorandum of Conversation with AB,* April 15,1806, Kline 2:962.) Although the memorandum was written, according to Jefferson, a month after the meeting, Jefferson's recollection was quite detailed and is quoted here almost in full. Read without a picture of Jefferson's deeper nature in mind, the letter reads like the beginnings of a thoughtful and carefully observed indictment of his former VP. It is, however, in fact brimming with suppressed and projected loathing. Jefferson wrote that Burr called on him, and:

> . . . entered into a conversation in which he mentioned
> that a little before coming into the office I had written
> to him a letter intimating that I had destined him for a

high employ, had he not been placed by the people in a different one, that he had signified his willingness to resign as V. President to give aid to the admn.

This was an accurate recounting of the exchange of letters between the two men. Burr's willingness to resign as VP and "give aid to the admn" in some other capacity must have seemed duplicitous to Jefferson after Burr had declined to resign if he had been elected President. Again, Burr was making fine distinctions. It is easy to interpret this apparent about-face as a manifestation of Burr's ambitions, i.e., that he refused to decline the presidency if he was chosen for that position, but he'd be quite happy to resign the vice-presidency, even when elected to it, allegedly to "give aid" to Jefferson's administration. How could Jefferson believe that? But to Burr, refusing to serve as President and resigning the vice-presidency were not comparable, because the presidency was an active obligatory role and the vice-presidency was passive and non-essential. In other words, to Burr, serving meant active, not passive, duty. He would have preferred to have taken any other active role within Jefferson's administration than to have been saddled with the tedious duties of presiding over the Senate and being utterly excluded from all active decision-making.

Jefferson records Burr's remarks:

> In any other place; that he had never asked an officer however,; he asked aid of nobody, but could walk on his own legs, & take care of himself: tht I had always used him with politeness, but nothing more: that he had aided in the bringing on of the present order of things, that he had supported the admn., & that he could do me much harm: he wished however to be on differt. ground: he was now disengaged from all particular business[,] willing to engage in something; should be in town some days, if I should have any thing to propose to him.

Again, Jefferson appears to have recorded without distortion. The wording is specific ("walk on his own legs," "take care of himself"). But the coldness in the reporting is detectable. And then there is the "he could do me much harm" phrase. Placed within this prosaic sequence of events, it has great impact. Had

Burr put his foot in his mouth again? Maybe, but he was saying he did *not* wish to do harm. Burr in opposition to Jefferson could indeed do harm to the political goals of the Republican President and to their joint cause. Jefferson took Burr's remark as a personal attack, rather than as a statement of fact about where things stood. Burr was asking Jefferson to collaborate with him, to put their heads together and figure out where Burr could be most helpful and useful to the Administration. Couldn't the President have found *something* to give him to do? He was putting himself at TJ's disposal. Instead, Jefferson commented:

> I observed to him that I had always been sensible that he possessed talents which might be employed greatly to the advantage of the public, & tht as to myself I had a confidence tht if he were employed he would use his talents for the public good: but that he must be sensible the public had withdrawn their confidence from him, & that in a government like ours it was necessary to embrace in it's admn. as great a mass of public confid[anc]e as possible, by employing those who had a character with the public, of their own, & not merely a secondary one through the Ex[ecuti]ve.

Jefferson was sensible that Burr possessed talents that might be employed greatly to the advantage of the public? But did Jefferson have confidence that Burr would use his talents for the public good? No. The impression one gets is that Jefferson was just being nice (treating Burr with politeness but nothing more) and that generates a feeling of sympathy with Jefferson and irritation toward Burr. How nice of Jefferson to give Burr that compliment while refusing him any outlet!

The following phrases increase the power of this sentiment, for if the public had in fact withdrawn its confidence in Burr, Jefferson was perfectly justified in treating Burr with mere polite distance. We feel the rectitude of Jefferson's position.

Not unless we know and can keep in mind that Jefferson had was deeply involved in the defamatory activities that caused the public to withdraw their confidence in Burr does the real meaning of the passage become clear. Jefferson knows what he has done to Burr, yet he blames Burr for it. And if Jefferson thinks that Burr knows what he did, he's rubbing it in, with salt. Jefferson continues:

> [Burr] observed tht if we believed a few newspapers it might be supposed he had lost the public confidence, but that I knew how easy it was to engage newspapers in any thing. I observed that I did not refer to that kind of evidence of his having lost the public confidence, but to the late presidential election; when, tho' in poss[essio]n of the office of V.P. There was not a single voice heard for his retaining it.

Wow. "Not a single voice" was actually a caucus of "congressional Republicans" (Kline 2:964n3) under the malicious control of DeWitt Clinton and Jefferson. And here Jefferson has to rub it in even more how low Burr had fallen, that not a single one of his former supporters was willing to come forward now. Given Jefferson's dedicated efforts up to this point to secretly gather the New York Clintonians and Livingstons under his benevolent and powerful wing against any efforts of the belittled Burr and his supporters, blaming Burr for it is completely backwards. But not a drop of sympathy here. How is it that readers can think Jefferson kind and benevolent, when his cruelty is almost monumental? It is Jefferson's legerdemain. We have been duped. Onward Jefferson continues:

> [T]hat as to any harm he could do me, I knew no cause why he should desire it, but at the same time I feared no injury which any man could do me: that I never had done a single act, or been concerned in any transaction, which I feared to have fully laid open; or which could do me any hurt if truly stated: that I had never done a single thing with a view to my personal interest, or that of any friend, or with any other view than that of the greatest public good: that therefore no threat or fear on that head would ever be a motive of action with me.

Again, wow! Jefferson ignores Burr's offer to take up any job Jefferson might see fit to offer him and instead turns Burr's alleged comment on its head. If Burr said such a thing, it would have been foolish but given his lack of social intelligence and his inclination to put bullies in their place when he could, it's possible that he did say it and it was in fact true that Burr's faction could have done damage to Jefferson. But if Burr said it, Jefferson certainly turned it around on him here, using it to create a malignant image of Burr. (In other words, maybe Jefferson did deserve to be harmed but that question is forgotten.) And Jefferson again presents himself as the kind and benevolent leader having to grapple with yet another mean distraction.

Despite Jefferson's remark about having nothing to fear, he had *much* to fear being "fully laid open." We need only think of Sally Hemings to know this. But when we think of what he had already done: his dealings with the Clintons, using Gideon Granger, John Armstrong, and James Cheetham to do his dirty work to publish wildly and viciously defamatory things over and over again in the papers, to spy on Burr, infiltrate his supporters and attempt to undermine them however possible, to find any ways and means possible to disrupt, detract, distract, disempower, dissuade, and undermine Burr and his supporters, we can be sure Jefferson did not want his hand in those doings fully laid open to the public. What Jefferson was really saying was that he was sure he had covered his tracks. (*See* "Knot of Knaves" chapter for details.)

Jefferson continues that Burr dined with him one more time before taking his leave and that Jefferson did not commit these things to writing before "but I do it now, because in a suit between him & Cheetham, he has had a depos[itio]n of mr. Bayard taken, which seems to have no relation to the suit nor to any other object but to calumniate me."

Thus, another arrow thrown, almost as an afterthought. Poor, poor Jefferson! He continues:

> Bayard pretends to have addressed to me during the pendency of the Presid[entia]l election in Feb. 1801 through Genl. Saml. Smith, certain cond[itio]ns on which my election might be obtained; & that Genl Smith after conversing with me gave answers from me. [T]his is absolutely false. [N]o propos[itio]n was ever made to me on that occasion by Genl. Smith, nor any answer authorised by me[,] and this fact Genl. Smith

affirms at this moment.

Would Jefferson lie outright? "Absolutely false." Well, the story of this episode is highly complex and here Jefferson capitalizes on that complexity. He had in fact agreed to terms but never overtly. It was done in true Jefferson fashion, via-via. That is, via one person to another to another, and by conveying his intentions in a way the Federalists would interpret agreeably, so that Jefferson was able to obtain in his opponents a *sense* that he had agreed with their terms without ever actually having said so himself.

After this outright denial of what he knew had in fact happened, Jefferson goes on to recount a chance meeting with Gouverneur Morris, in which Morris told Jefferson "the reasons why the minority of states were so opposed to my being elected" being that they apprehended Jefferson would "1. ... turn all federalists out of office[,] 2. put down the Navy[,] 3. wipe off the public debt & 4. [space in MS] that I need only to declare, or authorise my friends to declare, that I would not take these steps and instantly the event of the election would be fixed."

Jefferson benevolently remarks that he told Morris "that I should leave the world to judge of the course I meant to pursue by that which I had pursued hitherto; believing it to be my duty to be passive & silent during the present scene; that I should certainly make no terms, should never go into office of [the] President by capitulation, nor with my hands tied by any conditions which should hinder me from pursuing the measures which I should deem for the public good."

Well, of course he wouldn't be going into office by capitulation, with his hands tied, and so on, but that is not the same as secretly conveying terms. After recounting several other similar chance conversations he had during the election, Jefferson noted that "certain I am that neither [Samuel Smith], nor any other republican ever uttered the most distant hint to me about submitting to any conditions or giving any assurances to any body; and still more certainly was neither he or any other person ever authorised by me to say what I would or would not do." Not ever submitting to conditions or giving assurances but surely letting his opponents think so.

Samuel Smith was the one who wrote Burr in January 1801, after it became evident that Jefferson and Burr would be tied: "... the Feds will attempt to disunite us, we must not believe any thing that comes from them, we must be on our guards, for we shall be assailed in every direction – you mentioned that the Virginians had been abusing you, I told you that I did not believe it, I have enquired everywhere, & find the whole a fiction." (SS to AB, January 11, 1801, Kline 1:488.) And Burr later chastised Smith: "you seem to believe every lie you hear." (AB to SS, February 4, 1801, Kline 1:498.)

Smith and others, including Jefferson, saw plots everywhere, felt "assailed in every direction," and were suspicious and "on their guard" with everyone. They were not above engaging in intrigue. Another Republican wrote Burr in December: "The language of the Democrats is, that you will yield your pretensions to their favorite [Jefferson]; & it is whispered that overtures to this end are to be, or are made to you. I advise you to take no step whatever by which the choice of the house of Representatives can be impeded or embarassed. Keep the game perfectly in your hand; but do not answer this letter, or any other that may be written to you by a federalist; nor write to any of that party." (Robert Goodloe Harper to AB, December 24, 1800, Kline 1:474.)

Note that "the game," the plotting, was in Harper and Smith's minds, not Burr's. It was clearly also in Jefferson's mind. Burr thought these things "absurd alarms." (AB to SS, 12-29-1801; Kline 1:479.)

In such a climate, it was critical to maintain an image of impartiality and rectitude. It was imperative that Jefferson not be seen as meddling, intriguing, making deals, or negotiating for the office, but *it is clear that Jefferson wanted the presidency more than anything in the world.* The "tell" is his need to lie on even the smallest details. And it is also clear that Smith was not above conspiratorial thinking or maneuvering and that he refused to believe any ill of the Virginians toward Burr.

Later accounts of Bayard and Smith differed from Jefferson's. Jefferson denied talking with Smith or authorizing him to speak for him, but both Smith and Bayard make clear that there was some sort of conveyance. According to Bayard, Smith told him that he had consulted with Jefferson and "was authorized by him to say that [the three points] corresponded with his views and intentions, and that we might confide in him accordingly." Bayard stated that "The opposition of Vermont, Maryland, and Delaware was immediately withdrawn, and Mr. Jefferson was made president by the votes of ten states." (Bayard Deposition, April 3, 1806, in the "wager-suit" of *Gillespie v. Smith,* in Kline 2: 966, quoting from Davis, *Burr,* 2:130-32.)

According to Smith, events occurred more or less as Bayard testified, but Smith told Bayard that he "might rest assured (or words to that effect) that Mr. Jefferson would conduct, as to those points, agreeably to the opinion I had stated as his." (Smith Deposition, April 15, 1806, id. at 2:967, quoting Davis at 2:134-36.)

The issue of Bayard's deposition came up some 25 years later and Davis (who was responsible for bringing the wager-suit, which Burr claimed was "without my agency or knowledge") wrote that "Mr. Jefferson did agree to certain stipulations or conditions therein specified." (AB to Richard H. Bayard [son of the James Bayard discussed above], March 10, 1830, Kline 2:1199 and Matthew L. Davis to AB, March 18, 1830, id. at 1200, from Davis, *Memoirs of AB*, 2:103-106.)

Bayard's son, Richard, sought information about his father's deposition from Burr in order to clear his father's name from the aspersions he felt were cast upon it by Jefferson's above-quoted memorandum, which had been published "lately," according to the son. (R. Bayard to AB, March 8, 1830, Kline 2:1197.) In a second letter, the son explained further to Burr that he wished to show "Mr. Jefferson's error in the statement of the case" (which Jefferson referred to as the Cheetham suit brought by Burr but in fact was the wager suit brought by Davis) and "to refute [Jefferson's] assertion that the deposition had 'nothing to do with the suit, or with any other object than to calumniate [him]." (R. Bayard to AB, April 22, 1830, Kline 2:1203; Davis, *Memoirs of AB*, 2:110-11.)

The papers collected in defense of James Bayard by Richard and his brother James, Jr., appeared in a Philadelphia newspaper on December 23, 1830 and were issued the following year in pamphlet form. The Bayard brothers told readers that they meant to cast no aspersions on Jefferson but "[h]is most enlightened friends cannot but regret ... that [Jefferson] did not look beyond the duration of his own life, and restrain the publication of much that is contained in [his] 'Memoirs,' which, whether with reference to his own fame, or with a proper regard for the opinions, sentiments, and characters of others, *sound discretion* would certainly have prevented." (Quoted in Kline 2:1204.) (Emphasis in original.)

Jefferson's memo and the lies and myths it contains show something else, as well. Jefferson wrote the memo a month after meeting with Burr in 1806, when Burr was well out of office. He should have felt safe from Burr. What could Burr do to him now, after all that had transpired? Jefferson managed to remove all Republican support from him, boot him out of office, keep his followers out of positions or offices of importance, and had destroyed his reputation and his chances in his home state. Why did Jefferson feel such a strong need to write this debasing and defamatory memo, directly from his own pen? He says it was because of Bayard's deposition. Maybe he thought the truth of his intrigues would come out. If anyone could manage finding out what had happened, it was Burr. And Burr said (at least Jefferson says he did) that he could harm him! Whatever could he mean by that? Suddenly Burr must have again loomed very large in Jefferson's mirror.

As I have discussed elsewhere in this book, Jefferson had far more to fear than most men. For a good part of his public life, he hid his sexual relationship with Sally Hemings. His sexual needs were highly charged, obsessive, and deeply painful for him. He also hid, perhaps even from his own conscious mind, his homosexual feelings for Madison and other men. And he hid his malice and loathing, his involvements in "dirty work." As it happened, at the critical juncture when Burr's expedition was just getting on its way, another thing arose that Jefferson had to cover up: the unlawful Freeman/Custis expedition he had authorized and gotten funded by Congress, which intended to (and did) enter Spanish territory, nearly getting the men killed and almost starting a war with Spain. Jefferson buried this event, not even permitting the expedition journals to be published, and then turned the public eye away from it as quickly as possible by trumpeting the fictitious crimes of Burr, which Wilkinson conveniently supplied to him at just the right moment. Wilkinson knew all this, too, for he knew everything that was going on in that region and had been advising both Jefferson and the Spaniards as to the actions and intentions of the other. Wilkinson suddenly saw his destiny in front of him and leaped to save his own skin. Burr was a convenient scapegoat.

~

Jefferson Gathers Rumors

Edwd. Livingston tells me that Bayard applied . . .
to Genl. Sam. Smith & represented to him . . . that he
was authorised [by Burr to offer him a cabinet position].
TJ Memorandum, Notes, Feb. 12 & 14, 1801

Livingston says that Bayard says that Smith says that Burr says. Smith told Livingston who told Nicholas who told Jefferson. Right from the horse's mouth. Proof of Burr's perfidy!

In his 1806 memorandum, Jefferson notes: "for some matters connected with [the Smith negotiations,] see my notes of Feb. 12. & 14. 1801. made at the moment." (Jefferson, *Memorandum*, April 15, 1806, in Kline 2:963). Kline includes the notes, "as revised for his 'Anas.'" They are as follows:

> 12 Feb. 1801. Edwd. Livingston tells me that Bayard applied to Day or last night to Genl. Sam. Smith & represented to him the expediency of his coming over to the states who vote for Burr, that there was nothing in the way of appointm[en]t which he might not command & particularly mentioned the Secretaryship of the navy. Smith asked him if he was authorised to make the offer. [H]e said he was authorised. Smith told this to Livingston & to W. C. Nicholas [in New York] who confirms it to me. Bayard in like manner tempted Livingston, not by offering any particular office, but by representing to him L's intimacy & connextion [sic] with Burr, that from him he had every thing to expect if he would come over to him. [T]o Dr. Linn of N. Jersey they have offered the government of N. Jersey. [S]ee a

paragraph in Martin's Baltimore paper of Feb. 10 signed a Looker on, stating an intimacy of views between Harper & Burr.

> Feb. 14. Genl. Armstrong tells me that Gouvrnr. Morris in conversation with him to day on the scene which is passing expressed himself thus. How comes it, sais he, that Burr who is 400 miles off (at Albany) has agents here at work with great activity, while Mr. Jefferson, who is on the spot, does nothing? [T]his explains the ambiguous conduct of himself & his nephew Lewis Richard Morris, and that they were holden themselves free for a price, i.e., some office, either to Vote [?] uncle or nephew.

(Kline 2:967n6.)

Jefferson further notes in his memorandum that he spoke to Gouverneur Morris. Kline notes that Morris does not record having discussed the election with Jefferson but notes in his diary that Jefferson's friend, Wilson Cary Nicholas, called on him, "and to him I state it as the Opinion not of light and fanciful but of serious and consideration Men that Mr. Burr must be preferred to Mr. Jefferson. He is as I supposed much wounded at this Information." (Kline 2:967, n.7, quoting Gouverneur Morris, *Diary.*) If Nicholas passed this onto Jefferson, it would have provided more fodder to the rumors the candidate was gathering.

These notes were made in the middle of the electoral "crisis" and it is clear that Jefferson was not viewing Burr favorably, that in fact he was listening to rumors from others and apparently making his determinations of Burr's intentions based on those rumors. This in fact seems to have been Jefferson's habitual way of coming to conclusions.

If it was wounding to Nicholas, it would have been more wounding to Jefferson to know that Burr was "preferred." It was easy for Jefferson to ascribe to Burr the kinds of political maneuvering the rumors suggested, which were perhaps not far from Jefferson's own thoughts, to equate Bayard's alleged contrivances with Burr's intentions, and to conclude it was all Burr's doing. After all, Edward Livingston said Smith said that Bayard said that Burr had authorized him to make the offers. How could it be wrong?

It is significant that Edward Livingston was one of the few Burr "friends" who obtained an appointment from Jefferson (U.S. Attorney) and Samuel Smith became the temporary secretary of the Navy, which post was then transferred to Smith's younger brother, Robert, in July 1801, when Samuel resigned.

~

PART THREE:

The Conspirators

"All the world knew that not Cheetham, but De Witt Clinton thus dragged the Vice-President from his chair, and that not Burr's vices but his influence made his crimes heinous; that behind De Witt Clinton stood the Virginia dynasty, dangling Burr's office in the eyes of the Clinton family, and lavishing honors and money on the Livingstons. All this was as clear to Burr and his friends as though it were embodied in an Act of Congress." (Adams, *TJ Administrations*, 225.)

"Never in the history of the United States did so powerful a combination of rival politicians unite to break down a single man as that which arrayed itself against Burr; for as the hostile circle gathered about him, he could plainly see not only Jefferson, Madison, and the whole Virginia legion, with Duane and his [newspaper] "Aurora" at their heels; not only De Witt Clinton and his whole family interest, with Cheetham and his "Watchtower" by their side; but – strangest of companions – Hamilton himself joining hands with his own bitterest enemies to complete the ring." (Adams, *TJ Administrations*, 226.)

"I hope you will not hang me for what I may do."
Wilkinson to Jefferson, December 25, 1806
Founders Online.

Moving against Burr

Unacquainted myself with these and the other characters in [New York] state which
might be proper for those offices and forced to decide on the opinions of others,
there is no one whose opinion would command with me greater respect than yours if
you would be so good as to advise me, which of these characters and what others
would be fittest for these offices.
Jefferson to George Clinton, Governor of NY
May 17, 1801
(quoted in Lomask 1:303-04; Ford, *TJ Writings* 8:53)

After the election, one of Jefferson's first tasks was to
remove extreme Federalists from civil offices. Obviously,
Jefferson knew that keeping such extremists in essential offices
could cause problems for him. He did not wish to remove
every Federalist, just those who might create trouble. This was
a process Jefferson did not relish. Nonetheless, he used the
process not only to rid himself of troublesome Federalists but
to exclude potentially troublesome Burrites, to deny Burr the
fruits of his work for the party, and to "render [him] naked to
his enemies at home," as well. (Lomask 1:304.)

Behind Burr's back, he approached New York
Governor, George Clinton, soliciting his opinions on Burr's
recommendations for appointments. He told Clinton that he
had received letters that two of Burr's recommended
appointees (one being Matthew L. Davis, discussed earlier)
were unsuitable. Jefferson wrote Clinton on the advice of
others (Samuel Osgood and John Armstrong, both of whom
subsequently received appointments themselves) who had
written to Jefferson and Madison, "repeating tales of Burr's
attempts to rob Jefferson of the presidency and urging that
Clinton be consulted before any further appointments were
made." (Editorial Note: *Burr and Jeffersonian Patronage*,
Kline 2:536-37.)[86]

---

[86] In addition to Armstrong and Osgood, Marinus Willett, a comrade of Burr's in
the war and usually a Burr supporter, also wrote to TJ, speaking against
Matthew L. Davis, whom Burr had recommended. He told TJ he had suggested
to George Clinton "to let you know his mind respecting appointments in the
State." Clinton had "expressed an unwilingness which appeared to arise from a
Conception that your acquaintance with him would Induce you to make enquiry

Kline justifies Jefferson's action by saying that "George Clinton's return to the governorship meant that his opinion must be sought in settling the distribution of N.Y. Patronage." (Kline, *Editorial Note: Burr and Jeffersonian Patronage*, [post 17 March 1801], Kline 1:540.) Really?

Kline further suggests that Jefferson was "disgust[ed] with AB" because he had pressed the appointment of Matthew L. Davis. (Id.) Maybe. Jefferson seems to have felt disgusted with Burr from the start anyway. But Lomask, discussing Burr's patronage recommendations to the NY Council of Appointment around the same time, notes that "[a]gainst the thousands of jobs at the disposal of the council, his shopping list – the only one he ever submitted to the council – was amazingly modest, a mere squeak amid the howls and yammers for places at the public trough then resounding throughout the state democracy." (Lomask 1: 305-06.) The same could be said about his requests to Jefferson.

However, Kline writes, "[b]y September [1801,] Jefferson had been apprised of every doubt and suspicion felt by a Republican politician concerning Burr's motives and honor. Perhaps just as damning, Jefferson had learned how precarious Burr's political position was in his home state." (Kline 1:540.) Among those so-called Republicans, Samuel Osgood wrote: "We have strong evidence" that the men Jefferson had appointed to offices in NY already "are entirely devoted to the Vice President and had it been in their power we have reason to believe that Mr. Jefferson would not have been President." (Osgood to Madison, April 24, 1801, Madison Papers, Library of Congress, quoted in Lomask 1:303.)

Presumably, Jefferson sought information and took the best advice he could get in each state but in approaching George Clinton, he was seeking counsel behind his own Vice President's back, in his home state, in opposition to him, and from his enemies. After all Burr had done for the party and for Jefferson (who would not have come close to the presidency without Burr's "extraordinary exertions and successes," *TJ: Memorandum,* January 26, 1804, Kline 2:822), this was not the

---

if you should conceive it necessary." MW to TJ, May 4, 1801. (*Papers of TJ.*) Less than two weeks later, TJ wrote the governor. Thus did one of Burr's own "friends" set in motion the machine that was to destroy him.

way Burr should have been treated. If Jefferson did not agree with Burr's recommendations, he certainly was not obliged to fill them, but he could at least have taken the time to discuss them with his Vice President, rather than leaving him in the dark for months and then belatedly writing him a cold note stating: "Your favor of the 10ᵗʰ [of November] has been received, as have been those of Sept. 4 and 23 . . . These letters relating to office, fall within a general rule . . . of not answering letters on office specifically, but leaving the answer to be found in what is done or not done on them." (TJ to AB, November 18, 1801, *TJ Papers,* Library of Congress, quoted in Lomask 1:302.)

The "Republican politicians" whom Kline says expressed "every doubt and suspicion" about Burr to TJ did not comprise the whole of Republicans in New York. They were his opponents, Clintonians. Nor was Burr's political position "precarious" in his home state, as Kline suggests. The state had long been divided among several wealthy political families. For a young, independent newcomer, Burr had remarkably high standing and repute.

Moreover, Jefferson might have followed Burr's example in how to regard rumors of "strong evidence" of his running mate's disloyalty. Burr had even provided his example directly to Jefferson when he wrote him in February 1801 that it being "so obvious that the most malignant spirit of slander and intrigue would be busy, that without any enquiry, I set down as calumny every tale calculated to disturb our harmony [and] invariably pronounce[d] to be a lie, every thing which ought not to be true." (AB to TJ, February 12, 1801, Kline 1:501.)[87] Burr was not the one being disloyal, adhering to his colleague's enemies, or plotting behind the other's back.

Had Jefferson properly supported his VP, the in-

---

[87] Burr made a similar comment to Gallatin when the latter wrote Burr about what Burr described as "your very amusing history" of the electoral tie, which told how the "feds boast aloud that they have compromised with Jefferson, particularly as to the retaining certain persons in office," about which Burr remarked that "without the assurance contained in your letter, this would gain no manner of credit with me." (AB to AG, February 26, 1801, quoted in Lomask 1:296, citing to Gallatin Papers, New York Hist'l Soc.) Lomask observes that Burr's last remark "indicates that [AG] shared the belief . . . that [TJ] had stooped to deal."

fighting in NY would have become toothless and faded away. Whatever rifts existed, Jefferson's actions expanded them into wide chasms, permanently damaging Burr's reputation and changing New York politics for the worse. For Burr, who had long worked hard to find common ground between the three New York factions and had frequently formed *ad hoc* nonpartisan coalitions (that even sometimes included moderate Federalists), Jefferson's meddling probably would have made no sense had he known of it. TJ's maneuverings were certainly a major factor behind the so-called "Pamphlet Wars" that broke out thereafter, first making their appearance, on Clinton's behalf and with Jefferson's encouragement, with James Cheetham's accusations against Burr. Without Jefferson's behind-the-scenes support, the Clintonians would have had no wind in their sails.

Years later, Burr identified Jefferson's modus operandi: "One of their principal arts & which has been systematically taught by Jefferson is that of promoting state dissensions." (AB to Joseph Alston, November 15, 1815, Kline 2:166, spelling modernized.) Exactly.

Roger G. Kennedy, describing how Jefferson's silence forced Burr to pursue his appointment recommendations through Gideon Granger and Albert Gallatin, noted that with regard to patronage matters, "Jefferson appears to have enjoyed goading Burr into that activity he [later] described in his private *Anas* as badgering him for patronage." (Kennedy, 169.) Burstein & Isenberg conclude that "Madison and Jefferson were in agreement that they should not shore up Vice President Burr's patronage power in his home state of New York." (*Madison & Jefferson*, 370-71.)

No reply from George Clinton to Jefferson has been found but Jefferson's letter was the start of a *sub rosa* collaboration between TJ and the New York Governor's nephew and protégé, DeWitt Clinton, who had just been appointed to replace John Armstrong in the U.S. Senate, over which Burr was to preside.

Jefferson took advantage of the unstable politics in New York and further destabilized it, encouraging the growth of malignant and anti-libertarian activities, undoing years of work for the Republican cause on Burr's part. Jefferson wrote "We shall yield a little to their pressure but not more than appears absolutely necessary to keep them together." (TJ to Wilson Cary Nicholas, June 11, 1801, in Ford, *The Works of TJ*, IX: 266.) His actions did not keep anyone together. They were divisive.

Thus already, by late-1801, Jefferson had the New York Clintons and Livingstons in his pocket and in his service, operating under the influence of whatever spoils they could obtain from doing his bidding. Isenberg writes that Jefferson had to make a choice: "He probably saw it as safer, for him, to risk schism in New York than to allow Burr to continue as the Republican leader in that state, as he had been before 1801. Burr alone, among the party faithful, might mount a northern challenge to Virginia's preeminence among Republicans nationwide." (Isenberg, 231.)

The president's thought process was that "Burr had to be sacrificed – no matter what – if Secretary of State Madison was to have the way clear to move up the ranks to chief executive." (Id. at 230.) If Jefferson was not thinking ahead, a letter Albert Gallatin wrote him six months after the election brought the topic to his full attention. Gallatin asked Jefferson:

> Do [the Republicans] eventually mean not to support Burr as your successor when you shall think fit to retire? Do they mean not to support him at next election for Vice President? . . . [T]he danger would be great, should any unfortunate event deprive the people of your services. Where is the man we could support with any reasonable prospect of success? Mr Madison is the only one, & his being a Virginian would be a considerable objection.

(AG to TJ, September 14, 1801, Founders Online.) Gallatin outlined two ways to approach the problem of Jefferson's successor: "either to support Burr once more, or to give only one vote for President, scattering our votes for the other person to be voted for." (Id.)

Burr was thus, in the mind of Gallatin, a thing to be disposed of for the benefit of the Virginia Dynasty. No thought to how Burr might feel about it or to find a way to work together with Burr. Gallatin simply accepted that Burr was out. This means Gallatin also accepted the rumors of Burr's disloyalty (or accepted that Burr's actions showed such disloyalty). Either way, Gallatin had turned away from Burr's friendship and bought into the Jeffersonian doctrine: Burr was a traitor. So much for Burr's opinion that Gallatin was the best head in the country![88]

Gallatin clarified to TJ the risks of supporting Burr: "If we do . . . we run, on the one hand, the risk of the federal party making B. president; & we seem, on the other, to give him an additional pledge of being eventually supported hereafter by the republicans for that office. If we embrace the last party, we not only lose the Vice President, but pave the way for the federal successful candidate to that office to become President." (Id.) Well, at least here was some rational thinking. The fear that Burr would allow the Federalists to make him president was legitimate to a degree. They had tried.

But Burr had declined. Did Gallatin not know this? Federalist Rep. William Cooper had declared that "Had Burr done anything for himself he would long ere this have been president." (WC to Thomas Morris, February 13, 1801, in Davis, *Memoirs of AB*, 2:113.) Federalist Rep. James Bayard wrote Hamilton that the "means existed of electing Burr, but this required his co-operation. By deceiving one man (a great blockhead), and tempting two (not incorruptible), he might have secured the majority of the States." Bayard added: "He will never have another chance of being President of the United States; and the little use he has made of this one . . . . gives me an humble opinion of the talents of an unprincipled man." (JB to AH, May 8, 1801, quoted in Lomask 1:294, citing to *Hamilton Works*, 6:522-24.)

To TJ, Gallatin closed his discussion by concluding that the problems "would be remedied by the amendt. of distinguishing the votes for the two offices; & by that of

---

[88] There was a rumor that during the electoral tie, Gallatin had written to Burr exhorting him to ride post haste to Washington to secure the presidency for himself. Gallatin apparently later emphatically denied this. *See* Lomask 1:287-88 and note to p.287 (at pp. 403-04) (Years later, Gallatin when asked about this, stated "[Y]ou must be mistaken, I was always for Jefferson."). Lomask suggests AG may have believed Burr's presence in Washington would prevent a Federalist usurpation.

dividing the States into districts." (AG to TJ, September 14, 1801.) Such an amendment, of course, was enacted in 1804.

Gallatin was not privy to the thinking of Federalists Cooper and Bayard. But rather than talking directly to Burr and finding out the facts, he chose to heed rumor, and adopt Jefferson's beliefs. Certainly not the best head in the Union.[89]

Thus, almost immediately after he was elected, Jefferson began consciously and actively gathering and utilizing existing forces against Burr. In 1804, when Burr finally sued James Cheetham for falsely claiming he tried to steal the election, Burr gathered statements from several persons, including Bayard, who confirmed that Jefferson had agreed to Federalist terms in exchange for their votes for him. (*See* Kline 2:964-67, n5.)

Jefferson was using men, interests, as well as socio-political forces to build his "Revolution of 1800," his "empire of liberty," and to destroy Burr. His focus on Burr's home state is significant. It was not hard for Jefferson to conjure the dark powers there against Burr. It was easy for Jefferson and he had no qualms about doing it.

~

---

[89]   Burr said: "No one in the United States appreciated [British philosopher Jeremy Bentham's] ideas except himself and Albert Gallatin . . . who was the best head in the United States." (Kennedy, 156, quoting Parton 2:168-69 (2 vol. edition, Chelsea House, 1983), apparently paraphrasing an 1808 letter or verbal communication from Burr while he was in London to Pierre-Etienne-Louis Dumont, Bentham's editor and English-French translator.)

The Knot of Knaves

Gideon Granger   John Armstrong

DeWitt Clinton   Ambrose Spencer

The Knot of Knaves

There are "[l]ong-smothered jealousies and pent-up heart-burnings
between the CLINTONIANS or JEFFERSONIANS, and the BURRITES."
(Federalist) *NY Evening Post,* April 27, 1802
(quoted in Kline 2:724)

This knot of Knaves cannot long hold together – they begin already
to call each other lyars – the only truth they have uttered.
Burr to Pierpont Edwards, July 15, 1802; Kline 2:728

With a violence that startled uninitiated bystanders, Cheetham in his
"American Citizen" flung one charge after another at Burr.
(Adams, *TJ Administrations*, 225.)

     While scholars have been aware of the existence of the group of men who were responsible for the fall of Burr in New York and have identified the actors, none has placed those men in the context of a larger conspiracy to destroy Burr managed by Thomas Jefferson. This loose cabal was comprised of DeWitt Clinton, John Armstrong, Ambrose Spencer, James Cheetham, and Gideon Granger. Their collaboration was in part the result of similar temperaments and views, part circumstance, and part a conscious collusion against Burr initiated and encouraged by Jefferson. Three of them had started out as Federalists and switched sides, all became super loyal Jefferson flunkies who later opposed him.

     That they were part of the second phase of Jefferson's conspiracy is clear. None other than Granger, however, directly participated in the third phase. All but Granger participated only in what they considered to be legitimate destruction of Burr's reputation and political career. Granger (who became a cabinet member) went further and we therefore deal with him in a separate chapter. Ambrose Spencer appears to have joined briefly in political efforts to undermine Burr before the young man was appointed New York State Attorney and later a judge, but he introduced Armstrong to Clinton. Cheetham was the only one of the gang that Burr called out (sued).

DeWitt Clinton, through Cheetham's articles and pamphlets, and Burr, largely through the writings of William P. Van Ness ("Aristides") and one "Brutus," engaged in a two-year protracted mutual denunciation campaign, dubbed "the Pamphlet War." It started with Cheetham's charges of Burr's "suppression" of John Wood's *History of the Administration of John Adams*, but according to Kline, "Burr's enemies deliberately delayed their exposure of his role in the suppression" from December 1801 to the end of May 1802, because "Republicans could not afford to publicize the embarrassing division in their ranks until the polls had closed" on local elections. (Kline 2:724.) Then, "[i]mmediately upon [DeWitt] Clinton's return from Washington, James Cheetham began work on a pamphlet." (Id., 725.)

DeWitt Clinton was the core around which the New York cabal orbited, with respect to the destruction of Burr. He was born March 2, 1769 in New York (likely upstate in New Windsor). (Cornog, 14) He was the nephew of Governor George Clinton (who later supplanted Burr as TJ's VP). He studied law before becoming his uncle's official secretary in 1790. After the elder Clinton's retirement in 1795, DWC returned to legal practice and entered politics in 1797 when he ran with Burr on the Republican ticket for NYC assembly. From February 1802 to November 1803, Clinton served as U.S. Senator, during which time he solidified his ties with the Jefferson Administration. (Siry, 89.)

Isenberg identifies what may offer a partial reason for DeWitt Clinton's aversion to Burr: Burr's support of Edward Livingston in opposition to Clinton for Mayor of New York City. Burr wrote Livingston that he (Burr) "will never be forgiven," presumably by the Clintons. (AB to EL, February 12, 1801, Kline 1:502.)

Another event occurred in early 1803 during the time Clinton served in the U.S. Senate while Burr was presiding, which provides a better explanation for the depth of Clinton's hatred for Burr. Although the Pamphlet War was already in full swing by the time of this event and it involved the junior senator Clinton and Jonathan Dayton, not "the principal"

(Burr),[90] Dayton, although a Federalist, had been a friend of Burr's since childhood. (He was later a key player in Burr's expedition.) It is likely that Clinton attributed the agency of this humiliating event to Burr.

This was prior to the Louisiana Purchase. Spain still held New Orleans and the Spanish Intendant there had just decided to prohibit Americans from depositing their goods in that city. Clinton argued the Administration's line: negotiation. He "questioned whether Madrid had authorized the infraction, stated that negotiations should, in justice, precede any employment of force, and contended that the immediate use of force . . . would not be in the best interest of the United States." (Siry, 93.) Apparently Clinton's tone offended Dayton. Repeating Clinton's words, Dayton asked: "Where were those gentlemen" who argued for strong measures "when the British were committing their depredations? . . . I was at my post in the other House, and the advocate of measures as strong, nay stronger than those now proposed." Dayton was just getting started:

> Why did not the gentleman from New York carry his inquiries back to the far more gloomy and trying times of 1776? . . . Had he asked where we then were . . . I could have told him that we, or some of us at least, were employed in his own state, upon the interior frontiers, defending the very people whom he now represents, from the irruptions of savages and the devastation of the enemy. Where was then this honorable interrogator himself? Doubtless in some place of safety, perhaps dangling on the knee of the mother, or probably still in the egg-shell.[91]

(Annals of Congress, 7th Congress, 2nd Sess., p. 136.) Dayton observed: "To what do all such questions tend? Certainly not to elucidate the subject nor to conciliate parties." (Id.) Dayton continued:

---

[90]   These were the words Clinton purportedly used in reference to Burr, after he dueled Burrite John Swartwout, who had challenged Clinton for having called him a liar, scoundrel, and villain. After shooting Swartwout three times, Clinton supposedly said he was sorry he hurt Swartwout "but I wish I had the *principal* here. I will meet him when he pleases." (Siry, 68.)

[91]   Clinton was born March 2, 1769. Thus, he turned 7 in 1776.

> Severe in his strictures upon declaimers, [Clinton's] own language was that of declamation; reprobating asperity in debate, on the part of others, he had indulged himself in a style little decorous or becoming, and exhausted against his opponents his full cup of bitterness. He had declared with a boldness of assertion not unusual to him, that the resolutions under consideration contained declarations of war; but this was not the fact, they were merely intended as preparations for [war with Spain,] an event which some regard as inevitable, and all believe to be too probable.

(Id.) By this time, Burr had long known that Clinton was behind Cheetham's muckraking. He wrote his son-in-law: "It will, in due time, be known what [Cheetham and Wood] are, and what is Dewitt Clinton, their colleague and instigator." (AB to JA, July 3, 1802, in Davis, *Memoirs*, 2:205.)

The following session, Dayton and Clinton continued exchanging criticisms. During this last exchange in the Senate, Dayton wanted to strike out the part of the proposed constiutional amendment that concerned selection of a vice-president. Clinton and Armstrong (who was about to return to the Senate and take Clinton's seat) viewed this amendment as directed against Burr. (Cornog, 46-49; Skeen, 50.) Clinton suggested that Dayton "had no reason for opposing the amendment except that he wanted to deny to Clinton the honor of securing its passage." (Siry, 96.) Dayton then observed what he called "the custom of the gentleman from New York . . . to arraign motives instead of meeting arguments." (Id., 97, citing *Annals of Congress*, 8th Cong., 1st Sess., pp. 16, 21-22.) Clinton denied it. Finally, Dayton declaimed that "his high respect for the Senate restrained him from replying in those terms which were due to such rudeness and such indecency of language as that in which [Clinton] had indulged himself." (Id.)

Dayton was on the war path against Clinton. That night, he issued a demand for an apology. Clinton sent an apology to the *Senate* and left town to assume the mayoralty of New York City. (*See also,* Cornog, 48-49.) The matter was apparently settled in an "honorable, manly, and proper manner" by Clinton's Virginia friends, who lamented to Clinton "Who is to supply the talents that we lost by your removing from the Senate?" (Id., 97-98, quoting Wilson C. Nicholas to DeWitt Clinton, October 27, December 3, 1803.) On the other side of the aisle, though, Federalist Senator William Plumer wrote: "[Clinton's] absence will not be the subject of regret to a single member of the Senate. He is a man of violent passions, of a bitter, vindictive spirit – unfeeling – insolent – haughty – & rough in his manners." (*Plumer's Memorandum*, 25-26.)

According to Siry, "Clinton's effort to attain passage of the amendment indicated, in part, his strong desire during this time to please the Jefferson administration" and "during his twenty months stay in the Senate he was one of the twenty men that President Jefferson considered as Congressional leaders." (Siry, 98, 99.) Clinton wanted to return to New York in order "to deliver a decisive blow against Burr's political career." He "correctly viewed himself as one of the most powerful Jeffersonian Republicans in the North, and recognized that his ties with the administration were stronger than ever" by the end of his U.S. Senate term. (Siry, 99.)

Back in New York, Clinton wrote to his brother-in-law, Thomas Tillotson (who by then was New York's secretary of state):

> The abuse I have received is so general and so brutal that I can scarcely work myself up to a very high pitch of irritation – but viewing it as I do as an exhibition of the cloven foot of Burr, I have learnt it is possible to entertain a worse opinion of him that I had before.

(DWC to TT, December 20, 1803, quoted in Cornog, 42.) Cloven foot, of course, refers to the devil. Cornog writes that "the fury of the Clintonians would admit no clemency." (Cornog, 42.)

Both Clinton and Armstrong were initially enthralled by Jefferson and wished to ingratiate themselves with him.[92]

---

[92]   DeWitt wrote to Horatio Gates: "I am much pleased with our President. Never did I before see realized a perfect view of the First Magistrate of a republican nation." (DC to HG, February 25, 1802, quoted without source in Siry, *DeWitt Clinton*, 90.) Armstrong wrote his brother-in-law, Thomas Tillotson: "The nearer you approach Jefferson, the better you like him." (JA to TT, January 13, 1801, NYPL, Armstrong Papers, Misc., quoted in Skeen, *John Armstrong*, 45.)

Both later formed unfavorable views of the President.[93] Neither man, however, seems to have reconsidered his opinions of Burr or regretted his actions towards him.

Clinton and Armstrong were the "ambitious underlings" who "joined forces to destroy Burr's career." (Isenberg, 228.) Armstrong had been appointed U.S. Senator in November 1800 and arrived in Washington the first week of January 1801, but by the Fall, he was expressing doubts about staying. About the undeveloped new capitol town, he wrote: "A banishment of six months in Siberia would not be much more disagreeable, than a stay of the same length of time at that place." (JA to Major General Horatio Gates, November 22, 1801, quoted in Skeen, 48.) After that session, he never returned. However, he remained interested in curbing Burr's influence and supported De Witt Clinton's efforts against Burr, suggesting that a Clinton victory might "prostrate[Burr] and his ambition forever, and will besides be a useful admonition to future schismatics." (JA to DC, June 26, 1802, quoted in id., 49.)

Then in 1803, Edward Livingston resigned as mayor and Clinton, who had taken Armstrong's Senate seat, now resigned that and took Livingston's mayoral seat, prompting Governor George Clinton to appoint Armstrong again to the U.S. Senate. He accepted and returned to Washington quite quickly, because "the presidential election is approaching and measures were to be taken in relation to that object." (JA to Chancellor Robert Livingston [his brother-in-law], February 4, 1804, quoted in Skeen, 50.) In other words (Skeen suggests), Armstrong returned because he wished to assist Clinton and Jefferson in the removal of Burr.

Born in Carlisle, PA, in 1758, Armstrong had begun his political career as a Federalist but switched to being a Republican when he moved to New York and rather quickly found his way into Jefferson's inner sanctum as advisor and

---

[93] "In due course, [Armstrong] retracted his favorable impressions of Jefferson," writes Skeen. Armstrong wrote Tillotson: "Vigor does not seem to be the character of the man himself and … his Cabinet will not be much calculated to supply his defects," adding that "It has received my private and public reprobtion and it shall continue to receive it." (Skeen, 46.) As to Clinton, Siry writes: "[B]etween 1803 and 1807 Clinton became increasingly alienated from President Jefferson over maritime issues and related matters." (Siry, 105.)

confidante. He had attended the College of New Jersey, as both Burr and Madison had, but left the college to enlist during the Revolution. As Horatio Gates' aide-de-camp, he was the author of the Newburgh Address in 1783, which essentially threatened mutiny if the soldiers were not paid. "For a brief ten days the heroic defenders of liberty took on the hideous mask of a standing army that could bully a democratic government into doing its will." (Linklater, *An Artist in Treason*, 110.) Furthermore, "the Newburgh address's call to officers to play upon 'the *fears* of government' continued to haunt Congress." (Id.) Thus, one of Armstrong's earliest public acts was – on principle, of course – to attempt to "bully" his government and play upon its fears.

In November 1800, we find Burr writing to a colleague that "John Armstrong is chosen Senator *vice*,[94] John Laurance resigned – Mr. A[']s principles & Talents will prove an important acquisition to our Cause." (AB to Tench Coxe, November 6, 1800, Kline 1:453.) Burr was then still a member of the New York Assembly and participated in appointing presidential electors, as well as the replacement U.S. Senator. Thus, Burr assisted in elevating a man who returned the favor by plotting against him. Later when in exile, Burr described Armstrong, who was by then minister to France, as "for many years . . . my personal and political enemy." (AB to Volney, August 5, 1810, Davis, *Private Journal of AB*, 2:30-31.)

With respect to Armstrong's party loyalties, Robert Troup (a Federalist) wrote in 1800: "It is not unlikely that Armstrong will be appointed [Senator] who being weary of waiting for federal honors has at length declared that he has discovered that he has long worn the political coat the wrong side out and that he now wears the right side out. He has lately published some of the virulent & Jacobinical pieces ag[ains]t the administration [of John Adams]." (RT to Rufus King, August 9, 1800, quoted in Kline 1:454n1.) But John L. Livingston, Armstrong's brother-in-law, wrote his brother Robert Livingston in December that Armstrong had "prevent[ed] your being a Candidate [for governor], that under

---

[94] Vice - acting as deputy or substitute for; next in rank : *vice regent* | *vice-consul.*
ORIGIN from Latin *vice "in place of." New Oxford American Dictionary.*

the stale pretence of throwing every thing on one family[,] your popularity might be lessened." (Kline, id., quoting John L. Livingston to Robert R. Livingston, [Dec. 1800].)

Armstrong "inexplicably became a confidant of Jefferson's when he was sent to Washington in 1801 as senator from New York." (Isenberg, 228.) Jefferson's own notes show he relied on Armstrong and Clinton to undermine Burr's recommendations. Where a candidate was identified by either man as "not estimated," "not approved" or "devoted to Burr," his appointment was delayed or struck. (Editorial Note: *Burr and Jeffersonian Patronage,* in Kline 1:535-36.)

In 1804, Armstrong, then serving a second term in the U.S. Senate, wrote his brother-in-law Robert R. Livingston, who was in France as a special envoy, that of all the vice presidential candidates, "Burr has the most industry, the most talent, the most address – but will have the least support." (Kline 2:823, quoting JA to RRL, February 7, 1804.) Kline notes that Armstrong explained to Livingston that George Clinton's candidacy for vice president was something that he "took upon myself, in direct opposition to all our friends at *home*, and have brought it to this point, that if he will consent to serve, no doubt can be entertained of his being selected." (Id.) Kline states: "In this letter Armstrong presented as his own [a] scheme by which [George] Clinton would not only gain the nomination for vice president but also run for another term as governor in New York. Once elected to the vice presidency, Clinton was to resign the governorship." (Id.) Armstrong explained to Livingston, "This will give time for your arrival [from France] & for such arrangements as may be necessary to produce your succession" to the governorship. (Id.) Armstrong thus wished to take all the credit for destroying Burr's political chances nationally and locally. However, he was not alone in his work.

Armstrong's connection with DWC arose from his friendship with Ambrose Spencer. Spencer was born in Connecticut in 1765. He attended Yale, graduated from Harvard in 1783 (the year the war ended), and studied law in CT, thence moving to Hudson, NY and gaining admission to the NY Bar in 1788. He served in the state assembly and senate from 1794-1803 and on the Council of Appointment in 1797 and 1800. He was the assistant state attorney in several upstate NY counties in the late 1790's and served as NY Attorney General from 1802-04, when he was appointed to the state supreme court, becoming chief justice in 1819. (Kline 1:477.)

Spencer met Armstrong in early 1797 and the two men "were apparently attracted to each other immediately, and it began a warm and intimate friendship that lasted until Armstrong's death forty-six years later." (Skeen, 44.) Skeen claims Spencer and Armstrong were "compatible intellectually . . . outspoken, opinionated, and . . . gave no quarter in partisan politics," invariably agreeing on political issues. (Id.) It is interesting that Skeen characterizes the friendship as warm, since he defines Armstrong's personality as diffident and arrogant, noting Albert Gallatin's observation about him that "there is something which will forever prevent [him] having any direct influence with the people." (Id., 47, quoting AG to TJ, September 14, 1801.)

In any event, Spencer "soon became allied with another young rising politician" - DeWitt Clinton – when both were elected to the "all-powerful Council of Appointment, which controlled the patronage of the state." (Id., 45.) Kline notes that Spencer had begun his service as NY Senator as a Federalist but changed to the Republican ticket the next year. (Kline 1:477.) In any event, Spencer's service as attorney general and supreme court judge probably prevented him from further direct involvement in the campaign against Burr.

In February 1804, Armstrong reported that the Republican caucus had chosen George Clinton to replace Burr as VP, giving Burr not a single vote.[95] Armstrong was happy with the results. He wrote Spencer, now a New York judge, that this result was proof of the "ascendancy of republicanism . . . against the combined force of federalism and Burrism," which he declared had put "all their machinery of misrepresentation into action against us." (JA to AS, June 4, 1804, quoted in id., 51.) Thus, it appears that the two men merged Burr with "federalism" and their "machinery of

---

[95] This was the "not a single voice" that Jefferson claimed supported Burr. *TJ: Memorandum of Conversation with AB,* April 15, 1806, Kline 2:962.

misrepresentation" against Republicans. A very Jeffersonian view.

What did Jefferson have to do with any of this? He had taken both Armstrong and Clinton under his wing as soon as they had gone to Washington, taking their advice about appointments, specifically opposing Burr's recommendations. He had solicited their opinions, in fact, not merely accepted and heeded them. How do we know this? Because he had written Governor George Clinton back in 1801 asking his advice and Jefferson made notes that show the weight he gave their advice to him. (Kline 1:535-56.)

While Jefferson was as much a man of his time as anyone and thus not everything was within his agency, he took advantage of men and conditions with the knowledge and intent of doing harm to Burr. Jefferson could (and should) have avoided writing to the New York Governor out of respect for his VP. He could and should have avoided creating and/or capitalizing on the schism in New York, which he increased by giving the ambitious young New Yorkers power or the semblance of power over Burr, who was their senior, their superior in ability, experience, reputation, and credentials. He could and should have consulted Burr for his recommendations and could and should have heeded Burr's advice. He could and should have kept Burr close by him, rather than making an enemy of him. Even if Burr had done what Jefferson liked to have thought he did (although Jefferson knew Burr had not attempted to steal the election), Jefferson would have been wiser to keep counsel with him, especially if Jefferson thought him a dangerous or powerful man. But he should have known better. Jefferson created a divide where none had existed or needed to exist. It is remarkable that Burr did not become the enemy Jefferson treated him as.

Meantime, while in 1803 Armstrong was doing his part in the U.S. Senate, Spencer and DeWitt Clinton had done their part in the 1801 New York Council of Appointment and Legislature to obtain the passage of a resolution whose object was to affirm the Council's authority to remove and replace civil servants. (*See* Lomask 1:304-05.) Lomask notes that the NY cabal was "happy to let Burr break the long stranglehold of the Federalists in the Empire State [but] [n]ow that it was broken, now that Federalism was no longer a threat, they were determined to gather the reins of power unto themselves ... not all at once . . . but step by step, subtly." (Id., 306.) But, says Lomask, "[s]o far as can be determined, [Burr] was still unconscious of the elements marshaling against him. " (Id., 307.) Burr could have prevented this event, for he was president of the convention to amend the state constitution for Spencer and Clinton's purpose, but did not "use his influence ... to try to prevent a change ... that enhanced the powers and resources of his enemies." (Id.)

Jefferson was directly involved with Clinton and Armstrong. Although James Cheetham was hired by Clinton, Jefferson was also directly involved with him. In December 1801, the journalist provided to Jefferson an "account of the plans and views of aggrandizement of a faction in the City of New York," which listed "in outline form most of the denunciations of Burr" he planned to publish in the Clintonian newspaper *American Citizen.* (Lomask 1:316.) A few weeks later, Cheetham wrote Jefferson about Burr's attempt to "suppress" John Wood's *History of the Administration of John Adams.* Burr considered that the book contained "low scurrilities" that would do more harm than good to the Republicans. He told the publishers the book contained legally actionable libels and graciously offered to buy all copies. Though Burr's action was intended to protect the Republican party, Cheetham distorted it, accusing him of purchasing Federalist favor.

Henry Adams claims that Burr had "flung down a challenge to the Virginians,"

> . . . which De Witt Clinton, on their behalf, hastened to take up. With a violence that startled uninitiated bystanders, Cheetham in his "American Citizen" flung one charge after another at Burr: first his Judiciary vote; then his birthday toast; then the suppression of a worthless history of the last Administration written by John Wood . . . whose book Burr bought in order, as Cheetham believed, to curry favor with the New England Federalists; finally . . . Cheetham charged that

> Burr had tried to steal the Presidency from Jefferson . . . [But] [a]ll the world knew that not Cheetham, but De Witt Clinton thus dragged the Vice-President from his chair, and that not Burr's vices but his influence made his crimes heinous; that behind De Witt Clinton stood the Virginia dynasty, dangling Burr's office in the eyes of the Clinton family, and lavishing honors and money on the Livingstons.

(Adams*, TJ Administrations*, 225.)

After receiving Cheetham's outline, Jefferson wrote him back, thanking him for the account of his plans, noting with obvious pleasure that the information about Wood's *History* was "pregnant with considerations." A few months later, he asked Cheetham to send him copies of the publications and "add the postage to your bill." (Lomask, 1:314-316, citing JC to TJ, December 10, 1801; TJ to JC, December 29, 1801; TJ to JC, January 17, 1802 and April 23, 1802.)

For the next two years, Cheetham put out "a running fire on the Vice President" in the *American Citizen* and issued four more pamphlets. (Lomask 1:316.) Adams writes:

> Never in the history of the United States did so powerful a combination of rival politicians unite to break down a single man as that which arrayed itself against Burr; for as the hostile circle gathered about him, he could plainly see not only Jefferson, Madison, and the whole Virginia legion . . . not only De Witt Clinton and his whole family interests, with Cheetham and his "Watchtower" by their side; but . . . Alexander Hamilton himself joining hands with his own bitterest enemies to complete the ring.

(Adams, 226.)

~

The Middle Ground

"Political life was moving beyond the range of what both [Burr and John Jay] regarded as decency for gentlemen of their character, but, for a time, Burr and Jay held the middle ground against the excesses of their factions." Roger Kennedy, *Burr, Hamilton, & Jefferson: A Study in Character*, 108.

Gideon Granger

[Granger's] conduct towards me was ever friendly and faithful, and I on several occasions used his services to the advantage of the public.
TJ to Madison, March 10, 1814
Kennedy, 277.

At age 33, Gideon Granger was appointed by Jefferson as his Postmaster General. The appointment was the reward for having spied on Burr and for having put Jefferson "on guard" about Burr's purported dealings with Connecticut Federalists. Later on, he confirmed his value to Jefferson by "expediting the mails" in New Orleans and by firing any postal worker suspected of being a Burrite during the crisis created by Wilkinson and Jefferson's alarms about Burr.

Granger was born in Suffield, Connecticut on July 19, 1767. He was 11 years younger than Burr (and like DWC, died many years before Burr). Like Clinton and Ambrose Spencer, Granger did not belong to Burr's generation nor to Jefferson's but to the generation that came into adulthood after the war.[96] Granger was 8 years old when war was declared and 16 when it ended. The principles of the Revolution were abstractions not impressed into the younger generation in the same way they were in men who had shared responsibility for or risked their lives in the war.

These younger men had stirrings of industrial nationalism and a drive to commercial expansion quite opposite of the doctrines of southern agrarians like Jefferson. Their alliance with Jefferson seems to have centered largely around two objectives: the creation of a national Republican party and the destruction of Burr. That is even more odd, since Burr's beliefs were closer to theirs. He was not against commerce, expansion, industrialization, or land speculation.

According to Granger's biographer, he was much influenced by Oliver Phelps, who had been indentured as a child to a Suffield family, where he learned the mercantile

---

[96] Armstrong, on the other hand, was only two years younger than Burr and had served in the war, though he did no active fighting. He seems to have identified more with the men from the post-revolutionary generation.

trade. Phelps had later prospered in Granville Hills, Massachusetts, where he had settled, acquired much land and become a man of prominence in business and politics, then returning to Suffield in 1789 to take title to a house, which he made "the finest in town," with ionic pillars and a triglyph frieze. (Hamlin, *Gideon Granger,* 2-3.)

In 1789, Granger was admitted to the bar and in 1790 he married a local girl, Mindwell Pease. He was elected to the state legislature in 1792, where he served for most of the next nine years. During that time, Granger and Phelps "formed a syndicate to bid" on some large tracts of western Connecticut-owned land. This activity was similar to Burr's land speculation activities during the same period. In 1793, the partners purchased land in what is now Ohio and Granger was appointed a commissioner from Connecticut to resolve a dispute with Massachusetts over the dividing line between the two states west of the Connecticut River. (Id. 4.)

Suffield, like many semi-rural areas in New England, was highly religious and Granger was certainly raised into religion, for he was prepared for college by a reverend,[97] whom he supplanted in 1797 as the deliverer of the local July 4th oration. When the reverend learned of the assignment of such a role to "a Person so open and pointed in his opposition to the Gospel," he wrote Granger that he wished "that the appointment had fallen on some other man, or that you, Sir, had been altogether a Christian." (Id., 5.) But Granger's oration expressed:

> With hearts filled with gratitude to the Supreme Disposer of events, who, in the time of our distresses and dangers, reskued [sic] us from the jaws of tyranny, established and confirmed our Liberty and Independence, and gave us a name among the nations of the earth: Let us, my Friends and Fellow Citizens, unite in the celebration of this beloved day. (Id.)

This passage reads almost as though written by rote. One may suspect a slight tone of derision and deflection in describing

---

[97] This is again similar to Burr's education, for he briefly studied for the clergy with Connecticut Reverend Bellamy after he graduated from Princeton. For the rest of his life, Burr avoided discussing religion.

having to fill his heart with gratitude for having been rescued by the Supreme Disposer of events from the distresses, dangers, and jaws of tyranny (that he had not himself encountered) to live in a country that has a name among nations and to celebrate the beloved day, which in all truth Granger was unlikely to have been able to appreciate.

Hamlin writes that "Granger went on at length … to encourage love of country even though the country should 'spread over large tracts of country that it is not probable that everyone would be able to comprehend an interest so large. The country must be composed of Freemen, who are capable of devising and making their own laws.'" (Id. at 6.) But Granger nonsensically equated this freedom to make one's own laws with being "under the strongest obligations … of maintaining and supporting our civil Constitution." (Id.)

These passages sound like a young man longing to be free of the constraints of his "beloved" country, looking westward to large tracts of land too large to comprehend, where he could make his own laws, but still somehow remain an obedient son.

Hamlin concludes that: "The sentiments expressed by Granger [were] already beginning to show the influence of Thomas Jefferson," such that "[b]y the following year (1798) Granger was definitely aligned with the Republicans and was an unsuccessful candidate for Congress." (Id.)

In 1800, Granger was present at the formal organization of the Republicans in Connecticut that took place at the home of Burr's uncle, Pierpont Edwards in New Haven. Theodore Dwight, a Federalist who was also a nephew of Pierpont Edwards (and thus indirectly related to Burr) and was president of Yale College (where Granger had attended), wrote in words that illustrate Connecticut politics, that if Jefferson were elected "the Bible would be cast into the bonfire, our holy worship changed into a dance of Jacobin phrensy, our wives and daughters dishonored, and our sons converted into the disciples of Voltaire and the dragoons of Marat." (Id.)

Granger later put forward the idea that Burr would align with the "rabid" Connecticut Federalists. But Burr had left that fold of religious fanatics behind him in his adolescence when he ceased his studies with Reverend Joseph Bellamy (a friend and disciple of Burr's grandfather, Jonathan Edwards) in Bethlehem, Connecticut after only a few short months. (*See* Lomask 1:31-32.)

Granger occupied a significant place in Jefferson's ménage and his position and character were also to some degree created by Jefferson. Jefferson selected men for his cabinet and appointed posts who were loyal to him and his cause. Those who rose to favor were those who did special favors, who were in effect willing to be blind to Jefferson's disturbing contradictions and buy the song that despite those hypocrisies, Jefferson was exclusively a good man and did only good things. Madison, Dearborn, Gallatin, and Granger were those closest to Jefferson in office who were "in on the secret." (Jefferson's words about Granger in relation to Burr's alleged secret doings. Here I used it to mean the doings of TJ and his cabinet.) (TJ to JM, March 10, 1814, Founders Online.)

Wilkinson, whom Roger Kennedy claims later colluded with Granger, was never close to Jefferson but he was in on the secret, too, and Jefferson heartily embraced him the instant he was willing to declare his undying loyalty and subjugate himself before Jefferson's all-powerful person.

Jefferson did not, however, merely select malleable young men; he also shaped them, he made them. Many of these men might never have done such wrong but for the demands of their beloved leader. It was a society of men who looked out for each other. Jefferson in essence said "Do this for me and I will protect and elevate you for all posterity." He was true to his word. In return, the men protected Jefferson and his reputation by doing his bidding and never breathing a word about what was really going on. It was pretty nearly a secret society.

As Postmaster General, Granger has sometimes been identified as the creator of the "spoils system," but his biographer, Arthur S. Hamlin, deflects this dubious honor onto Jefferson. He writes that, Jefferson, in response to the midnight appointments of President John Adams, "by his recognition of party allegiance as a controlling factor in the appointment and removal of officers, introduced the spoils system into the Civil

Service." (Hamlin, *Gideon Granger,* 11.) Hamlin continues: "Thus it was that Postmaster General Granger carried out in 1802 the first of the many 'proscriptions' which have taken place in the history of the Department." (Id.)[98]

During the crisis over Burr, Granger wrote that Mr. Pease, his brother-in-law, was sent "on the route to New Orleans to expedite the mails and remove suspected agents [of Burr] of the Post Office." (quoted in Kennedy, 293 without source. *See* TJ to GG, March 9, 1814, Library of Congress, Granger Papers.) Kennedy quotes a revealing passage he unearthed in an official history of the Post Office published in 1879, by D.D. Leech, quoting as follows:

> A suggestion which this administrator [Granger] succeeded in having incorporated into the revised postal law of 1810, and which was not repealed till 1865 – though doubtless well intended, would have found latterly few advocates in Congress – the provision prohibiting Negroes from employment as mail carriers. He was of the opinion that they could not be safely trusted with such a duty, as it would enable the more intelligent of them to form schemes for the communication of intelligence detrimental to the whites.

(Kennedy, 293, quoting D.D. Leech, *History of the Post Office Department*, 1789-1879 (Washington: Judd & Detweiler, 1879), 14.) Granger's spoils system, then, involved *removing Burr agents and African Americans* – the two naturally being aligned in their ability to form schemes detrimental to southern whites!

Of the spoils system, Burr later observed: "The best citizens of our Country acknowledge the feebleness of [Madison's] administration – they acknowledge that offices are bestowed merely to preserve power & without the smallest regard to fitness . . . So long as the present System prevails,

---

[98] DeWitt Clinton is also credited with being responsible for utilizing the spoils system in New York. ("Good policy requires the removal [from federal service] of the greater part in this state as the creatures of Hamilton, and the implacable foes of republicanism ... Such is the situation of parties with us, that no responsible accommodation can take place." (DWC to Gallatin, July 21, 1801, in Siry, 60.)

you will be strugling [sic] against wind & tide to preserve a precarious influence – You will never be forgiven for the Crime of having Talents & independence." (AB to JA, November 15, 1815, Kline 2:1166-67.)

Despite being of such great service to Jefferson (or because of it), Granger later suggested he might blackmail Jefferson. Others before Granger had tried this and had ended up dead. (James Callendar and likely Meriwether Lewis, General William Eaton almost, but he was bought off at the last minute.)

So, this was a recurring theme for Jefferson: men who had done things for him who later ungratefully turned on him. It never seems to have occurred to Jefferson that maybe what he had asked these men to do, the opportunity for which Jefferson believed they ought to have been grateful, was wrongful conduct – deleting names and information from documents, destroying letters, unlawfully seizing property, unlawfully suspending habeas corpus, effecting martial law and illegally arresting and transporting "suspects," lying to people, spying on people, illegally entering foreign territory and attempting to subvert their laws, and, worst of all, conspiring to kill a political opponent.

But Granger never seemed to have minded doing his master's bidding, at least until Madison removed him. According to Granger, as early as 1800, he had "put Virginia on her guard against the designs of Burr." (TJ to Madison, March 10, 1814, in Kennedy, 277.) Jefferson wrote to by-then-President Madison, that Granger's "appeals to my very defective memory" were "*very painful,*" but Jefferson thought to accommodate him on friendly terms, "of justice to him personally," because "his conduct towards me" (that is, his espionage on Jefferson's behalf and his damaging activities against Burr) "was ever friendly and faithful, and I on several occasions *used his services to the advantage of the public.*" (Id.) (Italics mine.)

To what public advantage did Jefferson use Granger's services? Well, in 1802, Granger "at [Jefferson's] request ... communicated to DeWitt Clinton Burr's aspiring to the government of New York." Further, in 1806, Granger gave

Jefferson "the first effectual notice of Burr's Western projects by which we were enabled to take *specific measures* to meet them." Last, without caveat, Jefferson said that Granger "*expedite[d] the mails* and *removed suspected agents of the Post Office.*" (Id.) (Italics mines.)

Thus, Granger's friendly and faithful conduct that Jefferson used to "public advantage" involved colluding to obstruct Burr's New York gubernatorial campaign, taking "specific measures" against Burr's "western projects," rifling the mails (which is and was then a federal offense) and improperly removing employees. At least those were the items Granger had listed and Jefferson corroborated.

In 1804, Granger told Jefferson "from day to day of the communications that passed between Burr and the Connecticut Federalists" and "at the President's request Granger warned De Witt Clinton of Burr's intrigues with the Federalists." (Adams, *TJ Administrations*, 431.)

According to Kennedy, "[b]y the end of November 1806, Wilkinson and Granger became the principal instruments in Jefferson's campaign to rid himself of his rival. Acting together, Wilkinson and Granger provided forged and perjured evidence to support the fable of a Burrite 'conspiracy.'" (Kennedy, 293.)

Jefferson seemed markedly oblivious to the impropriety of the actions he acknowledges. In his reply to Granger, he denies his involvement only in the first item (rumors of Granger's alleged Burrism): "I am [sic] neither concerned nor consulted" on "the first article mentioned in your letter," and "never knew anything of it, nor would ever listen to such gossiping trash." (TJ to GG, March 9, 1814, quoted in Kennedy, id, citing to Arthur Hamlin's biography of Granger, 48-9). But listening to gossiping trash was exactly what Jefferson repeatedly did in forming his conclusions about Burr.

The rest of his 1814 letter to Granger offers advice on how Granger may avoid "universal reprobation" and public "indignation." (*Id.* at 277-8.) As to the first item, Jefferson advised Granger to "erase it from your memory" (and of course to "stand erect before the world on the high ground of your own merits, without stooping to what is unworthy of your or their notice"). (*Id.* at 278.) The charge to erase it from his memory is significant given Jefferson's propensity to bury his own unpleasant deeds. He also tried to erase Burr from memory.

The "specific measures" Jefferson took "to meet" "Burr's Western projects" were to send agents out to follow and spy on Burr and watch his movements, which bore no fruit and later to declare Burr guilty and set in motion efforts to stop him using the military. Perhaps Granger also encouraged the multiple prosecutions by Daveiss, alerting officials to the impending "insurrection," the arrests of Burr's friends and seizure of his property, for he certainly did recommend "expediting the mails" and "removing suspected agents."

But it didn't take long for at least one of *Jefferson's* "agents" -- not one he sent on Burr's trail but the one in command of Jefferson's army: General James Wilkinson – to concoct convenient stories (fabricating evidence and later committing perjury) for Jefferson by which to justify taking any and all measures against Burr, and when Burr disappeared into the southern forests, to send men out to find him and capture or kill him. And then, failing that, at least to arrest him and bring him to trial for treason – a hanging offense.

Granger's role in his work for Jefferson went far beyond managing the mail system. His contribution to the destruction of Burr, with Jefferson's encouragement and approbation, was directly and mutually supportive of Wilkinson's activities.

The New England Secession Movement

Henry Adams writes that by 1804, of the six Federalist senators from the eastern states, all but two thought inevitable a dissolution of the Union on northern/southern lines (Adams, 409) because of Jefferson's policies, and the New Englanders determined to secede from the Union rather than see the ship sink. Right at the outset of the year, several of these men set forth a plan of action to organize a secession movement.

Burr's own brother-in-law, the "eminent Judge Tapping Reeve, of Connecticut," (Adams, 415) wrote: "I have seen many of our friends; and all that I have seen and most that I have heard from believe that we must separate, and that this is the most favorable moment." (Reeve to Uriah Tracy, February 7, 1804, id, citing Lodge's *Cabot*, 442.)[99]

At least one of these men approached Burr and attempted to pull him into their plan. Senator Timothy Pickering of Massachusetts wrote that "New York must be associated ... She must be made the centre of the confederacy." (Pickering to George Cabot, January 29, 1804, quoted at length in Adams, 409-10, citing to Lodge's *Cabot*, 337.) But "how is her concurrence to be obtained?" he asked. (Id.) Roger Griswold (1762-1812), a "well-known lawyer of Lyme and Norwich, Conn. [who] served as a Federalist congressman 1795-1805" (Kline 2:863), wrote that "[t]he project which we had formed was to induce, if possible, the legislatures of the three New England States who remain Federal to commence measures which should call for a reunion of the Northern States." He added that "If any hope can be created that New York will ultimately support the plan, it may perhaps be supported." (Griswold to Oliver Wolcott, March 11, 1804, quoted in Adams, 410-11.)

The element that drew the confederation together was that "[t]he people of the East cannot reconcile their habits, views, and interests with those of the South and West. The latter are beginning to rule with a rod of iron." (Id., at 411, apparently quoting Pickering.) The New England secessionists knew that Burr shared this viewpoint. Griswold met with Burr, who told him "that the northern States must be governed by Virginia, or govern Virginia – and that there was no middle mode – that the democratical Members of Congress from the East were of this sentiment, some of those from NY ... and some of the Leaders in Jersey, and likewise in Pennsylvania." (*Rufus King: Memorandum of a Conversation between Burr*

---

[99]   Reeve (1744-1823) had married Burr's older sister, Sarah ("Sally") Burr (1754-1797). Reeve had been a tutor to Aaron and Sally when they were children in Elizabethtown. Reeve and Sally went to live in Litchfield, CT. Burr joined them there in May 1774 to study law, which was interrupted by the coming of the Revolution. Sally bore one son, Aaron Burr Reeve (1780-1809), but she died at the age of 43. Reeve was the originator of the "case law system" of legal education. (*See* Kline 1:liv, lx, 131n6.)

and Roger Griswold, April 5 [1804], Kline 2:862-63.)[100]

However, significantly, Burr specifically declined to ally with the Federalists. According to King's Memorandum, Burr told Griswold that "he must go on democratically to obtain the Gov[ernmen]t [but] that if he succeeded he sh[oul]d administer the Gov[ernmen]t in a manner that w[oul]d be satisfactory to the Federalists [although] no particular explanation was made on this head." (Id.)

The secessionist alliance was the secret referred to by Jefferson, some years later when he reminded Granger that he had been "in the secret." (TJ to GG, March 9, 1814, Founders Online.) "The conspirators dared not openly discuss the project," writes Adams. (Adams, 415.) One "conspirator" wrote: "There are few among my acquaintance with whom I could on that subject freely converse; there may be more ready that I am aware of." (Theodore Lyman to Pickering, February 29, 1804, Adams, id., citing Lodge's *Cabot*, 446.)

Why? Because, as New England Federalist leader George Cabot noted: "[t]here is no energy in the Federal party, and there could be none manifested without great hazard of losing the State government" for "[s]ome of our best men in high stations are kept in office because they forbear to exert any influence, and not because they possess right principles. They are permitted to have power if they will not use it." Cabot continued: "A separation is now impracticable, because we do not feel the necessity or utility of it. The same separation then will be unavoidable when our loyalty to the Union is generally perceived to be the instrument of debasement and impoverishment. If it is prematurely attempted, those few only will promote it who discern what is hidden from the multitude." (Cabot to Pickering, February 14, 1804, Adams, 412-13, citing Lodge's *Cabot*, 341.)

As noted above, several of the New England Federalists wished to ally with Burr. Adams writes that after a congressional caucus nominated George Clinton as the

---

[100] Although this is hearsay, it is supported by numerous other sources. *See for example,* Burr's overheard observations about Virginia, Kline 1:433 and Burr's direct remarks to his son-in law in AB to JA, November 15, 1815, Kline 2:1167. *See also* Griswold to Wolcott, March 11, 1804, quoted at length below.

Republican candidate for vice president in the 1804 election, "Griswold rightly argued that nothing could be done in Congress, – the formation of a Northern interest must begin at home, and must find its centre [sic] of union in Burr." (Adams, 423.) Griswold asked Burr to meet with him. His letter to Wolcott on the meeting is worth quoting at length:

> [Burr] speaks in the most bitter terms of the Virginia faction, and of the necessity of a union at the northward to resist it; but what the ultimate objects are which he would propose, I do not know. It is apparent that his election is supported in New York on the principle of resisting Virginia and uniting the North; and it may be presumed that the support given to him by Federal men would tend to reconcile the feelings of those democrats who are becoming dissatisfied with their Southern masters. But it is worthy of great consideration whether the advantage gained in this manner will not be more than counterbalanced by fixing on the Northern States a man in whom the most eminent of our friends will not repose confidence. If Colonel Burr is elevated in New York to the office of governor by the votes of Federalist, will he not be considered, and must he not in fact become, the head of the Northern interest? His ambition will not suffer him to be second, and his office will give him a claim to the first rank.

(Griswold to Wolcott, March 11, 1804, quoted in Adams 423.)

Griswold's letter indicates exactly the point of confusion over Burr. Burr could not be trusted by the radical Federalists because he insisted upon relying on democratic processes to obtain any office. He specifically refused to "conspire" with anybody (or to ally with Federalists) to obtain office. Burr agreed with some Federalist views and as strongly disagreed with Jefferson's practices, but he never abandoned his democratic principles.[101] The Federalists could not "repose confidence" in him and worried that if they supported him without concessions from him, he would become the head of the northern interest. In effect, what this was saying was that Burr would incorporate federalism into his democratic

---

[101] *See also,* Van Bergen, *Aaron Burr and the Electoral Tie of 1801.*

government. And it is true that Burr consistently attempted to find common, middle ground and build coalitions. But to the radical Federalists, who had lost all their power and offices to Jefferson, this meant the end of Federalism, the end of their party. It meant that "peace and order, freedom and property, would soon be [all] destroyed." (Adams, paraphrasing Justice Chase, 409.)

Meanwhile, "[i]n New York, the Clintons never ceased their attacks [on Burr], with the evident wish to drive him from the party." (Adams, 416.) James Cheetham, "after publishing in 1802 two heavy pamphlets [against Burr], attempted in 1803 to crush him under the weight of a still heavier volume, containing 'Nine Letters on the Subject of Aaron Burr's Political Defection.'" (Id.) Nearly all the other democratic newspapers followed this lead, "abandoning Burr as a man who no longer deserved confidence." (Id.)

Burr eventually replied to Cheetham's charges through William P. Van Ness's pamphlets and he sued Cheetham in court for defamation. The damage was done, however. Even Henry Adams concludes, without foundation, that "[a]s a politician Burr had played fast and loose with all parties," adding off-handedly "but so had most of his enemies." So, "none of them could show clean hands." (Id. 418.) But in fact, as we saw above, Burr did not play fast and loose at all.

Still, though, in a self-affirming circle, Jefferson saw what Clinton, Cheetham, and Granger saw in dutiful obeisance to what they knew their master wanted to hear: political defection. Jefferson later wrote to Granger:

> I mean the intrigues which were in agitation, and at the bottom of which we believed Colo Burr to be; to form a coalition of the five Eastern states, with New York & New Jersey, under the new appellation of the seven Eastern states; either to overawe the Union by the combination of their power and their will, or by threats of separating themselves from it. [Y]our intimacy with some of those in the secret gave you opportunities of searching into their proceedings, of which you made me daily and confidential reports[,] this intimacy to which I had such useful recourse, at the time.

(TJ to GG, March 9, 1814, Founders Online.)

Jefferson confirms to Granger in this same letter that although he did not recollect the particulars, he had no doubt that Granger was correct that "on my advice, you procured Erastus Granger to inform DeWitt Clinton of the plan to elevate Burr in N. York." And further Jefferson did have "a general recollection that Colo Burr's conduct had already at that date rendered his designs suspicious; that being for that reason laid aside by his constituents as Vice President, and aiming to become the Governor of New York, it was thought advisable that the persons of influence in that state should be put on their guard; and mr Clinton being eminent, no one was more likely to receive [sic] intimations from us, nor any one more likely to be confided in for their communication than yourself." (Id.)

What suspicious designs? That he and Griswold met, at the latter's request, and discussed a possible alliance, which Burr specifically declined? That the New England secessionists looked to Burr to save them from Jeffersonian democracy and that probably only Burr could do so? That Burr openly stated that he was unhappy and angry at the way he had been treated by the Jeffersonians (and Clintonians), and that this might give him good reason to ally with the Federalists? That he agreed with them that the Southern and Northern interests were irreconcilable and that separation "at some period not very remote may probably take place"? (Cabot to Pickering, February 14, 1804, in Adams 412.) But what did Jefferson or Granger really know about Burr's thoughts, principles, or activities? Their conclusions about him were not based on personal knowledge or reasonable inferences.[102]

Nonetheless, Jefferson felt beholden and grateful to Granger for upholding his oedipal fantasy and rewarded him accordingly. More importantly, we see here the alliance

---

[102] Interestingly, Granger later became involved attempts to prevent the continued domination of the Virginian presidential dynasty. In 1816, he wrote DeWitt Clinton: "I do believe that if the dominion of Virginia be continued or any Executive power given south of the Potomac, that before the close of the next administration we shall have war in the Gulph of Mexico with more than one of the principal powers in Europe." (GG to DC, March 27, 1816, in Hamlin, *Granger*, 60.)

between Jefferson, Granger, and DeWitt Clinton, and Jefferson's guidance to Granger to do what he could to undermine Burr.

Their alliance may well have been a sincere political attachment. Connecticut had a Federalist majority and Granger lost two attempts in 1801 to serve as a Republican U.S. Representative. But as the men became entangled, they jointly moved into a type of relationship that, as I discuss later, seems to have existed in many, most, or perhaps even all of Jefferson's relationships and is most easily understood as master-leader and servant-underling, with the morals of each becoming more and more diluted as the relationship progressed (that is, as the master's judgment and power increased unchecked and the servant became more obedient, lest he be excluded from the source of power) until the co-actors simply ceased to have any moral grounding (or the grounding was simply fallacious or delusional).

In Jefferson's first known letter to Granger, he explained the Republican platform in opposition to the Federalist one. This letter shows how TJ obtained and maintained control: by oversimplifying and polarizing. He wrote:

> [T]hough we may obtain, and I believe shall obtain a majority in the legislature of the United States, attached to the preservation of the federal constitution according to its obvious principles, and those of which it was known to be received; attached equally to the preservation to the States of those rights unquestionably remaining with them; friends to the freedom of religion, freedom of the press, trial by jury, and to economical government; opposed to standing armies, paper systems, war, and all connection, other than commerce, with any foreign nation; in short, a majority firm in all those principles which I have espoused and the federalists have opposed uniformly; still, should the whole body of New England continue in opposition to these principles of government, either knowingly or through delusion, our government will be a very uneasy one.

(TJ to GG, August 13, 1800, quoted in Hamlin, *Granger*, 7.)

Jefferson's claim that the Federalists would be opposed to the preservation of the Federal Constitution or basic freedoms went a bit far. Originally, those who by 1800 called Republicans were the anti-Federalists and were identified with opposition to the adoption of a federally-centered constitution. According to one newspaper, "The constitution[,] once adopted, the appellation [anti-federalist] should have ceased . . . A modern anti-federalist, then, is one who is sincerely attached to the constitution of his country, which proceeded from the people." (*New York Journal*, August 13, 1794, quoted in Isenberg & Burstein, *Madison and Jefferson*, 279.)

The Federalists initially were the supporters of George Washington's administration, who referred to themselves as "true friends of the constitution" and "friends to peace[,] freedom and government." (Id., source uncited, possibly *Gazette of the United States*, June 19, 1793, cited in their following footnote.) As one Federalist paper made clear:

> It might seem, from the outs, or Antifederalists, as they were called, that they are the only friends of liberty and the constitution, while the federalists are become enemies to liberty and the government . . . Instead of Antifederalist you are to use the word republican, and in place of federalist you are to use the word aristocrat.

(Id., quoting *Federal Intelligencer*, January 10 and January 12, 1795.)

Jefferson, in his passage to Granger, oversimplified, conflated, and presupposed opposing differences. This was one way he dominated and guided his followers. He divided and polarized people and their beliefs. Us versus them. You are either with us or against us. Good versus bad. There is no in-between, no room for one's own judgments.

The Yazoo Lands

Granger was involved in the fraudulent sale of Indian lands conducted by the state of Georgia. These were fraudulent because several tribes of Native Americans had lived on this large expanse for centuries but Georgia laid claim to it, despite treaties between the federal government and the Indians. The

Georgia legislators, many if not most of whom were members of the land companies, stood to make millions by the sale of these lands.

Julius Goebel and Joseph H. Smith, editors of Alexander Hamilton's law papers contribute a lengthy analysis of the so-called Yazoo or Georgia lands controversy. They write:

> Of all the speculative dealings in land during the early years of the Republic, none equaled in extent or in extravagance of risk the vast grants of western territory made in 1795 by the State of Georgia ... which was not only to agitate the citizens of Georgia but was to involve the federal government, echoing in the halls of Congress and raising constitutional issues that were ultimately to be brought before the Supreme Court of the United States.

(Goebel & Smith, *Law Practice of AH,* 4:356.) The editors continue: "Georgia's title to lands in the lower southwest, as against the title of the United States, was open to some doubt; nor was it fully conceded by the federal government." (Id.)

President Washington issued a special message to Congress, stating: "These acts embrace an object of such magnitude, and in their consequences may se deeply affect the peace and welfare of the United States that I have thought it necessary now to lay them before Congress." (Id., 368.) Theodore Sedgwick, Representative from Massachusetts, wrote "The Georgia sale of indian lands [is] as violent & infamous as any out of any Government." (TS to Ephraim Williams of Boston, February 24, 1795, quoted in id. at 369.)

Granger admitted his agency to Jefferson in 1810, who later acknowledged Granger's involvement to Madison. He wrote Madison in 1810, recommending Granger's appointment as a Supreme Court Justice, saying that although Granger had "been interested in Yazooism . . . [he] has long been clear of it," and Jefferson had "confidence in his integrity." (TJ to JM, October 15, 1810, quoted in Kennedy, 276, citing to Hamlin, 44.)

But while a member of Jefferson's cabinet, Granger had acted as agent for the New England Mississippi Company to secure the ratification of the Yazoo interests by Congress. John Randolph launched an extended philippic against Granger that continues to resound:

> His gigantic grasp embraces on one hand the shores of Lake Erie and stretches with the other to the bay of Mobile. Millions of acres are easily digested by such stomachs. Goaded by avarice, they only buy to sell, and sell only to buy. The retail trade of fraud and imposture yields too small and slow a profit to gratify their cupidity.
> . . . They buy and sell corruption in the gross, and a few millions more or less is hardly felt in the amount. . . [T]he game and the stake which is set upon their throw, is nothing less than the patrimony of the people . . . This same agent is at the head of an executive department of our Government . . . inferior to none in the influence attached to it. This officer, possessed of how many smug appointments and fat contracts . . . having an influence which is confined to no quarter of the Country . . . with offices in his gift amongst the most lucrative . . . this officer presents himself at your bar, at once a party and an advocate . . . Is it come to this? Are heads of executive departments of the government to be brought into this House with all the influence and patronage attached to them, to extort from us now what was refused at the last session of Congress? . . . [I]f they are, and if the abominable villainy practiced upon, and by, the legislature of Georgia, in 1795, is now to be glossed over, I . . . ask . . . what . . . they can offer. [Is] it . . . necessary to give the Cerberus of corruption, this many-headed god of Hell a sop . . . to pacify him – and this sentiment is re-echoed by his yells. Good God, Sir!

(Kennedy, 294, citing Russell Kirk, *John Randolph of Roanoke* (Liberty, 1951); also partly quoted in Adams, 445.)

Granger explained his involvement to Jefferson as follows, when he was soliciting an appointment to the Supreme Court:

> It may be objected that I am a member of a company

who claim Georgia lands . . . It is four years now since I resigned my agency, which you will please to remember was affirmed at the request of the Att'y Gen'l Lincoln, one of the Com'rs. Who believed it would insure [sic] a compromise, as he knew it was my opinion that the Company ought not to enter into a contest with Government and Mr. Gallatin must recollect that I informed him at our first interview that I would come to an immediate agreement with him; and that when I called the next time he informed me that on further reflection he did not think it would be for the interest of the United States to settle with the Company I represented because as things "stood" we should push the other companies to settlement.

(GG to TJ, September 27, 1810, quoted in Hamlin, *Granger,* 42.)

~

Jefferson's Cabinet

James Madison
Secretary of State

Albert Gallatin
Secretary of Treasury

Gen. Henry Dearborn
Secretary of War

Gen. James Wilkinson
Commander of Army

Jefferson's Cabinet

A *"colossal failure of statesmanship."*
Leonard Levy, **Jefferson & Civil Liberties,** 124.

In the case of Jefferson's cabinet, the question is not whether the members were involved in the conspiracy to destroy Burr, for as cabinet members, although they might advise, they had to carry out Jefferson's orders and meet his wishes, so they had to be involved with his efforts to destroy Burr. The question is what degree of knowledge each possessed of Jefferson's unlawful ends, whether they knew them to be unlawful, and whether they thought violating the law was justified and if so, on what legal basis. Jefferson went so far out on a limb that it would have been difficult for men of their education and intelligence (particularly Gallatin and Madison) *not* to know. How far were they responsible, then, for what they helped their boss do?

In conspiracy law, a co-conspirator is liable for the crime committed by the goal of the conspiracy, so long as he agrees with that goal, Even if he had only a small role in bringing about that end and did nothing illegal himself, he shares the same liability as the principal. The members of Jefferson's cabinet knew what was what and they continued to do their jobs to the end and beyond.

Gallatin

In late 1801, Albert Gallatin wrote Jefferson a long, revealing letter about New York and Burr and the future of the presidency. Formerly a friend of Burr's, but by the time of writing this letter, just six months into office as Secretary of Treasury, he was a near full convert, Gallatin asked Jefferson whether Republicans "eventually mean not to support Burr as your successor when you shall think fit to retire . . . [or] at next election for Vice President?" (AG to TJ, September 14, 1801, Founders Online, National Archives.) He added, "it seems to me that there are but two ways, either to support Burr once more, or to give only one vote for President, scattering our votes for the other person to be voted for. If we do the first, we run, on the one hand, the risk of the federal party making B. president; & we seem, on the other, to give him an additional pledge of being eventually supported hereafter by the republicans for that office." Burr was merely a chess piece.

Gallatin noted a "diffidence, I mean total want of confidence" in "a large majority of the republicans towards Burr" which he had discovered the previous winter, and says that if he had felt this previous to the election, he would not have given his consent to supporting Burr for VP. Gallatin's remark was either disingenuous or self-deceptive, for if there had really been a total want of confidence in Burr by "a large majority" of the Republicans, he would not have been nominated or have tied with Jefferson for the presidency.

Clearly, as someone who had been seated as a Republican appointee, Gallatin owed his job and his loyalty to Jefferson and to the party. In addition, he felt – as most Republicans did – that the Federalists had to be kept out of power at all costs. But Gallatin presented the sacrifice of Burr as an either/or dilemma (inherently a logical fallacy). He entertained no other alternatives than supporting Burr or sacrificing him. He made no suggestion that they consult with Burr, see what he preferred, strategize with him.

Kennedy believes that Gallatin felt friendship for Burr but this letter suggests otherwise. It shows that Gallatin was more concerned with (or valued more) popularity and public image than with Burr's friendship. He was perfectly willing to abandon his friend for the end of achieving or maintaining Republican ascendancy. This was as acceptable then as it would be now. Anyone who sincerely believed in the aspirations of their party would be expected to put their duty to their nation and their leader before their personal friendships.

In context, what it meant about Gallatin was that he had determined to follow Jefferson wherever he led as long as Gallatin could justify it to this purpose, which is to say, as long as Jefferson could justify it, and Jefferson always was able convince his followers of the purity of his Republican purpose, no matter what laws or principles he violated.

When it comes to adherence to a president who

declares a man guilty before trial, party is not a sufficient answer. It is one thing to justify snubbing a man or not endorsing him politically. But hanging him? Did Gallatin (and other members of the cabinet) believe that the future of Republicanism justified hanging Burr? Apparently so, for not one of them resigned in protest or issued a public statement against the prosecution. Did they really believe he had committed treason? Did they really believe there was a crisis in the west? That the Union would fall? That Burr was prepared to march on Baton Rouge and steal the armaments and then onto New Orleans? That he would then magically transport himself back to Washington and throw them all out to be guillotined or something? Or what? Had they all gone mad?

   Some believed Burr mad because of the improbability of the stories about him, but nonetheless believed the stories.[103] The conspiracy to destroy Burr thus relied in part on the lack or loss of judgment of educated men, on their susceptibility to rumor, their predisposition to believe the drama that was touted, over and above their own knowledge of Burr or the facts of his career.

---

[103] For example, John Adams wrote Benjamin Rush: "I never believed him to be a fool. But he must be an idiot or a lunatic if he has really planned and attempted to execute such a project as is imputed to him. It is even more senseless and extravagant than Miranda's. It is utterly incredible that any foreign power should have instigated him. It is utterly incredible that without foreign aid he should have thought that the trans-Alleghenian people would revolt with him; or even if they should revolt, that he and they could maintain themselves against the United States, who could so easily block up the Mississippi." (JA to BR, February 2, 1807, in Schutz, *Spur of Fame,* 82.)
    Adams suspected "this lying spirit [of the southern states] has been at work concerning Burr" but Rush concluded that "[t]he history of ... Burr's pursuits verifies" a remark made by Richelieu: "To be unfortunate is to be imprudent." Rush listed Burr's failures and told Adams about his college commencement address, which Rush had witnessed when Burr was 16 years old. Burr "spoke an elegant oration and with great spirit upon 'Building Castles in the Air.'" Rush concluded that "There is often something said or done by men in their youth that marks their destiny in life." (BR to JA, April 3, 1807, id., 84.) Adams then responded with an evaluation of Burr's successes as merely due to "the flattery of the Presbyterians" and others who venerated his father and grandfather. All the rest of Burr's accomplishments were "chimerical and without success." (JA to BR, April 12, 1807, id. 85.)

But Gallatin, the best head in the country? He showed his readiness to do what was necessary. Wisdom was for him what it is for most people: making good social calculations. He was being wise. But this shows exactly why social wisdom is a dangerous brand of ignorance that leads to utter lack of judgment when it is most needed. Follow this path and you will find that not only will men in power destroy their most able and faithful allies (preserving the worst men) but they will destroy anything else, even their very home and family to preserve the social structure to which they owe their position.

According to Leonard Levy, over the summer of 1808, Jefferson and Gallatin, "two of the three titans in the history of American libertarianism," exchanged a series of letters, which "confronted a major crisis that shook the democratic character of the Administration; and they responded by considering ways and means of assaulting liberty in a manner that matched the repressive imaginations of the Essex Junto." (Levy, *Jefferson and Civil Liberties*, 121.) Again, Gallatin saw only two possible courses of action.

Jefferson had laid an embargo against the great foreign powers France and England for their mutual restriction of American commerce to each other. That is, France prohibited America from "carrying anything to British territories" and England "after prohibiting a great proportion of our commerce with France and her allies, is now believed to have prohibited the whole [world] . . . and our vessles, their cargoes, and crews are to be taken by the one or the other for whatever place they may be destined out of our own limits." (TJ to John Thomson Mason, [circa December 1807], quoted in Adams, *TJ Administrations*, 1042.) Jefferson "submitted to the wisdom of Congress, who alone are competent to provide a remedy," the question: "If, therefore, on leaving our harbors we are certainly to lose [our ships], is it not better, as to vessels, cargoes, and seamen, to keep them at home?" (Id.)

Because, as Adams writes, "no official document could be produced in proof of the expected British interdict," Madison then redrafted Jefferson's message to Congress, which avoided this difficulty by relying on a prior decree by Britain and its Impressment Proclamation. (Id., 1043.) The rest of

Jefferson's cabinet "unanimously concurred" with the embargo by Jefferson and Madison, except Gallatin, who agreed in principle but wrote Jefferson that he wished the embargo to be limited in time, adding: "In every point of view – privations, sufferings, revenue, effect on the enemy, politics at home, etc. – I prefer war to a permanent embargo." He warned Jefferson: "Governmental prohibitions do always more mischief than had been calculated." (Madison's draft, id., 1043; AG to TJ, December 18, 1807, id., 1043-44.)

Nonetheless, over the summer of 1808, with the Burr trial in progress, Gallatin helped Jefferson put into effect a congressional authorization investing the Executive "with the most arbitrary powers," which Gallatin acknowledged were "equally dangerous and odious." (Levy, 122-23, quoting AG to TJ, July 29, 1808.) Gallatin was proposing that the power of port authorities to seize property be made "general," that rather than only being able to seize off the coast or at points adjacent to foreign territory, "legal authority [be given] to prevent, seize, and detain[,] [to which] must be added a sufficient physical force to carry it into effect." (Id.) Gallatin, however, said the decision must be Jefferson's alone. Presumably, as long as Jefferson bore responsibility for it, Gallatin was okay with this dangerous expansion of executive power. Jefferson's answer was "Congress must legalize all *means* which may be necessary to obtain its *end.*" (TJ to Gallatin, August 11, 1808, quoted in Levy, 124.) TJ "betrayed neither a shade of doubt nor a sense of the tragedy that hovered over his decision." (Levy, 124.) Levy points out that:

> Gallatin's letter and Jefferson's response revealed the colossal failure of statesmanship that afflicted the Administration. Neither one discussed the possibility of searching for means to alleviate the hardships resulting from the embargo. Neither saw any alternative other than war or measures of an arbitrary and military nature for enforcement against the American people. Neither considered the possibility of nonintercourse with Great Britain and France, a strong naval program (Jefferson built gunboats to enforce the embargo, but not a single frigate), the arming of merchant ships and protecting

them with convoys, a vigorous program of public education, and perhaps the issuance of letters of marque and reprisal against France and England.

(Id.)

These alternatives were ones that Burr likely would have considered and promptly adopted, had he been in the president's shoes.[104] While Burr was a military man, he did not prefer war. He was not afraid to use the military but he considered it as not only an offensive weapon but as a protective body. While he was certainly capable of giving orders, he preferred consultation and collaboration. He would also likely have found some way to outflank the great powers and bring back upon them some of their own medicine.

The colossal failure of statesmanship that Levy details was also a colossal failure of moral compass that extended well beyond considerations of politics or commerce, bleeding ultimately into the realm of criminal conspiracy to destroy a person's life. If you are willing to ruin the economy and livelihood of an entire region of your homeland,[105] ruining the life of a single man must seem much less significant an act. Gallatin, despite his prior collegial friendship with Burr and previous hesitations about how closely he wished to follow Jefferson's lead, was by mid-1808 well on board with Jefferson's program. In his attempts to guide Jefferson's policies and perhaps to limit Jefferson's misjudgments, Gallatin fell into the river of Jefferson's thought with waters deep and murky enough to swallow his own better judgment.

Months after Burr's acquittal, Jefferson wrote a note to Gallatin asking him to notify authorities in New Orleans to obtain a "writ . . . grounded on the [Ohio] indictment by which Burr may be arrested any where and brought back to trial." (TJ to AG, March 10 1808, quoted in Lomask 2:317.) Why he was asking his Secretary of Treasury to do this is not clear, but it suggests that Jefferson assumed Gallatin's agreement with his

---

[104] I have analyzed Burr's views on the superpowers, on the U.S., and on use of military in three chapters not included in this limited edition due to space constraints. I am happy to supply these chapters in electronic form to any Kickstarter backer upon request.

[105] The embargo nearly destroyed the New England economy, which was largely mercantile based, and almost caused civil insurrection.

continued persecution of Burr.

Dearborn

The role of Henry Dearborn, Secretary of War, was that of clerk.[106] He seems to have simply done whatever Jefferson told him to do. In 1803, Burr referred to Dearborn fondly as "our fellow-traveller through the wilderness" in a letter to another soldier of the march from Quebec. (AB to Dr. John Coats, February 23, 1803, quoted in Isenberg, *Fallen Founder*, 475, n. 6 (citing to Davis, *Memoirs of AB*, 2:220.))

Dearborn seems to have had the role of transacting business that Jefferson found distasteful or wasteful. After a ten-year correspondence with William Dunbar, whom TJ had asked to lead expeditions into the southwestern Spanish territories, once Dunbar began asking troubling questions and showing doubt in Jefferson's judgment, the President simply turned the correspondence over to Dearborn – and he and Dunbar never again communicated. Dearborn had to convey Jefferson's wishes to Dunbar, as he did also to Wilkinson, and to field their replies, when he had no authority to deal with the issues involved.

That Dearborn was Jefferson's hireling is further suggested by the difference between his eight years of favored treatment of Meriwether Lewis (TJ's nephew) and the haughty, mistrusting treatment Lewis received from his successor, William Eustis. When TJ left office, so did HD. "[F]rom then on, the attitude in Washington was changed. Lewis was no longer the gifted prodigy, the president's protégé. He was now just another political appointee in the field." Eustis refused to honor a $19 draft which "Dearborn would have honored ... without question."[107]

---

[106] General Gates recommended John Armstrong for the position but Armstrong (who was never approached by Jefferson) apparently determined not to accept, since "the qualifications expected were those of a mere clerk." (Skeen, *John Armstrong*, 46, paraphrasing Gates to TJ, February 10, 1801 and Armstrong to Tillotson, February 23, 1801.) Armstrong later served disastrously as Madison's Secretary of War.

[107] Chandler suggests that Lewis implied to Eustis that "he was being set up on false charges, as Burr had been," when Lewis wrote: "Be assured Sir, that my Country can never make 'A Burr' of me. She may reduce me to poverty; but she can never sever my attachment from her." (Chandler, 261-62, Lewis to Eustis, n.d. [post July 15, 1809], National Archives, Louisiana-Missouri Territorial

Further evidence is Dearborn's acquiescent affirmation of Jefferson's support of Wilkinson. (Adams, 916, see paraphrase of HD's words to Major Bruff at p. 229 below.)

Madison

The role of Madison, Jefferson's Secretary of State, in Jefferson's conspiracy is the most difficult to ascertain, because Madison kept his own counsel and when he advised Jefferson, his advice was usually intended merely to moderate Jefferson's message. Burstein and Isenberg write summarily: "There can be no mistake about it: Thomas Jefferson entertained grand expansionist plans, and James Madison was in favor of them all." (Burstein & Isenberg, 443.) As support for this conclusion, the authors state: "Madison's bold actions in 1810, as president, in the seizure of West Florida, provide ample proof of this."

With respect to the Burr expedition, the authors also remark:

> Whether Burr's design was in fact a quest to develop and populate western land, a staging action in case the opportunity arose to seize undergoverned Spanish territory, or a conspiracy to foment a war with Spain, it was an outright conspiracy in the mind of the president [and] Madison appears to have fundamentally agreed with Jefferson's assessment of the situation; he gave no one any contrary indication, though the written record is otherwise silent.

(Id., 445.)

Madison's character is not revealed in these larger pictures. Rather, one must look peripherally, as it were. For example, Madison advised Jefferson that utilizing the army against Burr was constitutionally problematical. Another indication of Madison's thinking was the fact that when he was President, he removed from office Gideon Granger – whom Jefferson had found useful in so many ways. Madison has his own mind, in other words, which he did not always reveal during Jefferson's rise and tenure.

Hamilton told a friend that Madison's "true character is

Papers, pp. 290-92, also in Daniel Jackson, *Letters of the Lewis & Clark Expedition, 1783-1854* (Univ. of Illinois Press, 1978), 2:456-61.

the reverse of that *simple, fair, candid one*, which he has assumed." (AH to Edward Carrington, May 26, 1792, quoted in id. 248.) This is an assessment that is corroborated by other peripheral evidence. Some of the most interesting and astute observations made about Madison come from one of the French ministers to the U.S.: Louis Marie Turreau. Immediately upon his arrival in Washington in 1805, Turreau became entangled in a dispute between Madison and the Spanish minister, the Marqués de Casa Yrujo, (aka "Yrujo"). He was obliged to become involved because Spain felt it necessary to side with France in their war with England caused by Napoleon's aggressions. Yrujo was very upset with the Jefferson Administration and Madison particularly. As Adams tells it:

> [Yrujo's] good-will vanished from the moment he saw that to save Florida [from being claimed by the U.S.] he must do battle with President, Secretary of State, Congress, and people. One insult had followed another with startling rapidity . . . The cold reception of his protest against the Louisiana cession; the captiousness of Madison's replies to his remonstrances; the armed seizure of New Orleans with which he was threatened; the sudden disregard of his friendship and great services; the open eagerness of the Government to incite Bonaparte to plunder and dismember Spain; the rejection of the [Spanish] claims convention in March, and its sudden approval by the Senate in January, as though to obtain all the money Spain was willing to give before taking by force territory vital to her empire; and above all, the passage of this law annexing the Floridas without excuse or explanation, – all of these causes combined to change Yrujo's ancient friendship into hatred.

(Adams, 476.) Yrujo angered Madison when he obtained the opinion of five prominent American lawyers on Franco-Spanish claims. (Among these was Burr's friend and Armstrong's brother-in-law, Edward Livingston.) Madison thought the lawyers should be prosecuted for violating the Logan Act, which prohibited interfering with official U.S.

foreign policies. But then Congress by a bi-partisan vote confirmed the Spanish claims, "causing in the end more embarrassment to the party in power than the most ingenious factiousness could have plotted." (Id., 477.) A lot was going on. In the end, Yrujo went in person to the State Department and exploded in Madison's face. Yrujo demanded that the law annexing the Floridas be annulled. As Adams writes: "Madison could neither maintain the law nor annul it; he could not even explain it away." (Id., 478.) Madison complained to Spain about Yrujo's conduct. Yrujo's subsequent note to Madison (Yrujo to Madison, March 7, 1804, State Dept. Archives) contained, among other impolitic things, "a rudeness which no government can tolerate," wrote Madison. (Madison to Robert Livingston, minister to Paris, March 31, 1804, State Papers, quoted in Adams, 478-79.)

Yrujo began publishing anti-Administration tracts in the papers. When Turreau arrived, he attempted to mediate a meeting between the two men. He wrote that "[h]e had no trouble in perceiving from the outset of the conversation that Mr. Madison and M. d'Yrujo cordially detested each other, and in the discussion that their passions took the place of reason and law." (Adams, 485, quoting Turreau to Talleyrand, May 13, 1805.)

When Turreau and Madison discussed the question of West Florida (which Spain held and Jefferson wanted), Madison attempted to assert that American title extended the eastern border of Louisiana "to the Perdido [River]" in West Florida because "we have a map" of it, to which Turreau retorted that he had one which included Tennessee and Kentucky in Louisiana, adding: "You will agree that maps are not titles." (Id., 486.) Madison then ended by saying that "if Spain had always conducted herself toward the United States as well as France had done, the difficulties would not have taken place" between them." (Id.) Turreau observed sardonically to Talleyrand: "I did not think myself called upon to appear very grateful for this kind of cajolery." (Id.)

Turreau observed that it was Madison's fault that his efforts at reconciliation with Yrujo had failed. "He is dry, spiteful, passionate, and his private resentments, still more than political difference, will long keep him apart from M. d'Yrujo" adding however that since Turreau was "on very good terms with Mr. Madison," he invited both men to dinner to make a second attempt. But "the Secretary of State cannot forgive," wrote Turreau. (Id., 486-87.)

Adams notes that "Madison seemed unconscious that Yrujo could have any just cause of complaint, or that his Government could resent the tone and temper of President and Congress." (Id., 477.) He determined to effect Yrujo's recall, but beyond that:

> [h]aving brought the government face to face with the government of Spain, in the belief that Spain and France must yield to peremptory demand, – finding that Spain not only refused every concession, but renewed depredations on American commerce and took an attitude of indifference to threats or entreaties, – Madison proposed no more vigorous measure than to "go every length the law will warrant" against certain Spanish land-grants.

(Adams, 652.)

Adams observes that "Madison's measures and conduct toward Europe showed the habit of avoiding the heart of every issue, in order to fret its extremities." (Id., 653.) "The same habit of mind," Adams continues, "made him favor commercial restrictions as a means of coercion." (Id.) Thus, Madison supported Jefferson's ill-considered and dangerous embargo idea. Madison thought "[t]he efficacy of an embargo cannot be doubted . . . it is more and more apparent to me that it can force all the nations having colonies in this quarter of the globe to respect our rights." (Id., 654, quoting Madison to TJ, September 14, 1805.) He meant to force the superpowers to respect infant America.

Madison's habit of mind "sprang from the same source as his caution, his respect for law, his instinctive sense of the dangers that threatened the Union, his curious mixture of radical and conservative tastes; but whatever its merits or defects, it led to a strange delusion when it caused him to believe that a man like Napoleon could be forced by a mere pin-prick to do Jefferson's will." (Id., 654.)

In the end, Jefferson's cabinet "agreed that Yrujo should be sounded through [Alexander J.] Dallas [a Pennsylvania Republican leader][108] whether he is not going away, and if not, he should be made to understand that his presence at Washington will not be agreeable, and that his departure is expected." (Id., 657, quoting Jefferson's Cabinet Memoranda (citing to Ford, *TJ's Writings,* 1:308.).) Adams concludes that "[t]his memorandum closed a record, unusually complete, of an episode illustrating better than any other the peculiarities of Jefferson and Madison, and the traits of character most commonly alleged as their faults." (Id., 656.)

Madison's lack of consciousness of his own spiteful and insulting attitude towards others whom he disliked or disfavored, his agreement with Jefferson's beliefs and policies, his willingness to conduct himself consistent with them, and his silence in the face of Jefferson's actions in relation to Burr show two things. First, that Madison, who was quite willing to say what he thought when he needed to and had great knowledge of and respect for the law (at least theoretically), said nothing about the Burr hunt or prosecution, probably did not fully agree with Jefferson's actions because Madison knew they were improper and unlawful. But he went along anyway. This failure to stop Jefferson must be seen as passive agreement and complicity.

Second, Madison agreed in principle with the destruction of Burr. If he had not, he would have told Jefferson so. His native spitefulness, which can be seen in many other situations and was identified both by Hamilton and Turreau, along with Jefferson's "gentle" guidance to Madison not to trust Burr too much, would have led Madison to wish the same for Burr that he and Jefferson had for Patrick Henry: devoutly for his death.

Thus, Madison knew Jefferson's goal (of destroying Burr's life and person) was unlawful and passively agreed to contribute his efforts towards that end.

~

---

[108] *See* Kline 1:453 for a short bio of Dallas. He was, Kline states: "one of the Republican party's most effective leaders in Pennsylvania."

PART FOUR:

THE CHARACTER OF

BAD MEN

Is it possible that a man, enjoying high command, and receiving daily marks of the confidence of his nation, should not only be tempted to betray it, but for days, and months, and years should continue in her service – wear the honourable livery of her household – eat her bread, and yet be continually plotting her destruction, exciting her enemies to the attack, pointing out the defenceless places, and meanly receiving the wages of such depravity[?] How did he dare to issue a command to men of whom the meanest had twenty thousand times his worth? How did he dare to punish crimes when the blackest criminal might come and whiten by his side? – Did he dare to punish drunkenness whose life was a continued scene of debauchery? Did not his hand tremble when he signed the sentence for desertion? – or what crime in the catalogue of military offences could he punish without thinking of his own?
Daniel Clark, *Proofs of the Corruption of*
General James Wilkinson, 42-43

[On President Jefferson's message to Congress of October 27,1807]:
I have nothing to do with its pouting fretfulness against Great Britain, its abject humiliation of this country to Spain, through the frowns of those in the French Ministry or the insidious misrepresentation of the financial prosperity of the United States . . . [T]he whole piece is replete with all the ambiguity and duplicity which have ever characterized the pen of this timid but crafty statesman.
Harman Blennerhassett's Journal, October 27, 1807
Fitch, *Breaking with Burr,* 140.

This fear that the "principal" [Burr] would escape became so intense that the sane and benevolent Jefferson was driven to deeds he must have repented in his calmer hours.
Walter F. McCaleb, *Aaron Burr Conspiracy*, 281.

Jefferson's Layers

The judgment of mankind in general is like that of Father Bouhours, who says, "For myself, I regard secret persons, like the great rivers, whose bottoms we cannot see, and which make no noise; or like those vast forests, whose silence fills the soul, with I know not what religious horror. I have for them the same admiration as men had for the oracles, which never suffered themselves to be understood, till after the event of things; or for the providence of God, whose conduct is impenetrable to the human mind." - **John Adams to Benjamin Rush, January 25, 1806**[109]

For [Jefferson] will never act as he speaks or writes, he will always counteract his political professions by the back-stairs committees 'til [John] Randolph shall finally sever him from them. - **Blennerhassett's Journal, October 29, 1807**
Fitch, *Breaking with Burr,* 145.

Many scholars have noted the sphinx-like qualities of Jefferson. These qualities appear contradictory because Jefferson had different distinct personality layers or parts, which he kept separate and used in different parts of his life. These contradictory qualities or behaviors become more understandable when viewed as separate parts of him, whether conscious or unconscious, whether actual dissociated personality parts[110] or merely different aspects of himself that he chose to reveal only to person's appropriate to that part or to its goals. And whether dissociated or by choice, one may find the nucleus in them when they are considered together. The boundaries between these layers were to some extent fluid and my identification of the content of these layers, while not arbitrary, is, of course, suggestive only.

---

[109] Schutz, *The Spur of Fame,* 49. (Thanks to Michael Drexler for this source.) This quote is sometimes found with the vivid preceding phrase: "Jefferson was like a shadow man..." I have been unable to find the source of that phrase. It is quoted in Brooke Adams, "John Adams: Realist of the Revolution," *The Hudson Review,* vol. 55, no. 1, 2002, pp. 45–54, at 51, without source. Similarly, the source of the Bouhours quote has not been located. (*See* Schutz, 49, n.65.)

[110] In psychiatry, dissociation is "the separation of normally related mental processes, resulting in one group functioning independently from the rest, leading in extreme cases to disorders such as multiple personality." *Oxford American Dictionary.*

The first layer was the surface layer. This was the enlightened **civil libertarian** whom we all know and admire, the author of the Declaration of Independence. This was the man who wrote "a summary of human rights and a justification of revolution on behalf of them, [which] it is doubtful if it has ever been excelled." (Malone, 224.) This is the man who, with Madison's help, developed an entire philosophy of government that remains the framework for much of what Americans believe. (*See* Koch, *Jefferson & Madison,* for an excellent survey.)

The second layer, which was the first subsurface layer, just under his skin close enough to the surface that he was willing to reveal it to close friends, was the **anti-libertarian autocrat**. Jefferson was able, in his own conscious mind at least, to reconcile these two opposing parts and justify them to others – though his justifications were thin and revealed his hypocrisy immediately to those inclined to see them. What he initially revealed only to friends (and primarily only at first to James Madison) became increasingly visible to his followers during his second administration.

This subsurface layer was the first to be revealed after the surface image began to fade over time. But this layer was translucent enough itself that through it, if one knew what to look for, one could espy the shades of the some of the deeper layers. Put another way, when the enlightened libertarian is grafted on top of an anti-libertarian, it suggests a deeper bias, a darker intent, although we might not yet see what that darker element is comprised of.

In a sense, then, this second layer is also a window into the deeper layers. Leonard Levy grapples with the two sides of this window in his excellent book *Jefferson and Civil Liberties: The Darker Side*. Levy notes six different subject matters, which he captures in phrases used by Jefferson: (1) In Times that Tried Men's Souls, (2) A Few Wholesome Prosecutions, (3) A Dictatorship in Extreme Cases, (4) Passive Resistance Enforced by Bayonets, (5) Any Means to the End: Embargo II, and (6) On Guard Against Political Heresies.

The third layer, or second subsurface layer, was the **man who had secrets** and engaged in activities – soliciting, supporting, funding, badmouthing, slandering, copulating, dominating, dictating – that he didn't want the public to know about. This layer encompasses his support of Blount's filibuster, funding western and southwestern "exploratory" expeditions, guiding the New York "knot of knaves," keeping slaves, and keeping Sally Hemings as his concubine, among other things.

I suspect that this was where his sexuality resided. For whatever reasons, Jefferson felt he had to keep hidden this and other manifestations of his manliness. This layer is also where his petty errant and miscreant behavior is found – his intriguing, his willingness to go beyond the law, even break the law, to do or enable something he thought was good or right that he felt was not permitted. It is also the part of him that engaged in his secretive adolescent commiseration with his man-friend, Madison, in sharing insults about others.

The <u>fourth layer</u> (third subsurface layer) was the part of him that contemplated and paid for others to do black **dirty work** that never could be revealed. This part may also be divided into two sub-parts: (a) the part of Jefferson that *solicited* criminal activity from others, and (b) the *projected* part of him that imagined and *did* the dirty deeds. Both character assassination and actual murder were contemplated here. Jefferson buried this layer so deep that nobody ever suspected it and even now over 200 years later, it is hard to believe, and the proofs require a great deal of careful piecing together.

The fifth or <u>deepest part</u>, however, which Jefferson never himself admitted, probably even to himself (meaning Jefferson was not conscious of it), was what Luther Martin called the *"hunter of men," the killer.* This part may be considered distinct from the imaginer of dirty deeds because this is the part that *contemplated and relished* the *hunting and killing.* It is one thing to decide one has just cause to go capture and kill a man (or to pay someone to do so) and quite another to feel the satisfaction Jefferson admitted to feeling in doing what he did to Burr. Jefferson's July 1807 letter to Pierre Samuel DuPont de Nemours captures something of this sentiment, where he writes "It has given me infinite satisfaction that not a single native Creole of Louisiana, and but one American . . . were in [Burr's] interest [and] [h]is partisans there were made up of fugitives from justice, or from their debts, who had flocked there from other parts of the United States . . ." (TJ to DuPont, July 14, 1807, Koch & Peden, *Life & Selected Works of TJ*, 536.) The entire letter shows Jefferson's immense pride in his work of destroying Burr. It is a remarkable, carefully constructed, and almost beautiful mixture of factual and imaginary material. The incongruencies are almost bizarre and yet the rhetoric is so perfect and poetic, it is only with great reluctance one dissects or deconstructs it.

While this part of Jefferson clearly emerged into the daylight and resembles in some ways his adolescent histrionics with Madison, it comes from a deeper well. This is the part that concerns us most because it was the part Burr confronted. It was to this deep, dark, murderous part of Jefferson that Burr lost everything.

Burr came to see and know this part of Jefferson and was unable to access the other more liberal, tolerant, and benevolent parts of the President. The wall was shut. As Burr said at trial, "The government may be tender, mild and humane to every one but me. If so, to be sure it is of little consequence to any body but myself. But surely I may be excused if I complain a little of such proceedings." (Robertson, 1:78, May 25, 1807.)

This part of Jefferson was not perceived by others, or to the extent it was, it so jarred with the other known and admired parts of Jefferson – even the hypocritical parts – that they could not make sense of it and tended simply to avoid seeing or grappling with it – and for Jefferson adherents, they did what Jefferson did: simply denied its existence.

Even while Burr stood there in court elaborating in detail on what he meant by persecution, adding almost as an afterthought "what was then to be said of those and other measures, such as the suspension of *habeas corpus* act, which concerned the whole nation? If in the island of Great Britain, such a measure was calculated to produce so much disturbance, what kind of sensation ought it to produce in this country?"[111] (id.), George Hay, the deputy Attorney General, declaimed:

> Sir, it was natural to supposed that such a serious charge [as treason] would have made a most serious impression upon Aaron Burr's mind; that he would have roused all the energies of his understanding to his service, in vindicating himself, and not in casting imputations upon the government. Why then does he turn from defending himself to attack the administration? Why these complaints of persecution which have fatigued our ears? I most solemnly deny the charge. I most confidently avow that there is not a tittle of evidence to support it . . .
>
> But, sir, when this cry and yell of persecution is once excited, it is not easy to set bounds to its fury. Not contented with inveighing against the pretended persecution of the government, *a government which never did persecute, a government which cannot persecute, and which will forever stand firm in the affections of the people, from the integrity and intelligence which mark its measures* . . . the counsel for the prisoner have . . . turned against the humble instruments who conduct the prosecution.

(Robertson 1:64, May 25, 1807.)(Emphasis mine.) Burr might have said nothing at all and gotten a better response!

I believe that the Burr event (the threat of Burr, his expedition, the accusations by Wilkinson, Jefferson's own several western expeditions, the danger of war with Spain, Burr's trial) pulled this buried part up out of Jefferson and brought it into the daylight for the first time in Jefferson's life (or at least his public adult life).

Like most monsters of the deep, this part of Jefferson lived and moved in the dark places where no one could see it. To see it, one must use reflections and projections, as with the mythological monster Medusa. We must look for evidence of it in its effects, in inferences and connections.

We can find evidence of the monster in some of his

---

[111] See Burr's full quote at the start of the chapter on "Character & Circumstance."

earlier involvements and contributions. (See the chapters on "Jefferson's Mirror.") We can also see it in some of the more unsavory characters to whom Jefferson seemed repeatedly and irresistibly to be drawn – like James Callendar, James Cheetham, De Witt Clinton, John Armstrong, James Wilkinson, Gideon Granger, and certainly others whose services he bought. The mysterious death of Meriwether Lewis, his nephew whom he had raised and trained to co-lead one of his expeditions (Lewis & Clark), may have been the flip side of the monster manifestation. Lewis was on a trip back eastward and was carrying a secret that he may have been murdered for. (*See* Chandler, *Jefferson Conspiracies.*) Note also Callender's mysterious death in three feet of water, which occurred not long after TJ rebuffed him and he published his revelations about Sally.

These men all knew something(s) about Jefferson that had to be kept secret. When they became uncomfortable keeping those secrets and threatened to speak out, odd things happened – mysterious deaths, disappearances, payoffs.

Callendar was a journalist/character assassin who later turned against Jefferson. Wilkinson became Jefferson's instrument of destruction against Burr and possibly Meriwether Lewis. Gideon Granger, as Jefferson's postmaster general, performed many indispensable services for Jefferson (spy/informant, burglar, conspirator). There were others, like the persons who committed perjury against Burr in order to gain favor from Jefferson. Col. George Morgan lied under oath; he had some large unsuccessful land claims Jefferson might help obtain for him. General Eaton succeeded by his perjured testimony to finally get paid the $10,000 he felt the government owed him for his Tripoli expenses. Jefferson attempted to turn Burr's friend, Erich Bollmann, by offering him a pardon, which he refused.

We ask why was Jefferson drawn to such people? Why did he make use of them? Why did he feel he ought to make use of them? Why would a refined, educated man like Jefferson want to have anything to do with such people? The answer is one any psychologist would know: because he was externalizing something that was inside of him.

The monster in Jefferson is discernible, too, in his outrageous and malicious vendetta against Burr: the unspoken, never admitted, "uncommon activity" (as Burr put it) of the prosecution in Burr's case and the harassment and persecution of Burr before he was even arrested or charged with anything, which Burr called "another small feature in a picture of oppressions and grievances" by the government, which led him to remark during the trial, quite mildly considering, that "there seemed to be something mingled in those proceedings which manifested a more than usual inclination to attain the ends of justice." (Robertson, *Trial of AB*, 1:77, 76, 78, May 25, 1807.)

But at that time, Luther Martin was the one who saw and articulated it most clearly. He said that Jefferson had "let slip the dogs of war, the hell-hounds of persecution, to hunt down my friend." (*Id.* 1:128, June 10, 1807.) It was only several years later that Burr was able to articulate what Jefferson had done to him. He wrote Jeremy Bentham:

> From any man, save one, if I cannot vanquish, I can escape. In the hands of that one, I am just what Theodosia is in mine. This was perceived after the first two hours; and seeing no retreat, nor anything better to be done, I surrendered, tame and unresisting, to be disarmed, stripped, hacked, hewed, dissected, skinned, turned inside out, at the will and mercy of the operator. Much good may it do him.

(AB to JB, January 31, 1809, Davis, *Burr's Journal*, 1:169.)

Burr's words clearly show the violence of what he experienced. This is the only declaration of its kind in Burr's own words in which he used such strong, vivid imagery. Specifically, the words "stripped, hacked, hewed, dissected, skinned, turned inside out, at the will and mercy of the operator": these are not just words of violence; they are words of death, of being killed in a particularly cruel and horrid manner.

The one who did this to him was Jefferson. That was Burr's experience of what happened and Burr did not imagine it. We may impute to Jefferson the intent to cause to Burr that which he in fact did cause – "stripped, hacked, hewed, dissected, skinned, turned inside out." This doesn't simply mean, as Jefferson said, "*I did wish to see these people get what they deserved.*"[112] It means Jefferson stripped Burr, hacked him, hewed him, dissected him, skinned him and turned him inside out. Survival was not an option in this equation and Jefferson did not want it to be.

Jefferson may have justified this by saying he wished only for what he, in his unilateral judgment, thought Burr deserved, but the fact is that Jefferson caused and intended to cause what did happen to Burr, whether he consciously meant to or not, whether Burr deserved it or not. TJ set the stage and created the choices, forcing Burr into a channel not of his choosing and then TJ nailed him for having walked that way.

What kind of man does this? What kind of man does this to another man who had been one of his strongest supporters and advocates? What kind of man does this to anyone, even his worst enemy?

If we were to apply to Jefferson the kind of justice he applied to Burr, we ought to say "an eye for an eye" and do to Jefferson what he did to Burr: destroy his reputation, his political and professional career, his life, withdraw all human support from him, all friendship, all possibility of love, erase him and his name from the archives of history except as an evil-doer, erase all his good deeds, all his hard-won accomplishments, take away his beloved home, his land, his children, all the things that made his life dear – Jefferson would have nothing left. We would probably not even know he ever existed. That is what Jefferson wanted to do to Burr and what he mostly succeeding in doing.

Burr did not deserve the justice Jefferson dispensed, but Jefferson may have deserved the vengeance Burr never wrought on him.

The yardstick, remember, is not the one Jefferson wanted to be measured by (what he said he intended) but the one that is manifest from the *result* of Jefferson's actions. And again, not incidental actions but those carried out over a substantial period of time with multiple opportunities to reconsider, redirect, retract, withdraw.   ~

---

[112]   TJ to James Brown, October 27, 1808, Founders Online.

Wilkinson:

The Making of an Assassin

He could do this without remorse; his mind is framed for treachery, and possesses a peculiar apathy that enables him to speak of his crimes as if they were virtues, and which takes away all hope of amendment and all sense of shame.
Daniel Clark, *Proofs of the Corruption of General James Wilkinson*, 42-43

But, sir, will it be forgotten that this man has already broken the constitution to support his violent measures; that he has already ground down the civil authorities into dust, and subjected all around him to a military despotism?
Martin Luther (attorney for Burr),
June 10,1807, Robertson 1:129.

Wilkinson and Jefferson

As I have mentioned, Jefferson seemed to have an attraction to a certain type of unsavory character. Not that this was the only kind of person he associated with (obviously not) but simply that he had an attraction to a type of person we wouldn't expect him to associate with. In fact, he didn't really associate with those unsavory people in a social sense. He kept them on the fringes of his life and never let them into his parlor, so to speak. But he certainly did associate with them – and use them – when it came to doing things he didn't want to be caught doing.

Clearly, somewhere in his mind, he found justification and cause for doing this. If he did justify such activities, his conscious reasons were probably as topsy-turvy as those he found to justify engaging in anti-libertarian actions. Already having decided that someone had relinquished all right to be part of the society in which good and upright people moved, it was not a big step for him to decide to have them removed. Or, if it had once been a big step, he had overcome it in the dark part of his mind a long time ago.

As Jefferson had said, "No one doubted that society had a right to erase from the roll of its members any one who rendered his own existence inconsistent with theirs; to withdraw from him the protection of their laws, and to remove him from among them by exile, or even by death if necessary." (TJ to L.H. Girardin, March 12, 1815, quoted in Levy, *Jefferson & Civil Liberties,* 40, citing to Lipscomb, 24:271-78.)

He repeated this sentiment about Burr, too, when he told James Brown that he did wish Burr and his followers to get what they deserved, "under the maxim of the law itself, that *inter arma silent leges.*"

There it is: if someone rendered his existence inconsistent with society's (that is, in *Jefferson's* better judgment, which is to say with *Jefferson's* existence), society (Jefferson) had the right to remove him and even to kill him. Having justified killing for the "public advantage" in theory, it was only another small step to soliciting someone to do the deed. Jefferson didn't have to have blood on his own hands. But the murderous intent originated and resided in *Jefferson.* It makes sense, therefore, that he would be drawn to people who were capable of and willing to commit murder. They fit like hand and glove.

And having resolved to justify murder, it was not hard thereafter to remove and discard the bloody glove once it had completed its task - that is, to find someone else to get rid of the assassin (who might one day talk and whose very existence might be used to prove Jefferson's involvement.) This requires a second evil-doer, of course, who is then twice removed from Jefferson – a much safer distance than the first one, who is tangentially associated with him.

Some of the men Wilkinson hired were the killers of killers. Just as there were levels of darkness within Jefferson, there were shades within the darker shades of those who did his dirty work. There were those at Wilkinson's level – those whom Jefferson solicited to arrange the deed. Wilkinson was an arranger. He hired the men who did the actual hunting and killing. Wilkinson then also often hired other men to obstruct and sometimes kill those he had hired. Usually the division was between the United States and Spain. Wilkinson did his job for the U.S., hiring and commanding men to carry out various tasks for his president or commander, and then undid those tasks for Spain by hiring other men to cut off and "dry-gulch" the Americans.

Wilkinson and his men were the most complete manifestation of Jefferson's murderous alter ego, so it is well that we spend a good amount of time with him, separately and in his relation to Jefferson.

The Making of an Assassin

Anyone who reads about Burr knows generally who Wilkinson was. Most know that he was a Spanish pensioner and that he betrayed Burr. The term "betrayal" is unfortunate since it may also mean to give up the secrets of. Wilkinson did not give up Burr's secrets. He betrayed Burr's friendship. He lied about Burr and was a traitor to his own country doing so.

But all that is the top icicle on the tip of a big and deep iceberg. Intrigue, conspiracy, and betrayal are what Wilkinson is known for. While many scholars have mentioned Wilkinson's role in various attempted assassinations, none has called Wilkinson what he was. Wilkinson was a destroyer and killer of men. And he wasn't born one.

Doctor Wilkinson

We will probably never know exactly what combination of things made Wilkinson what he was but we can ascertain some things. Knowing now what he was, knowing how he fit into things (how he used others and was used by them), we can piece together some, maybe even most of the elements of the template of who he was.

The first thing Wilkinson pursued when he was of age was a medical degree -- which he completed. If we go back in our minds to the medical theaters of late 19th century England, we might get some idea of the activities in which a medical student engaged in the late 18th century America. It was an profession of ghastly sights. You don't practice medicine, you don't complete your medical degree – especially in the late 18th and early 19th century America – if you can't stand the sight of blood, infection, disease, and dead bodies. Although Wilkinson didn't stay in the medical profession long because the Revolution and the military called to him, the effect of this beginning on the development of the man he became was likely far greater than anyone has imagined. Neither the military nor the frontier life of a merchant (nor certainly his double life as spy for Spain) relieved him of that bent of mind. Rather, they seem to have solidified his dark habits.

If Wilkinson went into the medical profession with the mental illness that later grew into his capacity for plotting and killing, the medical profession externalized what was up to that point internal only. It literally gave physical substance to – and perhaps release of – horrors that had resided previously only in his imagination and subconscious.

The combination of medical training and military is a dangerous mix for a sensitive man like Wilkinson. He had to have come into adulthood with some pre-existing sociopathy, a predisposition to cruelty and betrayal, an unconscious need for bloody revenge. He was very likely seeking release of an already fixed unresolvable combination of terror and rage. He seems to have had a tendency to get himself into situations where he was going to be blamed, going to be made to take the fall for something, and always somehow managed to just escape. To look at that as coincidence is silly. To see it as mere manifestation of a character trait without looking at the underlying cause and origins is remiss.

He was going to be crucified for some terrible deed that at the outset, when he had first become involved in it, was a simple expression of natural need. The theme is played over and over again in his life. He wrote to Daniel Clark on Oct. 27, 1807: "assailed as I am by the worst, the meanest demons that ever infested the earth." (Clark, *Proofs of the Corruption of General James Wilkinson*, "Notes," (Appendix) p.18.)

It is an unenvious situation to be in. Wilkinson was going to be killed. Over and over again, that's the situation in which he found himself. He was going to be killed just for trying to make his way, for trying to find the way to survive, for allying himself with those who nurtured him and agreed with his assessment of his situation and wanted to join with and help him. His entire life, Wilkinson got himself into these situations, over and over again, and the only way out was to betray and sometimes to kill.

If he found it necessary to go over to the other side in order to survive, was that his fault? If he had to stay behind and live a double life in order to make ends meet?

His assessment of the situation was not incorrect. Out in Kentucky, he saw what the American government was not doing, how it was putting its own countrymen in harm's way and failing to offer any protection. He (like many others in Kentucky) felt he had to ally with Spain but that alliance, if it became known to the U.S. government, could have gotten him hung. As time passed, this divide only widened. He told Spain:

> I hope it may never be said of me, with justice, that in changing my allegiance from the United States to the honorable Court of Madrid, I have broken any of the laws of nature or of nations, nor of honor and conscience . . . [T]he policies of the United States having made it impossible for me to obtain this desired end under its government, I am resolved to seek it in Spain.

(Kennedy, 132, citing Wilkinson's "famous expatriation declaration" ("Wilkinson's Memorial").) He was speaking truth.

We can view this declaration as treason but in the context it was common sense. Most westerners felt betrayed and abandoned by their leaders and felt they were free to choose their loyalties. Indeed, Thomas Jefferson even acknowledged and expressed his support of the right of Kentuckians to go their way.

Wilkinson saw every American administration (and official) pretty much the same way. As he wrote the Spanish governor of Louisiana in the early 1790's, the United States had "an incompetent secretary of war, an ignorant commander-in-chief, and a contemptible union." (Chandler, *Jefferson Conspiracies*, 108, quoting Wilkinson to Carondelet without citation.) He was talking about Henry Knox, George Washington, and the United States.

Wilkinson wrote Burr in May of 1802:

> . . . the treatment I have experienced in & about Congress has awakened me as from a dream, after the race of perils & hardships, of suffering, & services which I have run for the last eleven years, shall men of yesterday, a set of prating puppies & coxcombs, who

have learned how to mangle truth & to garnish falsehood, reproach me with being a drone & the only one of the political hive? . . .

(JW to AB, May 16, 1802, Kline 2:720-721.) Again, no joke.

In 1803, he wrote Daniel Clark that the new American governor of Lower Louisiana (aka Orleans Territory), William C. C. Claiborne (a Jefferson appointee): "is a mass of duplicity, meanness, envy, ignorance and cowardice – Yet you must not make any attack on him at present." (JW to DC, June 9, 1803, Clark, *Proofs,* Notes (Appendix), 197.) In 1794, he called the Secretary of War, Henry Knox, "a weak, corrupt minister" and General Washington "a despotic, vainglorious, ignorant general." (JW to John Brown, August 28, 1794, Kennedy, 131.)

Viewing Wilkinson's remarks in retrospect and in light of his intrigues, scholars tend to see them as exaggerations. But what if they weren't? What if he was right? At least from Wilkinson's perspective, what if he was right in viewing these people as ones who would as soon harm as help him, people whose ethics were dictated not by moral right but by self-interest? Was he supposed to just let them hurt him? Mangle truth & garnish falsehood and call him whatever names they pleased? He had, after all, risked his life for his country more than once. But that counted as nothing to such "men of yesterday," such "prating puppies & coxcombs."

In order for Wilkinson to consistently see his superiors this way, he probably had to possess a fairly thin skin for criticism and a sense of confoundedness or disturbance at normal social and political maneuverings. He must have perceived it all as an evil game. He would be the victim unless he learned how to play the game better than his abusers.

Both Wilkinson's emotional sensitivity and his narcissism mirrored Jefferson's quite closely. Both men perceived themselves as the center of the universe. Neither man could tolerate criticism. Both were vengeful for perceived emotional hurts and were hurt easily.

Wilkinson's Modi Operandi

Wilkinson lived in a world where random death and killing constantly occurred. Frontier life in Kentucky was similar to what Burr's mother, Esther, had so vividly described in her journal the year of his birth (1756) on a visit she made to her father up in Stockbridge, Massachusetts. While her father, Jonathan Edwards, lived among and preached to the Stockbridge Indians, who were peaceful, there were other tribes who were far less passive about the incursions of white men into their ancestral territories. A week or so after Esther arrived, there were reports of an Indian attack at Oswego, New York. Her journal entries convey the constant fear families experienced on the frontiers. She wrote:

> This place is in a very defenseless condition – not a solider in it . . . this is a place that the enemy can easily get at, and if they do we can't defend ourselves. Ten indians might with all ease destroy us entirely. There has been a number seen at about 30 miles distance from this place.

(Karlsen & Crumpacker, *The Journal of Esther Edwards Burr*, 221 (journal entry date September 8, 1756).) (Spelling modernized on all Esther's entries).

Esther said she was "Almost overcome with fear . . . O how distressing to live in fear every moment." Over the course of the few weeks of her visit, she was in continual distress. "I want to be made willing to die in any way God pleases, but I am not willing to be butchered by a barbarous enemy." And "I could not sleep for fear of the enemy." Esther felt a sense of gloom: "O how dark do things look! I fear I shall not be able to take any comfort in my friends nor they in me." "[I]f the Indians get me, they get me, that is all I can say . . . All is dark as Egypt!" she wrote. "I grow worse and worse, more afraid than ever – if I happen to drowse I am frighted to death with dreams." *Id.*, 220 (Sept. 2-3), 222 (Sept. 10), 220 (Sept. 1), 223 (Sept. 13), 221 (Sept. 7). (Esther died only two years later.)

Esther might excused for being so fearful. She was an unprotected woman with a young child. Men, of course, especially military men, were supposed to be fearless but the dangers along the frontiers were very real and for an intelligent, sensitive man like Wilkinson, who grew up feeling unprotected and now had a family of his own to protect, the effect cannot be exaggerated. This was Wilkinson's world.

Andro Linklater describes the stages of JW's development into an "artist in treason." Although Linklater seems unaware of JW's transformation into an assassin, the stages he describes clearly show the progress of his deeper disorder.

The opening episode begins with Wilkinson "wooing" General Gates. Linklater notes: "There was something of the seducer in the way James Wilkinson set about winning the hearts of his generals." (Linklater, *Artist in Treason,* 24.) While Linklater suggests that the affection he exhibited was "too intense to be pretended" and "suggested how much he missed his father," Linklater quickly notes that JW had admitted that Gates won him "by his indulgence of my self-love" and JW "responded by encouraging the older [man's] taste for intrigue," which Linklater declares "a dangerous exchange." (Id.)

If JW's relationships with "his generals" were modeled on his relationship with his father, this description takes on a greater significance, as it illustrates the original driving force that ultimately led to what JW became.[113]

What in those days was "a taste for intrigue" today would be spy-craft, and in the world of espionage, lies and betrayals are the norm. The wearing down and ultimate destruction of the soul that happens through the habitual practice of lying about who one is, about what one wants, and what one will give – the smoke screens, veils, reversals, playing on people's weakness and needs, using them for purposes neither humanitarian nor humane, always with the ominous truth threatening one's safety – the effect of these cannot be over-estimated. The public today adores spy stories and reveres the manly James Bonds who live luxurious lives with women hanging at the heels, always managing to out-trick or out-gun the evil enemy. But what happens to the soul of real spies cannot be fathomed by ordinary people. The spy becomes

---

[113] Or his mother. These relationships had homosexual undertones in which it seems the two men frequently switched roles, the older one first playing the father figure and the younger playing the doting, servicing mistress; then the older one switching to the woman in distress needing rescue by the young, dashing man. A confusing and potentially volatile exchange indeed.

so completely nameless and bottomless – doing terrible things to others (who are as likely innocent as not) in the name of God or country with no sense of remorse or accountability. To operate continually outside moral values is, however, an intoxicating and addictive drink that may be hard to give up once the taste has been acquired.

The homosexual element should not be forgotten here either. Homosexuality contains one form of reversal (gender reversal). Lies and betrayals embody other forms.

Wilkinson's first step into the world of betrayal on the road to becoming an assassin was when (by a strange twist), in Linklater's revealing words, he "proved his devotion [to Major General Gates] by the way he … neatly *disposed of* his former patron," Major General Benedict Arnold (who as we all know, later betrayed America and defected to Great Britain – another interesting reversal). In a quarrel between the two generals, Wilkinson had to choose. He made no attempt to mediate or find a middle ground. Instead, he betrayed his former patron (Arnold) in favor of his current one. As Linklater puts it, when push came to shove, he simply "neatly disposed of" Arnold – gave him up, abandoned him, got rid of him. (Linklater, 38.)

What we have then is someone who has learned or decided to prove his devotion to one father figure by "disposing of" the other. Deriving from this framework, we find that this is someone who has learned that proving his devotion, his love for a father figure, necessarily involves doing away with another (a lesser father figure). He gets rid of the former (and now lesser, or less useful) father figure to prove his devotion to the greater (present, more useful) father figure. ("Useful" being not only that which JW felt would best satisfy him ambitions but that which was more useful in enabling him to survive.)

The phrase "disposing of" is Linklater's but it speaks of something we can discern throughout Wilkinson's life – his repeated decisions to get rid of people who had previously been of service to him but no longer were. He did not simply walk away from them. In Arnold's case, Wilkinson came to the rescue of Gates and turned squarely against and betrayed Arnold. Later, he literally got rid of inconvenient or no longer useful people by having them killed.

Interestingly, though Wilkinson consciously betrayed Arnold in favor of Gates, he later *inadvertently* betrayed Gates' trust. While drunk, he casually divulged a passage from a letter between two generals. This ultimately became known as the Conway Cabal, which was supposed to unseat George Washington and elevate Gates to commander-in-chief. When Gates found out about Wilkinson's indiscretion, it provoked Gates to call his actions "positive treason," which Linklater notes was "the first time the charge had been laid against Wilkinson, and unique in being the only occasion it was wholly unjustified." Wilkinson had a "murderous reaction." He wrote in his *Memoirs*: "I was ready to have laid down my life for him, yet he had condemned me unheard for an act of which I was perfectly innocent." He then twice called Gates to duel. Linklater notes: "There was an edge of hysteria in James Wilkinson's uncontrollable rage as though what Gates had done to him was so unbearable he had to be blotted out. But the urge to destroy Gates had only succeeded in destroying his own desire for military glory. When he finally recovered his composure, his career as an officer in the Revolutionary War was at an end." (Linklater, 54, 56, 59, citing Wilkinson, *Memoirs of My Own Times* (Philadelphia: A. Small, 1816), 1:385.)

In this episode, we can discern the emotional disturbance that Wilkinson suffered in his attachment to the men in his life. Linklater calls this "an edge of hysteria" in his "uncontrollable rage" and "urge to destroy" Gates. One of Wilkinson's fellow staff officers wrote Gates about him: "I ever was sensible of Wilky's volatility and open heartedness..." (Linklater, 55.)[114]

It is not hard to see where such a disturbed attachment relationship could lead. Abraham Clark, a New Jersey delegate to the Continental Congress, wrote presciently: "If he betrayed

---

[114] Linklater cites to a letter from Walter Stewart to Gates in Gates, *Memoirs* 1:390, apparently meaning Wilkinson's *Memoirs*. (*See* Linklater, 337, note at beginning of footnotes for Chapter 3.) Linklater chose not to include in his main text a remarkable statement from Gen. Charles Lee to Gates of March 29, 1799: "With respect to Wilkinson, I really think he had been a man more sinned against than any." (Quoted at Linklater, 341, in the fourth footnote to page 55.)

the Confidence of his Patron he may do the same by his Country." (Linklater, 55, quoting Wilkinson, *Memoirs*, 1:390, 341 (fn. to p. 54, quoting Abraham Clark to William Alexander, Jan. 15, 1778)).)

But what has been missed in Wilkinson's behavior, even by Linklater, is that this disturbance not only provided the predisposition to betrayal but to murder, as well. The betrayal was, in fact, a form of destruction of his former male love object. At the end of this era, Wilkinson "had neither command nor patron, and too much pride to seek either again. He had trusted Gates and, in his own mind, been betrayed, and the experience had erased a small but curiously childlike innocence." (*Id.* at 59.)

The stage had been set for Wilkinson. Having accidentally betrayed his general and been falsely accused of treason (thus feeling himself betrayed), Wilkinson thereafter became the betrayer. He would betray before he could be betrayed. This is a fairly typical behavior for someone with a volatile, sensitive nature in situations such as Wilkinson's, but for the victim-turned-perpetrator, something more must happen to become a killer.

Motive is the first part, opportunity the second. Third, there must be impetus to physically act. That impetus came, for Wilkinson, out of the heat of battle. He always had felt happiest and most at ease in his skin when he was in the midst of battle, where emotional betrayals could be projected outward onto the field and enemy and resolved directly there. The act of killing is sanctioned in war, but for Wilkinson, as for many battle-tried warriors, the permission, the necessity to act swiftly and resolutely became internalized. The initial need for moral justification for killing fades as the need for personal resolution takes over.

Return to Civilian Life

How, then, does one accustomed to war become a husband, father, and businessman? Because JW never returned to medical practice, his medical training is usually overlooked and forgotten. Doctors today follow diagnostic models that were not in existence in Wilkinson's time. Now, doctors are trained to identify sets of pre-established diagnostic criteria and to choose the most correct diagnostic answer from the presented symptoms. They are trained not to think or come to independent conclusions.

But doctors in Wilkinson's time were independent thinkers who often had a scientific bent. Apparently neither were of interest to Wilkinson, but that doesn't mean his exposure to the medical field left no marks on him. Rather, to the permission to take physical action to do battle and kill one's opponent and to his experiences with attachment and betrayal, we may add the two incongruously conjoined conditions of medical training: the desire to heal and the physical invasion of another person's body. The latter was limited to prescribing medicines, other times extended to small incursions like visual inspection, manual palpitation, or blood-letting, but sometimes involved surgical procedures and amputation.

In a much later famous U.S. Supreme Court case, the Court made clear that surgery was a physical invasion of the patient's body, which would be considered a battery without "informed consent," in which the patient is informed about the nature of and need for the procedure, the benefits and risks, before giving consent. Since that decision, "informed consent" is required to perform surgery, invasive medical procedures, or treatment. Doctors today view this as a perfunctory but annoyingly necessary step to performing surgery on a patient.

In Wilkinson's time, the informed consent doctrine did not exist. Instead, one went into the medical profession, viewing the practice as a science and healing profession. Wilkinson never seems to have contemplated returning to the profession. Maybe it was easier for him to kill than to heal. Or maybe he preferred the power of command and killing to the closer physical intimacy and touch of healing.

In any case, he became a merchant where had no luck either. Or rather, he was plagued with repeated bad luck. Eventually, he came up with a plan that involved giving allegiance to Spain in order to get preferred status for passage of his goods into New Orleans. This began what Linklater calls "an astonishingly firm friendship" with Don Esteban Miró, governor of New Orleans and Louisiana, "the most enduring of Wilkinson's oddly dependent relationships, and one that

seamlessly evolved into that between spy and handler."
(Linklater, 96.)

The Killer

Wilkinson was involved in several attempts to assassinate individuals, beginning with an attempt on the life of General "Mad" Anthony Wayne. Interestingly, Linklater ignores this event. JW hated Wayne like he hated others for suspecting him. Apparently the plan was to keep supplies from reaching Wayne's troops (which were at that time engaged in battles with the Indians) – the idea being to prevent Wayne from succeeding in the campaign – and if that failed, to kill him.[115] The attempt on his life occurred when a tree fell on top of his tent while he was sleeping. Wayne found out about JW's agency with the British and involvement in the plot via a convoluted series of events, described in detail in Kennedy.[116] Unfortunately, Wayne died (apparently of an ulcer) before JW could be tried. (Kennedy, 134.)

Kennedy lists three other Wilkinson conspiracies to attack an army under his own command:

> He had arranged for the ambushing of one of his own detachments in Tennessee by the Creeks. In 1806, he notified the Spanish authorities that his own troops were advancing across Texas. Most astonishingly, a year earlier he sent a force including his own son on a mission against which he stimulated a Spanish attack.

(Kennedy, 132.) Kennedy concludes that "Wilkinson's tactics against Wayne in 1794 . . . demonstrate most horridly his willingness to use extreme measures." (Id., 133.)

---

[115] Kennedy says JW's correspondence with the British is reported in Simcoe 2:243 but he does not list Simcoe in his bibliography. Kennedy may be referring to Lieutenant-Colonel [John Graves] Simcoe, *A Journal of the Operations of the Queen's Rangers From the End of the Year 1777 to the Conclusion of the Late American War* (Originally published 1789).

[116] Wayne's quartermaster and spy, Robert Newman, was picked up by the British. He pretended to be a deserter and learned of the involvement of JW with the British Elliot brothers to get rid of Wayne and bring the Ohio Valley back into British control via JW. Newman nearly didn't make it back to Wayne but when he did, Wayne learned of the plot. Kennedy cites to Timothy Rusche, "The Battle of Fallen Timbers: Securing America's Western Frontier" (Senior Thesis, University of Pennsylvania, April 1997). Rusche found a letter from JW to one of the Elliots and the account of Newman in the Wayne Papers in the Philadelphia Historical Society, 34:13 and 38:79. (Kennedy, 133.)

Another example of his use of extreme measures was an encounter with another British agent, John Connolly, who approached JW in 1789, offering money, ammunition, and ships to "open the navigation of the Mississippi." Instead, JW told the Spanish that he "employed a hunter, who feigned attempting his life." Since Wilkinson held "the commission of a Civil Judge, it was, of course, to be my duty to protect him against the pretended murderer, whom I caused to be arrested and held in custody," telling Connolly that he could not "answer for the security of his person and I expressed my doubts whether he could escape with his life," at which point Connolly begged JW to provide him an escort out of the territory, to which he "readily assented." (Linklater, 98.)[117]

When it came to arresting Burr, JW first attempted to hire Silas Dinsmore, to whom he promised $5000 if he would "cut off" Burr. When Dinsmore didn't act, JW hired several others, including two army officers, "armed with dirks and pistols" to get Burr. (Chandler, 230.) Meanwhile, at JW's behest, the Spanish intendants were plotting the doom of TJ's explorers: Pike, Lewis & Clark, and Freeman/Custis. (Chandler, 165-66, and *see below*, chapter on Dunbar, Freeman & Custis Expeditions.)

Wilkinson's attempts to kill Burr were nothing new for JW. Nor was Wilkinson's nature unknown to Jefferson. President Washington knew directly from General Wayne what Wayne had learned. Washington called him "that vile assassin." Jefferson, who was Secretary of State, would have known through Washington, as far back as 1795. (*See* Kennedy, 134.) Loosing Wilkinson on Burr was neither accidental nor unintended. Jefferson knew exactly what Wilkinson's capabilities and propensities were.

~

---

[117] The story is also told by James R. Jacobs, *Tarnished Warrior: Major-General James Wilkinson* (Macmillan, 1938) 89, citing to JW to Miro, February 12, 1789, Archivo General de Indias, Seville, Papeles de Cuba, legajos 2374. Linklater cites to Papeles Procedentes de Cuba, JW to Miro, February 14, 1789, legajos 3893.

The Madison-Jefferson Bond

[H]*is judgment is so sound and is heart so good.*
TJ to Peter Carr, December 11, 1783 (about Madison)
(Burstein & Isenberg, 104.)

Madison's *"true character is the reverse of that simple, fair, candid one, which he has assumed."*
Hamilton to Edward Carrington, May 26, 1792
(Burstein & Isenberg, 248)

In 1791, Madison, Jefferson, and Burr first met in New York City. Years later, Jefferson stated that from the outset he had mistrusted Burr and had repeatedly warned Madison not to trust him. Jefferson misidentified the time of that first meeting, stating that he didn't know Burr until the New Yorker entered Congress and that his opinion was formed through observing Burr's work in Congress. But Jefferson and Madison had specifically sought Burr out and met with him privately months before he served in the U.S. Senate. First meetings are generally memorable. Apparently Jefferson didn't want his readers to know that he and Madison had sought Burr out.

By the time Jefferson met Burr, he and Madison had been working together for ten years. They had developed a powerfully close friendship and working relationship. Their socio-cultural backgrounds were similar. Both men were landed gentry from slave-owning Virginia families. Jefferson was Madison's senior by eight years. He had been raised and educated in Virginia. Madison grew up several hundred miles from Jefferson but received his college education at Princeton, then the College of New Jersey (where Burr's father had been President), graduating a year ahead of Aaron Burr. Evidently, both Madison and Burr were strongly influenced by the progressive ideals of Princeton's president, John Witherspoon.

In Madison's case, however, those ideals fused with the more conservative culture of his upbringing.

Had it not been for Madison, the Jefferson most of us know would have been lost to history. Madison understood both Jefferson's weaknesses and strengths. He tolerated the parts of Jefferson that others found distasteful, foolish, or alarming, and he patiently and repeatedly redirected Jefferson to continue the great theoretical work Madison knew was in him. But even so, without Madison's practical application of Jefferson's theories, neither man would likely have achieved anything near the supremacy they did. In that decade, the two men not only developed theories and made plans; they developed and practiced a method of working together that made the best use of both of their unique talents.

But their relationship had another side to it that is relatively unknown. The two shared a coded lingo of mutually-encouraged cruelty and slander. Alexander Hamilton (who engaged in his share of nasty rhetoric) discerned this side of Madison. He noted that Madison's "true character is the reverse of that *simple, fair, candid one*, which he has assumed." (Burstein & Isenberg, *Madison and Jefferson,* 248, quoting AH to Edward Carrington, May 26, 1792.)

To a large extent, historians (and even biographers) do not explore the deeper psychological dimensions of their subjects, the wellsprings of personality and character – what I like to call "the secret life." The secret lives of all men and women are full of deep psychological drama. Life and death issues are always at the core, love and survival always the primary drives. Most people by the time they reach adulthood have sublimated these issues into culturally higher and socially more acceptable activities. By the time we reach adulthood, few of us remember the drama and trauma of our childhood and because we adapt and sublimate, we believe we have rid ourselves of those "problems." But, those issues continue to haunt and drive us, largely unconsciously.

The extent to which an individual traverses the treacherous stages of child development and functions as an adult in a mentally/emotionally healthy and socially acceptable way depends on many factors. And these two ends –

mental/emotional health and socially acceptable behavior – are not synonymous or necessarily mutually supporting. High social contribution does not necessarily mean fully successful resolution of childhood issues. Unresolved childhood issues can continue to color and direct the personal, interpersonal, social, political, cultural contributions and activities of even the most highly regarded men and women. Nor will all activities that society views as productive necessarily be good for an individual's psyche. There is nearly always a psychological cost to social adaption. Where there are unresolved issues and repression, there is projection: what one cannot accept in oneself is projected onto "the dark other."

In Jefferson and Madison's case, the deep psychological drama of their intersecting and merging secret lives contained repressed and unresolved homosexual and dominant-submissive elements. These elements are essential to understand, as they create the context for Jefferson's subsequent projection onto and ultimate vendetta against Burr, and for Madison's acceptance of this projected/fabricated image of Burr, and the acceptance by the rest of the cabinet and eventually by the rest of the world.[118]

In the late 18th century, it was not unusual for educated gentlemen to form close male friendships and to express love and affection warmly and openly. There was nonetheless an unspoken and invisible line one did not cross without social consequences. Sexual intercourse between two men, for example, or a man's overt sexual preference for another man, were not acceptable behaviors in gentlemanly circles and would have led to social and political disgrace and downfall. Men were supposed to be manly: forthright, bold, brave, strong, and firm. Feminine traits in a man were viewed as weak and cowardly.

In the northern states, a married man who got another woman pregnant had a social obligation to support the woman and child and arrange for the child's education. Such a

---

[118] My analysis of homosexual elements accepts the view of homosexuality as gender preference but does not conclude there. My interest is in viewing the circumstances of these men from inside their experiences. Love and acceptance of different human conditions does not require lack of analysis. Every human behavior and condition has an outcome.

situation, even if frowned on, did nothing to ruin his social or political standing (though the woman fell into disgrace). In the southern states, it was not unusual for men to have children by their slaves and that didn't damage their standing either, but in both the north and south, such relationships were rarely openly acknowledged.

Evidence of Jefferson's intimate/sexual life presents an interesting picture. He appears to have been happily, even blissfully married to his wife of twelve years, Martha.

In the months just prior to her untimely death in 1782, Martha copied a selection from *Tristram Shandy* that reveals her feelings about her own imminent demise. Biographer Fawn Brodie writes about Martha's copying of this passage:

> That she singled these out for copying, omitting what was not appropriate to her own condition, tells us much about her intelligence, her sensitivity, and above all her necessity to communicate her ow feelings with an eloquence she could not herself command but felt compelled to express.

(Brodie, 167.) This passage is revealing on a number of levels. The part she copied reads:

> Time wastes too fast: every letter I trace tells me with what rapidity life follows my pen. The days and hours of it are flying over our heads like clouds of [a] windy day never to return – more everything presses on –

(Id.) (Brodie does not identify the location of the document but notes: "That the lines came from *Tristram Shandy* and were not written [i.e. invented] by Martha Jefferson was established by Professor Edward L. Hubler. *See Papers*, Boyd, VI, 196-97n.) (Id., 515n23.)

Brodie states: "At this point, her hand must have faltered, for the remainder of the passage, copied in darker ink, is in Jefferson's clear, firm hand." (*Id.*)

> --- and every time I kiss thy hand to bid adieu, every absence which follows it, are preludes to that eternal separation which we are shortly to make!

Brodie quotes the remarkable account of his eldest daughter, then ten, written over forty years later, who witnessed her father's intense grief after his wife's death:

> The scene that followed I did not witness but the violence of his emotion, of his grief when almost by stealth I entered his room at night to this day I dare not trust myself to describe. He kept his room for three weeks and I was never a moment from his side. He walked almost incessantly night and day only lying down occasionally when nature was completely exhausted ... When at last he left his room he rode out and from that time he was incessantly on horseback rambling about the mountain ... in those melancholy rambles I was his constant companion, a solitary witness to many a violent burst of grief ...

(*Id.* at 168-69, citing to George Tucker, *Life of Thomas Jefferson* (2 vols., Philadelphia, 1837) 1:158).)

Brodie observes: "One sees here a grief that bordered on the pathological, a truly symbolic dying, followed by a binding of father and daughter." (*Id.* at 169.) Brodie adds insightfully that

> Jefferson seems to have no such inner fortification as most people develop in caring for a dying loved one. His wife's many illnesses, inevitably associated with pregnancy, had been in the most literal sense caused by him. With every illness he must have feared her death, and also fought off the guilty reflection that certain freedoms would come to him if she did die. The greater his love the more guilt about these intrusions. Jefferson paid for such conflict first in absolute insensibility, then in insomnia and in a total incapacity for work.

(*Id.*)

Brodie notes that five days after Martha's death, Jefferson wrote in his Garden Book about how to preserve birds: "So he transmuted the inevitable imaginings of the dissolution of his wife's body into a scientific account of how to preserve for display a beautiful dead bird. Such was one of the defenses of a sensitive man who could not handle his grief as other men did." (*Id.*)

I see several things here. One is that "the defenses of a sensitive man who could not handle his grief" involved a morbid effort on his part to physically handle a dead animal in order to preserve it. His "scientific" account was his way of handling his grief. To me this manifests emotional disturbance.

I also see that this joint pre-death copying is like a duet of death sung by two weeping/singing voices, each in agreement with the other. The complete agreement, partnership, and mutual support in the creation of this duet is astounding. They each agree she is dying, but at the point of the copying, could either Jefferson or his wife be absolutely certain of her death? She had been close to death many times before this. Immediately after her death, witnesses recorded that Jefferson was "in a state of insensibility" and grief that continued for months. So whatever Jefferson anticipated or agreed with, he was not prepared emotionally for the loss. It struck him like lightning and utterly prostrated him.

But here both Martha and Tom seem to be expecting, almost inviting and welcoming her death, as if both were giving permission for her to die. As well, the exquisite preciousness of the emotions they shared is remarkable, the experience of which had to have been nigh unsurpassable in terms of intimacy and love.

In such an equation, death and the terrible suffering and grief accompanying it become merged with the greatest love and intimacy. For Jefferson, who felt everything deeply, sexual and emotional intimacy were literally life-threatening to his beloved, turning his love into unintended violence and death. His sex drive literally killed her.

That love involved sexuality for Jefferson is clear from the fact that Martha gave birth six times in twelve years. However, quite literally, his sexuality was also responsible for her death. That his sex drive continued unabated after her death is indicated by his long-standing sexual relationship with Sally Hemings, his mulatto slave and deceased wife's half sister, who bore him at least four children.[119]

These relationships indicate that Jefferson had difficulty managing his sexual appetites and experienced tremendous emotional suffering as a result. After the death of his wife, apart from his short-lived affair with the much younger Maria Cosway in France, which began as an forbidden

---

[119] *See* Gordon-Reed, *Thomas Jefferson and Sally Hemings.*

love with a married woman (which Jefferson never even mentioned to Madison) and dissipated when Jefferson came to understand that she cast him as her father/rescuer, Jefferson never again engaged in a male/female courtship of social equals. Instead, importantly, he pursued two other paths: ongoing forbidden sexual relations with a black female slave (almost by definition a dominant/submissive relationship) and close intellectual intimacy with male social equals, which contained veiled elements of homosexual dominance and submission.

Dominant/submissive relationships often exchange and reverse roles within foreplay, intercourse, and consummation (whether literal or metaphorical). In a male/female, dominant/submissive sexual relationship, the male may act out a submissive, female role and the female may become dominant. (This is where the typical "dominatrix" is found.)

Similarly, in homosexual male/male relationships, men may freely exchange the male/female and dominant/submissive roles. The relationships may be inaugurated with a courtship period during which one or both men exhibit subtle (or not-so-subtle) gender reversed behaviors to the other. These courtships may occur quite publicly where such behaviors have alternative meanings: such as in late 18th century, post-revolutionary America, when men were openly affectionate. They might be conveyed openly through purposeful double entendre. Or they may be exchanged in coded language between the two suitors or openly only in private.

Other identifying and bonding messages may include shared secrets, mutual secret jibes or criticisms of others, use of violent images or hyperbole, or even collusive plotting against others.[120] The bonds between partners in such a homosexual, dominant/submissive relationship can be incredibly powerful, founded as they are on perennial, mutually-driven escape or rescue from annihilation.

Dominant/submissive relationships can be found throughout Jefferson's social and political life. There were those that involved class differences (master/slave

---

[120] As in Jefferson's exhortation to Madison to pray for Patrick Henry's death. (TJ to JM, 12-18-1784, quoted in Burstein & Isenberg, *Madison & Jefferson*, 112).

(white/black); older/younger; aristocrat/yeoman-peasant; leader/lackey (public figure/right arm), and those in which physical violence and even murder occurred. He utilized these types of relationships before and during his presidency by hiring men who were younger, foreign born, socially marginalized, and/or lower class to carry out his political dirty work.

If one uses the earlier identified sequence (Jefferson engaged in homosexual/dominant-submissive relationships after the death of his wife = his sex drive killed "her" = sex only with "the dark other female" and latent homosexual "male/female" [dominant-submissive] relationships with men) as a template to frame Jefferson's childhood issues, we find that *in Jefferson's unconscious mind*, his forbidden Oedipal wish to be his mother's mate, his natural male love for and drive to sexually "have" her, is the thing that kills her. The danger to her is genuine and literal, even if Jefferson's mother did not actually die. For Jefferson, the connection between his sexual drive and her death is total and absolute. Since a boy's relationship with his mother is what frames everything he knows about men and women and is indeed a matter of life and death (for without his mother, he would literally not have come into existence and might not survive), it becomes the template for all his relationships with women thereafter. *She*, the mother, becomes she, all women.

Such a psychological/developmental framework, once formed in the child's mind at the appropriate moment(s) in his development (up to and at the Oedipal stage), does not change throughout life.

Jefferson, the small boy, was faced with the untenable choice between loving/wanting to have his mother = killing her (being a male kills the female) (thus also incurring the murderous wrath of the father), or not loving/having her (not being a male, not surviving = his own death).[121]

---

[121] To an extent, this dynamic necessarily exists within all men (and women). Why some men (or women) grow up stuck at one or another place in their psychological development, while others with apparently identical situations and timing, are not, is a matter of other factors or circumstance, temperament, happenstance. Suffice it to say that when we see a manifestation of childhood, we may be able to figure out what caused it, but we cannot reverse that and say that the cause always leads to a particular manifestation of behavior.

Having killed her, *the female*, Jefferson had only two choices: (1) continue to be male only with "the dark other female," in secret, and using coercion (inherently violent), and/or (2) stop being the male or become a celibate male, which is tantamount to not being a male, become the female and engage only with men. We know that Jefferson did both.

Any public expression that in Jefferson's mind was equivalent to "being the male" (loving a woman, wanting to have her sexually, or expressing his masculinity in any endeavor) would have immediately created a subconscious terror of great violence to and the imminent death of someone (either a female or a person in the position of a female [e.g. dependent, possessing female characteristics such as weakness, frailty, highly refined emotions and verbal ability, whininess, softness: whatever attributes Jefferson's mother may have had in his mind] *or of himself*, the young, untested male who hasn't yet had a chance to mature, prove himself, make his way).

Dorothy Bloch, a certified psychologist and psychoanalyst who practiced in New York City in the 1960's and 70's, described in her book *So the Witch Won't Eat Me* what she had discovered in child patients who insisted they belonged to the opposite sex. Bloch found that in each instance, "the child had commenced acting out the fantasy" that he or she belonged to the opposite sex, "when a specific incident jeopardized his already precarious situation and convinced him that his life was endangered." Bloch noted that: "In all instances, [the children] had been exposed to the actual violence of one parent, so that they had to defend themselves not merely against the fear, but against the threat of infanticide." (Bloch, 50.)

In addition, "the only refuge offered by the other parent against this danger was at most detachment and a seductive facade." In all cases, the child was convinced that the parent of the opposite sex preferred him instead of the other parent and felt that this preference would make the other parent enraged at the child for being preferred. (Id.)[122]

---

[122]   Science does not require hundreds of samples to define a rule or principle. Bloch's observation of specific repeating parent-child patterns in multiple children with the same condition (gender reversal) provides us with a template for understanding hidden dynamics in TJ and JM.

The specific dynamics of the parent/child relationship Bloch describes provides us with an interior picture of Jefferson's subconscious psychological wiring, which is mirrored by the dynamics of his relationship with his wife, her death, and Jefferson's subsequent relationship choices.

Both Jefferson and Madison were known to have exhibited identifiably feminine characteristics. Madison was small, physically frail, and had an almost laughable self-conceit and prudishness. His reverence for Jefferson was great and lifelong. Jefferson, though tall and robust, was delicate and vulnerable emotionally. His love for Madison was equally strong as Madison's for him. Despite the division between head and heart that Jefferson delineated in his famous essay, he had great difficulty separating his intellect from his emotions. If he felt something, that made it true. A painful but inadvertent slight was felt by Jefferson as intentional and cruel; having been felt as such, Jefferson concluded it was intended so and he determined to respond in kind.

Madison was almost paternally careful with Jefferson's delicate emotions. He declined Jefferson's veiled offers of greater intimacy but received his friend's forays without judgment or aversion, and seems to have helped to turn Jefferson's mind to better uses. Jefferson remained forever grateful to Madison, believing always that "his judgment is so sound and is heart so good." (TJ to Peter Carr, 12-11-1783, quoted in Burstein & Isenberg, *Madison & Jefferson,* 104.)

Neither Madison's actual marriage to Dolly Payne Todd nor his refusal to consummate his partnership with Jefferson by becoming his "next door" neighbor, as Jefferson offered (or later, as Jefferson again suggested, to move into the presidential mansion with him) negated the homosexual elements or changed the meaning of their relationship. Indeed, Madison's reticence appears to have strengthened their bond and enabled them to do their best work. But the characteristics of that bond also led on more than one occasion to them doing unnecessary harm to others. In more than one instance, their actions may have been responsible for the loss of lives. And in one case, it resulted in the loss to America of one of its greatest public servants: Aaron Burr.

By the time Jefferson met Madison, both men were mature adults and Jefferson was a widow with children. Both were prominent politically and well aware of social prohibitions. To my knowledge, neither man ever declared either publicly or privately that he possessed homosexual feelings, that he was sexually attracted to men (or to each other), or that he saw himself as a woman. But the homosexual undertones in the language between them is hard to miss.

Jefferson's first homosexual overture to Madison followed not long after his wife's death (almost as if, with *her* gone, Jefferson could become "her" and was free to show his devotion to *him*). Jefferson wrote Madison to try to persuade him to move closer to Monticello. He told Madison that Monroe was already in the process of doing so and another friend, William Short (who later joined Jefferson in France as his secretary) was also considering it.[123]

In that letter, having just suffered the death of his wife, Jefferson turned the subject of death on its head, as it were, when he suggested that they pray for Patrick Henry's death. His wife's death had deeply wounded him. Now he was using death to imaginatively wound someone he disliked.

Turning immediately from his wish for Henry's death to his wish for intimacy with Madison, Jefferson suggested that if Madison joined the others in moving closer to Jefferson, they would make it a "partie quarree" – a *partie carrée,* which meant a four-way male/female dance unit.

Burstein and Isenberg write that "[c]oncerning bonds of love and friendship, with or without political overtones, Jefferson was emotionally demanding and a hard bargainer." (113) Placing his imagined four-way unit first, Jefferson argued that "[a]greeable society is the first essential in constituting the happiness and of course the value of our existence." (Id.)

Interestingly, although Madison never did move his residence near to Monticello but remained at Montpelier (his father's estate, in distant Orange County, Virginia), Jefferson did eventually get his wish for a four-way unit when he formed his administration. There, he had Madison, Gallatin, and

---

[123]   Short, who himself was engaged in a long affair while in France, was one of the few people who knew of Jefferson's affair with Cosway.

Dearborn to form the core of his cabinet. The three men stayed in close loyal lockstep throughout Jefferson's two administrations and in 1806 closed ranks against Burr (although all three were former "friends" of Burr's) after Jefferson predetermined Burr's absolute guilt of crimes against the nation.

Thus, the Jefferson-cabinet conspiracy against Burr was founded on the four-way homosexual, dominant-submissive relationships between the members of Jefferson's cabinet. This was the core *partie carrée* unit. The outside accomplices who joined the conspiracy on the periphery were Wilkinson and Granger (and outside this ring was another ring of those "employees" hired for the hands-on dirty work). Those outside the inner circle were never privy to the full conspiracy as the principal cabinet members were.

According to Burstein and Isenberg, starting in the early 1780's Madison and Jefferson began "testing ... a confidential vocabulary about the people who surrounded them. In public, the two Virginians came across as cordial and proper; in private, they could sound hypercritical and even cruel." (95) Burstein and Isenberg mention this in the context of a shared derision of John Adams, without giving further consideration of the meaning of their "confidential vocabulary." But it is good to remember that this private language was foundational, permeated their relationships, and contained keys to their characters and explanations of later reactions and behaviors, as in their reactions to the accidental interloper into their private world: Aaron Burr. They had, in essence, established not just a private language or a four-way dance but a secret relationship, an impregnable bond, a closed circle around each other with impenetrable walls. The intense secrecy of this bond is illustrated by the level of punishment for an unwanted intrusion: death.

The code was not only a shared language; it was a way to approach political problems, based on a practice of molding opinions and thereby securing alliances. Burstein and Isenberg make note of a letter from Jefferson to George Rogers Clark that the authors conclude "is meaningful as a template, because this was how Jeffersonian-Madisonian politics would be constructed in coming years." (100) In the letter, Jefferson gave Clark "a guide to who Clark's friends were and who was secretly undermining him. To do this meant resorting to invective without sounding petulant." (99)

Burstein and Isenberg's description is worth quoting in full:

> Writing to one whose susceptible nature he had earlier flushed out, Jefferson stepped gingerly across the page. Clark would, of course, know that Henry was meant when Jefferson damned a certain someone as "all tongue without either head or heart," whose "schemes" were "crooked" (meaning wily and unpredictable). Exposing Henry's betrayal of Clark, Jefferson feigned surprise at Henry's hostile turn; he inserted the clause "as far as he has personal courage to shew hostility to any man" to show the courageous soldier that he could write off his political rival with one deft twist of the knife.

(Id. at 99-100.)

As noted earlier, "crooked" was the word Jefferson later used when he referred to Burr as "a crooked gun." (TJ to William Branch Giles, April 20, 1807, National Archives.) Apparently Burr was not the first "crooked" man in Jefferson's ideology. The phallic implication of the terms crooked and crooked gun is noteworthy. A man who could not be trusted was crooked, bent. Ostensibly, a man who could be trusted was not bent; he was upright, erect. This would mean that an untrustworthy man was not trustworthy because he was not manly, not a man. In an interesting double reversal, tall Jefferson, having been playing the part of the foolish female supplicant to little Madison's wise paternal male, perhaps was too eager to call another man crooked. (Tall normally would be the man; little would be the woman. It was a reversal for Jefferson to take on the female role and Madison to take the male one. It was another reversal to then call another man crooked, when Jefferson was the one who was "bent" – lying about his gender.)

Although in jest, it is of passing interest that Henry "Light-Horse Harry" Lee, called James Monroe a "Benedict" –

after the traitor Benedict Arnold – to Madison for having betrayed their close-knit fraternity of single men by marrying before they did. (Id., 127) (So, it was treason to marry a woman.)

In the template Burstein and Isenberg identify, Jefferson began by "first identifying friends and enemies; then molding opinions, building alliances, and forging plans in coded letters or in small conclaves; and last, presenting those well-formed plans to large deliberative bodies." (Id., 100.) Burstein and Isenberg add: "In general, it would be Jefferson who issued the controlling statements, goading their allies, while approving Madison maintained a temperate pose in all his prose." (Id.)

What Burstein and Isenberg politely do not say is how close to slander "molding opinions" could be. Or how polarizing and divisive "identifying friends and enemies" is. The kinds of derogatory secret remarks they made to each other and those that they then cautiously spread, often also in private correspondence and likely in private meetings, did not merely "identify" or "mold." To mold opinions was often to create what today we would call a slant (or slanted view), a memorable image, an appeal to emotions without reference to fact. Logical fallacies. Either/or propositions. So that "While Mr. Henry lives, another bad constitution would be formed and saddled forever on us." And Adams was "not remarkable for any thing unless it be a display of vanity." Burr was a "crooked gun or perverted machine."

These kinds of remarks did the opposite of building coalitions, finding common ground, or unifying. They were divisive, damaging, and defamatory. They were far from principled. They were dirty politics. Truth was irrelevant.

And yet Jefferson could without any sense of irony say about Madison: "His judgment is so sound and his heart so good." And Madison could, while engaged in creating emotional and ideological divides, concern himself deeply with building national consensus. Both of these are co-equal opposites, reversals. Should one perceive the discrepancy between the two men's "cordial and proper" public demeanor and their "hypercritical and even cruel" private demeanor, the added discrepancy between their declared policies and actual behaviors (as in, concern for building consensus versus actually causing contention and division) would be confounding, for it was reversal on top of reversal, piling up and shunting back and forth.

Not that either man consciously intended it (at least at first), confounding the opposition often works better than logical argument or brute force. And where the latter do not work anyway, the former may be the only choice.

Under the premise that everything means everything it can mean, where we find social, political, logical, ideological, or positional reversals, we must include the possibility of gender reversals, and visa versa. Gender is an ontological matter. With extremely rare exceptions, biology and evolution dictate that humans *are* either male or female, not both. To insist on a reversal of one's biological gender is to insist on both an ontological impossibility and an act of the greatest violence to one's actual gender: the death of what one *is*. Thus does the issue of one's imminent annihilation arise repeatedly, if unconsciously, in gender-reversed relationships.[124] For such persons, either "to be" or "not to be" are both matters of life and death, for to be what one feels one is, if that is the opposite of one's biological makeup, is death, but not to be what one feels one is, is also a death.

And thus the need for absolute secrecy, closing of the ranks, perpetual vigilance, and the willingness to strike down any perceived threat to oneself, to the relationship or to anything allied to oneself or one's people. Anything that intrudes into the secret or threatens to expose it is a dire threat.

And for Jefferson, once he was president, allied to him and to his secret, in his mind while he was the nation's leader, was the entire nation. A perceived threat to him or his self-contradicting views was a threat to the nation.

To say that Jefferson (or Madison) *was* a homosexual would not be accurate. It is clear he engaged throughout his life in relations with women and had a strong sex drive. But his relations with his slave, Sally Hemings, illustrates another

---

[124] This also suggests, as Bloch observes, that gender reversal may be a result of fear of infanticide.

crucial facet of his makeup, for as noted earlier it was by definition a dominant/submissive relationship. It is fine to say that once in France where slavery was abolished, Jefferson permitted Sally to choose either to stay and remain free or to return with Jefferson to America, where she would remain enslaved – and she chose to return. But there was no actual choice there for her. Both she and Jefferson knew it. She was a woman of color, uneducated, with no means of support, with children and completely dependent on her master. She was subject to his wishes and whims. She had to go where he told her and if he was permissive, it was still his choice, not hers. She had to do what he wanted her to do and that obviously meant submitting to sexual intercourse with him.

In that relationship, Sally had to be submissive and Jefferson was necessarily dominant, which is interesting because in his relationship with Madison, while both men tossed ideas and words back and forth, in some ways it was Jefferson who seems to have more often taken the submissive, feminine role – letting Madison manage him. But as noted earlier, in dominant/submissive relationships, as in homosexual ones, roles are often exchanged, passed back and forth, as it were. Thus, it is quite possible that Jefferson permitted or even solicited Sally to take the dominant role during sexual relations. If so, the couple may well have engaged in what we nowadays call bondage and discipline. Indeed, in a shifting dominant/submissive relationship between master and slave, it would perhaps have been unusual if the couple did not.

In any event, these underlying factors were the stage upon which Burr entered and played his part, one which could only lead to one result: failure, loss, self-destruction.

~

PART FIVE:

PRETEXT &

COMPLETION

Jefferson had always envisioned his explorers as American envoys to the Indian nations of the West, and a diplomatic mission to the very considerable numbers of native inhabitants of what had been Spanish Louisiana was of utmost importance to the takeover and eventual settlement of the province. *** In one important sense, Indian diplomacy was merely a means to an ultimate end, and it provides the first glimmer of the American imperialistic drive later known as Manifest Destiny.
Flores, *Jefferson & Southwestern Exploration* 24.

Ultimately, [Jefferson's] exploration of the Southwest would assume the status of an international incident, one which came precipitously close to involving the United States in a war with Imperial Spain.
Flores, 9.

Preceded by messengers bearing news of the confrontation [with Spanish troops] on the river, during the last week of August, 1806, the disappointed members of the Exploring Expedition of Red River straggled into Natchitoches on borrowed Indian ponies. They found the frontier town virtually seething with excitement and outrage over the incident . . . To both Americans and Spaniards, the war that had been looming like a storm cloud since the purchase of 1803, now seemed an imminent reality.
Flores, 281.

Although, the facts clearly show that the administration wanted as little attention drawn to the Southwestern expedition as possible, a suspicion persists that perhaps Jefferson was content to have the American public assume that the Burr Conspiracy was actually responsible for the uproar [along the Red River].
Flores, 293-94.

Maps

(Map borrowed from Kline 2:599)

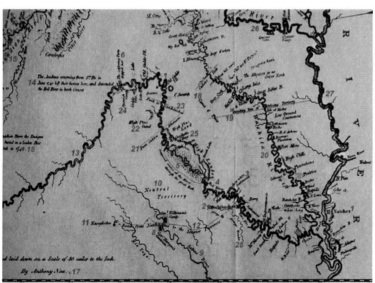

*Contemporary map by Anthony Nau of
Red, Washita, and Mississippi Rivers*

The Dunbar & Freeman/Custis

Expeditions

There is *"no better proof of the good faith of the United States
[toward Spain] than the vigor with which we acted ... in suppressing
the enterprise meditated lately by Burr against Mexico."*
Jefferson instructions to James Bowdoin (U.S. minister to Spain)
April 2, 1807 (Lipscomb 11:279)[125]

By sending explorers up the Red River, Jefferson "not only risked
the destruction of a team of scientific explorers but a possible war over it.
Jefferson was literally courting disaster."
Flores, *TJ & Southwestern Exploration*, 70-71.

Blennerhassett said he had written several essays for the *Ohio Gazette*
*"to divert public attention from scrutiny into contingent plans or operations
against Spain, which, whilst kept secret, government would not disapprove,
but when exposed, [they] would be obliged to frustrate,
as [they] had done at New York in the case of Ogden and Smith."*
Fitch, *Breaking with Burr*, 196 [HB's Brief].

Jefferson's Southwestern Expeditions

In the spring of 1804, the start of the last year of Aaron
Burr's career as Vice President (the last time he served in a
public capacity, having served his country since 1775) and
around the time that Lewis & Clark were setting off on their
famed exploration up the Missouri River, President Jefferson
hired a Scottish-born mathematician and astronomer, Sir
William Dunbar, who was by then a resident of Natchez,
Mississippi, to explore the Red River in lower Louisiana.

What is important about this mission for our story is
both the nature of the expedition (like Lewis and Clark's, for
botanical and geographic purposes, but also unacknowledged
espionage against Spain) and an example of Jefferson's modus
operandi. Dunbar's observations set Jefferson's actions in relief,
providing a way to discern what otherwise would be (and
largely has been) lost to history: what Jefferson was really up
to and what he really intended at the crucial moment when
Burr, believing he had Jefferson's permission, was preparing

---

[125] Also quoted in Lomask 2:201 and Kennedy, 311 (citing to Wandell, S.H. &
Minnigerode, M., *Aaron Burr* (G.P. Puntnam's Sons, 1925) 2:178.)

and setting out on his own expedition – a lawful one – down the Mississippi and up the Ouachita. These events give us the final missing pieces as to why Jefferson responded to Burr's expedition as he did.

Dunbar came to wonder about Jefferson's decisions and might also have come to suspect General James Wilkinson, the man who betrayed Burr, who performed the functions of both the U.S. military commander and civilian governor of Upper Louisiana, while also serving as a secret paid informant for Spain, and whose maps, which he gave to Jefferson, made the Red River exploration possible, while his "advice [to Spain] also ensured that a troop of two hundred Mexican cavalry were being dispatched from Nacogdoches ... to intercept [the American explorers]." (Linklater, *Artist in Treason*, 212, 236.)

Dunbar's correspondence with Secretary of War Henry Dearborn throughout this period establishes Jefferson's methods. It was Dearborn who encouraged Burr and Wilkinson, separately and with Jefferson's sanction, to pursue the objects of their activities – until those became inexpedient to the government, whence he later retracted, denied, and covered up. Dunbar saw Dearborn and Jefferson do this with the near-disastrous Freeman/Custis Red River expedition.

In the Freeman/Custis expedition, Jefferson was pushing for confrontation. As Dan Flores wrote: Dunbar "must have been astounded at the administration's stubbornness" in insisting upon sending an expedition up the Red River after Dunbar's repeated warnings, "which not only risked the destruction of a team of scientific explorers but a possible war over it. Jefferson was literally courting disaster." (Flores, *Jefferson and Southwestern Exploration,* 70-71.) Indeed, the Freeman/Custis expedition nearly did provoke war with Spain.

In Burr's case, Dearborn had told Burr that his proposed settlement of the Bastrop lands in Louisiana would "render a very great service to the public and afford pleasure to the administration" (AB to Tupper, November 21, 1706, Kline 2:1002) but later both Dearborn and Jefferson denied this and pretended the administration had given no encouragement or sanction to Burr's activities. Jefferson even stated publicly that the settlement was one of Burr's tricks to lure young men to his cause.

Wilkinson, having had much experience with betrayal, seems to have anticipated it from Jefferson and by betraying Burr, avoided risking himself.

But this is all method; we get ahead of the story.

When Jefferson hired Dunbar, it had been exactly a year since Jefferson had purchased Louisiana from Napoleon, who had re-acquired it from Spain and by selling to the United States, had violated the acquisition treaty with Spain. Spain was not happy. From Spain's point of view, there was now nothing to keep the Americans from expanding westward into Spanish territory. And from America's (and Jefferson's) viewpoint, Spain was not only in the way but was openly obstructive of American needs and wishes, as well as oppressive to its own colonists. As Andrew Jackson put it: with a few thousand volunteers under "firm officers and men of enterprise [we] will look into Sante Fe and Mexico, give freedom and commerce to those provinces, establish peace, and a permanent barrier against the inroads and attacks of foreign powers on our interior, which will be the case so long as Spain holds that large country on our borders."(Lomask 2:134-35, citing AJ to "a friend" (n.d.) in Robert V. Remini, *Jackson and the Course of American Empire: 1767-1821* (1977), p. 147.)

We know that Burr, who was friends with Andrew Jackson, shared Jackson's opinion. According to Charles Biddle, Burr told him that as part of his expedition plans: "He would have collected a number of military men round him near the [Spanish] lines, [and] formed a barrier between us and the Spaniards which would have prevented them from disturbing us." (Charles Biddle, *Autobiography*, p. 314.)

"Do You Know the Way to Santa Fe?" – The Dangers of the Three Rivers

Congress funded two expeditions on these rivers during this period: (1) the Dunbar Washita River Expedition of 1804-05, and (2) the Freeman/Custis Red River Expedition of 1806. After the second expedition almost ended in war, Congress withdrew funding for any further exploration of the region.

The exploration of the area formed by the three rivers (the Red, Washita, and Arkansas) was one of several at

Jefferson's behest into what was then Spanish territory. These three rivers flow down from the northwest (the headwaters of the Arkansas are in the Rockies in present-day Colorado and of the Red in present-day New Mexico) into the lower Mississippi. They are like three fingers or tentacles. The upper two attach directly to the Mississippi and the third (the Red) attaches to the middle one (the Washita).

Also roughly parallel and to the southwestward of the Red is the Sabine River, a fourth tentacle, which, however, flows directly into the Gulf. The Sabine became the temporary boundary between American and Spanish territories and forms most of the border between present-day Louisiana and Texas.

The stated purpose of these explorations was to make precise maps of the waterways and geographic features (for scientific reasons and to determine the boundaries) and to categorize the flora and fauna. But these were reconnaissance missions. Jefferson used these to make forays into Spanish territories with the ultimate intent of expanding U.S. territories. Spain was well aware of it, due to the reports by the duplicitous General Wilkinson and Baron Bastrop, both of whom warned Spain about the expeditions and about American intentions, advising the colonial regime to quell any incursions.

From an American political-military viewpoint, there were three critical strategic locations in the Spanish Territories: Santa Fe (in present-day New Mexico), Vera Cruz (Mexico, on the Gulf a few hundred miles directly east of Mexico City), and Mexico City. As Lewis and Clark's expedition was expected to find a northern river route (through Spanish territory) to the Pacific, Jefferson hoped Dunbar's Red River trip would provide "information on the most direct waterway route to that remote but fabled outpost of the Spanish Provincia Internas: Santa Fe." (Flores, 17.)

When asked by General John Adair "how far is it, and what kind of way from St. Louis to Santa Fe, and from thence to Mexico?," General James Wilkinson replied "Do you not know that I have reserved these places for my own, triumphant entry, that I have been reconnoitering & exploring the route for 16 years; and that I not only know the way but all the difficulties & how to surmount them. I wish we could get leave, Mexico would soon be ours." (Adair to JW, January 27, 1806 and JW to Adair (date uncited), quoted in Abernethy, *Burr Conspiracy*, 45-46.)

The Red River was important to the Spanish because the colonial officials in Texas believed that when "inevitable war" with the Americans came, the Red River would furnish one of the primary avenues of attack. (Flores, 30.)

According to the editors of the Dunbar-Hunter journals, President Jefferson "had come to believe that the Red River, 'next to the Missouri [was] the most interesting water of the Mississippi' [and] was the key waterway to the southern [Louisiana] Purchase. He also believed that the United States had some claim to part of the Texas territory held by Spain. A trip up the Red, Jefferson believed, might test Spanish resolve and place pressure on Spain during the newly opened negotiations with the United States concerning such areas as West Florida [still held by Spain] and the true extent of the Louisiana Purchase." (Berry, *The Forgotten Expedition,* xxxii, quoting from one of Jefferson's annual messages, without attribution.)

Texas historian Dan L. Flores notes that until the limits of Louisiana "were definitely set, [Spain's Royal] Council cautioned, the Americans should not be allowed on the Western rivers, whether to mark the boundaries or on any other pretext." (Flores, p. 27.) Flores states that "The royal council's decision was communicated to the commandants of the Provincias Internas in a letter [dated] April 22, 1804," a year before the Freeman/Custis expedition, which obviously flouted the Spanish rule. (Id. fn. 35.)

Flores continues that "The Spanish officials distrusted the Americans on the boundary issue, for they believed that despite its libertarian principles, the young American Republic was expansionist at heart. This attitude would soon be exacerbated by American newspapers reports, several of them forwarded anonymously to Texas officials, that the United States was ready to go to war over the boundaries issue." (Id. at 27-28.)

The Marquis de Caso Calvo, a former governor of Louisiana and now Spain's commissioner to settle the boundary question, learned of Jefferson's "daring undertaking" to send explorers up the southern Louisiana rivers, which he thought Spain could easily "divert and even destroy." (Id. at 28.) Manuel Salcedo, the last Spanish governor of Louisiana before the Purchase, wrote to his superiors in August 1804 that "...with great activity and care [the Americans] are sending expeditions to the Upper Mississippi, Missouri, Arkansas and Red Rivers in order to reconnoitre their sources and courses, examine the lands, and attract and conciliate the Indian nations to them, which with study and with cautious skill they will separate from our friendship..." (Id. at 29.)

Spanish Texas governor Bautista was "less than confident about Spain's right to stop all American examinations of Southwestern rivers. According to his information, the sources and mouth of the Arkansas River lay within the bounds of Louisiana, and there Spain had no grounds for interference. But while the Americans now owned the Red River's mouth, Spain was in clear possession of its sources, and in his opinion 'any expedition to the Colorado [i.e. Red] would be a hostile act.'" (Id. at 29-30.)

So, for these and other reasons (increase in hostilities with the Indians, for one), the Dunbar Red River expedition was postponed at Dunbar's suggestion in favor of a shorter exploration of the Washita River, just north of the Red, which commenced in October 1804 and was completed without incident by the end of January 1805.

As noted, Dunbar knew the Red River was more dangerous for American explorers and predicted that an exploring party could encounter Spanish obstruction.[126]

The Freeman/Custis Red River Expedition

Dunbar was correct in his apprehensions. A short description of what happened on the 1806 Freeman/Custis Red River expedition illustrates the actual danger. The Freeman/Custis expedition set off on April 28, 1806. About halfway up the river, a local Caddo Indian Chief told the Americans that "upwards of about 1000" Spanish troops had

---

[126] *See* Berry, *The Forgotten Expedition,* xxxii fn.63; Flores, 70n108; *and* Rowland, *William Dunbar,* 131, 149,174-75, 177, 329-32, 192-93. *See also,* TJ to Freeman, April 14, 1804 and TJ to Dunbar, March 28, 1806, Dunbar to Dearborn, March 28, 1806 in *TJ Papers,* Library of Congress.

invaded his village, "insulted the Chief [and] said they were going after the Americans on the Red river, whom they would serve in the same manner, and, if resistance was made, either kill them, or carry them off prisoners, in irons." (Freeman Journal entry, in Flores, 193.) The Chief said the commanding officer was "a Cross and bad man, who would do all the mischief he could to the party" and advised the Americans to turn back. (Id., 194.)

When the following day, the Freeman/Custis group encountered a Spanish military detachment of about 150 horse, the commander, Captain Don Francisco Viana, told them that "his orders were not to suffer any body of armed troops to march through the territory of the Spanish Government; to stop the exploring party by force, and to fire on them if they persisted in ascending the river, before the limits of the territory were defined." (Id. at 203-204.) Freeman told Viana they would turn back the following day, which Viana allowed. No coward, Freeman – who had men in the bushes already pointing guns at the Spaniards – assured Viana that if his party were disturbed or prevented from leaving, they would shoot on Viana's men. Only thus were Freeman and his corps able to return home safely. Had a battle ensued and had Spanish soldiers killed any of Freeman's part, it would have been difficult for Jefferson to avoid escalation. Jefferson had thus knowingly put these explorers in harm's way and had knowingly attempted to provoke Spanish aggressive response, while he maintained plausible deniability.

The danger inherent in Jefferson's western explorations is also illustrated by the murder of Philip Nolan in 1800, who was one of Wilkinson's protégés. (JW referred to him as "a child of my own raising" [JW to Miro (date and source uncited), quoted in Linklater, *Artist in Treason,* 91]; *see also* Flores, p.33, n44, quoting from JW to TJ, May 22, 1800 (source not cited): JW "implied that 'the Mexican traveller' had been reared in his household."].)

Nolan was not one of Jefferson's scientists on an alleged exploratory mission. He was a gunrunner and horse trader and a former employee of Wilkinson's. But he was also a mapmaker and a secret agent for Wilkinson. He had made four expeditions into Spanish Texas to capture mustangs, the wild descendants of the Arabian and Barb stock of the early Spaniards. Nolan had been on his way to bring Jefferson a horse but for unknown reasons seems to have turned back at Lexington, to mount a fifth western expedition. Flores says: "The Spaniards now suspected, probably correctly, that Nolan was gathering information for the United States, and early in March 1801, Lieutenant Miguel Musquiz and a Spanish calvary surrounded Nolan's camp on the Grand Prairie, killed him, and captured more than half his party ..." (Flores, 32.)

Given Wilkinson's repeated betrayals of his own colleagues and Jefferson's peripheral involvement in the suspicious deaths of others who threatened to expose him (like Meriwether Lewis and James Callender)[127], as well as his involvement in the attempted killing of Aaron Burr, Nolan's death ought to be viewed with suspicion.

Nolan's guide and traveling companion, Joseph Lucas, was an expert in Indian sign language and was later employed for one of Jefferson's southwestern expeditions, and Nolan's maps and discoveries eventually found their way, via Wilkinson, into Jefferson's hands, which "convinced the administration that the North Fork of the Red was the correct highway to the Rockies." (Id., 33, 34.)

After the Red River expedition, however, when Jefferson wouldn't follow Dunbar's advice or exercise more care with the lives of those he expected to go unlawfully into foreign territory to "explore," Congress "fully cognizant of the perilous nature of Southwestern exploration ... [in 1807] ended Jefferson's cherished dream of sending scientific expeditions up all the major rivers of the West by the very effective withholding of funds." (Id., 313.)

Dan Flores notes that one development worth taking note of with respect to his last southwestern expedition:

> is that Jefferson allowed Dearborn to assume virtually sole responsibility for it, which may explain why Congress was allowed to 'overlook' the appropriation for it. A second [development] is Jefferson's strange

---

[127] That Jefferson portrayed these men (Lewis, Callender, and Burr) as either drug addicted or depressive (Lewis) or "ripe for Bedlam" (Burr) is of interest here, too.

failure to personally notify Dunbar, a correspondent for most of the preceding decade, of the cancellation. In fact, Jefferson and Dunbar *never* corresponded again after the failure of the Red River expedition in 1806. (Id., 313 n49.)(Flores' emphasis.)

Dunbar's Doubts

From the start of his correspondence with Jefferson and Henry Dearborn, Jefferson's secretary of war, Dunbar showed his awareness of the difficulties associated with proposed expeditions up these rivers. In May 1804, he wrote Jefferson: "on the first intimation of the business it struck me that it would not be inexpedient to discover in what light this expedition might be viewed by the neighboring Spanish Gov...," adding that "the Com[mander] of the Spanish post [at] Nacokdosh about 125 [miles] west of Nackitosh has the most positive orders not to suffer any american or other Stranger to pass beyond what they conceive to be the limits of Louisiana." (WD to TJ, May 13, 1804, in Rowland, *William Dunbar*, 131. *See also* WD to HD, May 4, 1805, id., 149.)

A year later, when preparing for the Freeman/Custis expedition up the Red River, which Dunbar decided to "promote" but not lead, he wrote Dearborn "Last year I informed the President of the Spanish opposition we were to expect on the red river. You do not say that measures have been taken to remove this." (WD to HD, May 4, 1805, *Life and Letters*, p. 149.) Dunbar wrote about George Hunter (a Scottish-born chemist, apothecary, Kentucky mineral explorer, and land speculator)(id. at xxi), the man he recommended to lead the expedition: "I doubt whether [he] will consent to make the tour of the two rivers [Red and Arkansas.] [H]ad the determination been to explore each river apart, the agreeable accounts we received of the arcansa river appeared to dispose him in some measure to incline to visit it." (Id. at 149.)

In response, Dearborn wrote Dunbar: "It is doubtful whether it will be expedient or safe for the party to ascend the Red river, farther than the first considerable ridge or high land, through which it passes. It being presumed that the source of this river is but a small distance from the Spanish settlement about Sante Fe, the party might be detained if they should advance too near them." (HD to WD, March 25, 1805, id. at 151.) Even that acknowledgement was sugar-coating things.

But on May 24th, Dearborn wrote Dunbar: "Your remarks and further reflection, have induced the President of the United States to confine the object of the proposed exploring expedition to the Red river, and some of its principal branches, together with the country immediately adjacent ... and instead of pursuing the course of said river to the first ridge only of high lands or mountains, to explore its main branch to its utmost source ..." (Id., 153.) This was an odd response, given Dunbar's expressed misgivings about a Red River expedition and Spain's claim the source was in its territory.

Dearborn added that Jefferson had asked the American governor of Louisiana to write to the Marquis de Casa Calvo "on the subject of the expedition," the object of which, Dearborn stated, "being merely to obtain geographical and other information, which will be equally useful to the Spanish and American governments." Without any reason for optimism, Dearborn "hoped that the Marquis will feel disposed to aid, rather than retard our views." (Id.)

Yet, despite the Royal Council's prohibition, the Marquis granted the passport, "which stipulated a scientific exploration into the Southwest by Dunbar and Spaniard Thomas Power (a one-time confidential agent between Spanish officials and General Wilkinson)." (Flores, p. 72.) Casa Calvo's superiors, however, informed him they had no intention of honoring such a passport. The Commandant of the Internal Provinces stationed at Chihuahua in Mexico, Nemecio Salcedo, even issued orders to a contingent from the garrison at Nacogdoches to stop the American "invaders," make them fall back or be taken prisoner. (Id., 73-74.)

Casa Calvo wanted a passport for himself in return from the Americans so he could conduct his own exploration. However, when he arrived at the American outpost, he was treated with rudeness and on his return found himself expelled from New Orleans, so that when the Americans later requested a similar passport for the Freeman/Custis expedition, Casa Calvo "promptly and haughtily refused." (Id., 75.)

Interestingly, considering that one of the accusations

made against Burr was that he lured many young men to his expedition,[128] Dunbar wrote in June 1804: "I cannot doubt that many young officers would be extremely ambitious of going upon this expedition." (WD to Thomas Freeman, June 14, 1804, Rowland, 138.) However, in May 1805, Dunbar wrote Dearborn: "I am surprised that young men of talents unencumbered by family affairs are not found in numbers with you who are solicitous to go upon so inviting an expedition; it may be perhaps the fatigues of an uncertain and unknown land journey which is to be made between the two rivers that deters persons who might have no objections to perform the expedition by water." (WD to HD, May 4, 1805, id. at 149.) Perhaps it was that the expedition was setting out to unlawfully entering hostile foreign territory.

In Dunbar's letters to Jefferson, he "emphasized that the Arkansas River might be a better avenue for ascent and the Red the better one for descent," reasoning that the Spaniards – who still claimed all the territory west of Louisiana and all of Mexico and were threatening to make war on the United States for incursions into their territories – "would be less likely to detect a boat traveling quickly downstream through territories they claimed." Dunbar's warnings turned out to be correct, for the Freeman/Custis expedition was stopped and fortunately turned back rather than the men being arrested or shot. Jefferson was fully aware of these dangers but he nonetheless "decided on and pushed for an ascent of the Red River." (Berry, xxxii)

The Freeman/Custis Red River expedition nearly ended in disaster and caused a diplomatic outcry that hit the newspapers, leading Jefferson to deflect attention from it. (See Flores, 281-84.)

Dan Flores suggests that "the play of circumstances that conspired to almost completely obscure the Red River expedition hints at more than simple political embarrassment; it may indicate that Jefferson wished to prevent a connection in the public mind between [his] exploration and the Burr-Wilkinson plot" and "[a]lthough cover-up is perhaps too strong a word, the facts clearly show that the [Jefferson]

---

[128] See Abernethy, *The Burr Conspiracy,* 67, 78, 85.

administration wanted as little attention drawn to this Southwestern expedition as possible." (Flores, 292-93)

Cover-up is not too strong a word, for Flores notes that Jefferson had passages redacted from Freeman and Custis's accounts. He had deleted "from the accounts several references implying that the expedition was attempting to win the Indians and was preparing for a military showdown with the Spaniards." (Id., 293.)

Flores says "a suspicion persists that perhaps Jefferson was content to have the American public assume that the Burr Conspiracy was actually responsible for the uproar in Texas." (Id., 294.)

In January 1807, "the *National Intelligencer*, the official [newspaper] voice of the administration, ran a detailed front-page article explaining the crisis in the Southwest, alluding to troop movements (without explaining *why* there had been a Spanish mobilization)," – which of course was caused by the Freeman/Custis encounter – "the diplomatic correspondence, and the Neutral Ground Agreement" which was made by Burr's betrayer General James Wilkinson, "without a single reference to the President's exploring expedition or its confrontation with the Spanish army." (Id., 294-95.)

The same month (which was a month after Jefferson announced Burr's guilt to the world), Jefferson said that "he knew of no evidence sufficient to convict [Burr] of either high crimes or misdemeanors."[129] But in April 1807, Jefferson wrote to the American minister to Madrid, Spain that "no better proof of the good faith of the United States could have been given [Spain] than the vigor with which we acted … in suppressing the enterprise meditated lately by Burr against Mexico." The letter was one of the diplomatic dispatches that Jefferson was unwilling to let the grand jury see as it considered whether to bring charges against Burr. (Kennedy, 311.)

When a major in the army (Major Bruff) declared to

---

[129] Kennedy, 310, cites to Plumer, at July 4, 1807, but there is no such entry. TJ said similar things on several occasions. *See* Lomask 2:178 (TJ Cabinet Memorandum, October 25, 1806: "he is committing no overt act against the law") and id., 2:198 (TJ to Thomas Mann Randoph, November 6, 1806: "as yet we have no legal proof of any overt act which the law can lay hold of.")

Henry Dearborn, Jefferson's Secretary of War, that he could prove that James Wilkinson was a spy for the Spanish, Dearborn explained that "there had been a time when General Wilkinson did not stand well with the Executive, but his energetic measures at New Orleans had regained his confidence, and he would support him," adding that "there might be an inquiry after the present bustle was over; but at present he must and would be supported." (Major Bruff's Testimony, Burr's Trial, *Annals of Congress*, 10th Congress, 1st Session (Senate), 1807-08, 598-600; also quoted in Adams, 916.) The United States Attorney General, Cesar Rodney, who was present with Dearborn, told Bruff: "What would be the result if all your charges against General Wilkinson should be proven? Why, just what the Federalists and the enemies of the present Administration wish, – [I]t would turn the indignation of the people from Burr on Wilkinson; Burr would escape, and Wilkinson take his place." (Id., 599; Adams, 916; Kennedy, 317.) What a terrible result that would have been! Henry Adams writes:

> Rodney did not add, what was patent to all the world, that if Wilkinson were to be convicted, President Jefferson himself, whose negligence had left the Western country, in spite of a thousand warnings, at the General's mercy, could not be saved from the roughest handling. The President and his Cabinet shrank from [Chief Justice John] Marshall's [ie. Burr's] subpoenas because under the examination of Wickham, Botts, and Luther Martin [Burr's counsel], they would be forced either to make common cause with the General, or to admit their own negligence. The whole case hung together. Disobedience of the subpoena was necessary for the support of Wilkinson; support of Wilkinson was more than ever necessary after refusing to obey the subpoena. (Adams, 916-17.)

> *Oh! what a tangled web we weave*
> *When first we practise to deceive!*
> **Sir Walter Scott**, *Marmion.*

> ~

Burr's Map

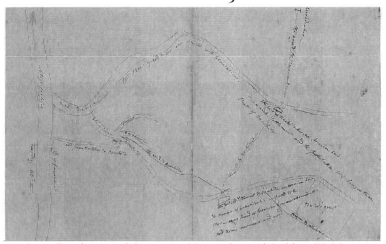

Aaron Burr letters and documents. Manuscripts and Archives Division. The New York Public Library. Astor, Lenox, and Tilden Foundations.

This is Burr's map of the way into the Bastrop Grant (which is the square on the far lower right), the land he purchased in lower Louisiana (Orleans Territory) on the west side of the Mississippi River, just prior to making his expedition. The map was clearly drawn to give directions to the location. It is upside down from most modern maps. On the left is the Mississippi, flowing from the bottom upward (which would be "downward" on most maps, towards New Orleans). The Red River is the wide one that comes out of the Mississippi, bending upwards. The Washita (Ouachita) flows "down" from the Red.

The other lines are indications of roads. The one going somewhat horizontally from the Mississippi to the Washita is labeled the "road from Natchez [which Burr notes is at 32 degrees] to Ouachita," which crosses the Ouachita River by ferry and continues onto "the fort and settlement of Ouachita, an American fort" and from there heads upward (SW) to "the post of Nachotoches, an American fort." The small rectangle on the Red River is that post. The road continues upward toward Nagodoches, in Tejas, in the "Interior Provinces" of Spanish territory then.

Burr notes that the post at Natchotoches is larger than that at Ouachita (which has 1500 inhabitants) but the latter one has "every kind of provision" and "horses (?) are numerous and good."

Burr acquired the 350,000 acre tract indirectly from Felipe Enrique Neri, the self-styled Baron de Bastrop, who had warned the Spanish of "movement of [American] forces to invade the dominions of [H]is M[ajesty, merely awaiting the movement for running the boundary." (Flores, 84, quoting Bastrop from Cordero to Salcedo, September 24, 1805, Bexar Archives.)

~

On Jeffersonian Ways

*[The Virginia Dynasty] are hostile to all freedom & independence of suffrage – A
certain junto of actual and factitious Virginians having had possession of the
government for 24 years consider the U.S. as their property and by bawling
"Support the Administration" have so long succeeded
in duping the republican public. . . .
. . . One of their principal arts & which has been systematically taught by Jefferson
is that of promoting state dissensions – not between republican and federal – that
would do them no good, but schisms in the republican party. . . .
The moment is extremely auspicious for breaking down this degrading system – The
best citizens of our country acknowledge the feebleness of our administration – they
acknowledge that offices are bestowed merely to preserve power
& without the smallest regard to fitness . . .
. . . Exhibit yourself then & emerge from this state of nullity – You owe it to yourself
– You owe it to me – You owe it to your country – You owe it to the memory of the
dead.*
**Aaron Burr to Joseph Alston (his widowed son-in-law),
November 15, 1815**
Kline 2:1166-67.

~~~~

*The president's declaration of Burr's guilt is unconstitutional. I deny his right to
make such a declaration against any man or to make such an inference from
statements made to him. The constitution gives him no such right and its exercise by
the president would be dangerous. It may and must excite unjust prejudices and
create a powerful influence against a man who is really innocent.*

*The constitution very wisely withholds from the president a power so unfavourable
to a fair trial between the public and individuals accused and so dangerous to the
liberties and lives of the citizens. I hope it is no rebellion but I hope our objection to
this dangerous and unconstitutional declaration of the president will be handed
down to posterity to prevent his conduct in this respect from being imitated.*

*Congress did not call upon him for his opinion. They would have been satisfied with
his statement of public transactions without his opinion. He is to see that the laws
be faithfully executed and to give information with respect to the state of the Union,
but he is not to give opinions concerning the guilt or innocence of any person.*
-Edmund Randolph [counsel for Burr], June 11, 1807;
Robertson, Trial of Aaron Burr, 1:159.

*It seems the stream of turpitude is unbroken in this country
from the President to his lowest retainers.*
Blennerhassett's Journal, October 7, 1807
Fitch, *Breaking with Burr*, 124.

Acknowledgements

From the early 1980's, when I began this project, through 2000, I had access to New York City's vast collections, from the research library at my alma mater, New York University, to the New York Historical Society collections to the New York Public Library holdings. I may still have the names of some of the folks who assisted me but, if I do, those papers are buried deep in some file box. I am grateful to all for their help.

Thanks to Meredith Mann in the Manuscripts and Archives Division of the New York Public Library, the librarians at the Dearborn collection in Detroit, MI, John Deeben at the National Archives, and the employees in the Alachua County Public Library system, especially Jeff Dreisin, for assisting me to obtain books via interlibrary loan.

More than anyone in my life, I am indebted to the late Bettina Olivier, theoretical scientist, of New York City, whose influence on my life and work has been incalculable, without whose genius I would never have looked for or found Burr.

I owe a great deal to my friend, David Patrick Ford. A man with a full life and many talents and abilities – actor, writer, dancer, musician, teacher and much more. David repeatedly offered his good will, ideas, and suggestions, nearly all of which I consistently rejected, whence David and I settled into an easier alliance doing repairs and construction on my dilapidated property and cat sanctuary, talking now and then about Jefferson, Burr, and the state of the world. I am thankful for his steadfast friendship and assistance.

I also wish to thank Don DeBar of Ossining, New York, my hometown, whose unexpected friendship, acumen, depth of understanding, and affirmation of my work has meant a great deal to me.

To Michael Drexler and the late Roger Kennedy, both brilliant thinkers and writers, whose work has been central to mine and who were kind enough to engage in occasional email exchanges with an irritable and insufferable writer, I owe further thanks.

To my daughters, Sarah and Giselle, who have, each in their own way supported my dedication to this project for as long as they have lived: *obligati.*

Finally, I must acknowledge and give thanks to my Kickstarter backers, who originally funded the promised private publishing of this limited edition eight years ago. Since quite a few of my backers are eminent book authors, academics, scholars, lawyers, whistleblowers, and/or civil rights activists, many of whom have spoken out at great risk to themselves, I must acknowledge here that while I do not credit their work anywhere in this book and none specifically provided me with support of any kind beyond the Kickstarter campaign, their examples have inspired and catalyzed my work. Thank you for contributing to this project and for so patiently waiting for the book.

Namaste.

Bibliographic Note

Websites – Many letters and documents from the different collections of the papers and works of Jefferson and other founders are available online. Founders Online contains material from the National Archives. Its general URL is https://founders.archives.gov/. The Library of Congress (LOC) materials are at www.loc.gov. American State Papers: Miscellaneous, and Annals of Congress are at http://memory.loc.gov/ammem/amlaw/lwsplink.html & /lwsjlink.html, respectively. I do not cite to specific URL's in these collections since the documents are easily findable by googling the author, recipient, and date.

Note on sources and citations – I cite to the source I have used and sometimes to its source (particularly to provide reference to a primary source that I have not been able to view). Where I have found citations in other works absent or incorrect, I say so and attempt to track down and supply the correct primary source, especially where it is important to my thesis.

Where my citation is long or has multiple references, I put it in a footnote. Otherwise, citations are in parentheses directly following the text to which they apply. Footnotes are numbered consecutively from start to end of the book (not by chapter).

Note on citation form – In the text, I use varying short forms sufficient for the reader to quickly identify the source and locate the full author and title in the bibliography. Where I have already cited to the author's last name and short title, I use only the author's last name (without the book title) in the following citations, unless it has been some pages since the author and title are cited. The full author, title, and publication information for every short citation I use can be looked up in the bibliography. Where I have not used a work referred to by one of the authors I cite but where I think their source is important to know, I cite that source after my citation, but do not list their source in my bibliography.

Latin – Generally I have avoided using Latin (legal) terms, except as follows. *Id.* (from Ibid. - Latin *ibidem* - *"in the same place"*) means "same as previous citation." *E.g.*, means "for example" (from Latin: *exempli gratia* - *"for the sake of an example."* *Op. cit.* means "in the work already cited."

Note on spelling in quoted material – Frequently but not always, I modernize the spelling and punctuation to enable easier reading.

Abbreviations: Thomas Jefferson = TJ; Aaron Burr = AB; Alexander Hamilton = AH; Harman Blennerhassett = HB; James Wilkinson = JW; James Madison = JM; Theodosia Burr Alston (Burr's daughter) = TBA; Joseph Alston (Burr's son-in-law) = JA; Theodosia Prevost Burr (Burr's wife) = TPB.

Dictionary – I cite to the New Oxford American Dictionary, Version 2.1.3 (80.4), Copyright © 2005–2009 Apple Inc.

Bibliography

Abernethy, Thomas P., *The Burr Conspiracy* (Oxford University Press, 1954).

Adams, Henry, *History of the United States of America during the Administrations of Thomas Jefferson* (Library of America, 1986, originally published in 9 vols., 1889-91).

American State Papers: Miscellaneous, *A Century of Lawmaking for a New Nation: U.S. Congressional Documents and Debates, 1774 – 1875,* at http://memory.loc.gov/ammem/amlaw/lwsplink.html.

Annals of Congress, *A Century of Lawmaking for a New Nation: U.S. Congressional Documents and Debates, 1774 – 1875* (same URL).

Barron's Law Dictionary (*Steven H. Gifis, 3d Ed., 1991*).

Berry, Trey, et al, eds., *The Forgotten Expedition 1804-1805: The Louisiana Purchase Journals of Dunbar and Hunter* (Louisiana State University Press, 2006).

Biddle, Charles, *Autobiography* (1883).

Bloch, Dorothy, *"So the Witch Won't Eat Me": Fantasy and the Child's Fear of Infanticide* (Houghton Mifflin, 1978).

Bowers, Claude G., *Jefferson and Hamilton: The Struggle for Democracy in America* (Houghton Mifflin Co., 1925).

Brodie, Fawn M., *Thomas Jefferson: An Intimate History* (W.W. Norton & Co., 1974).

Burstein, Andrew and Isenberg, Nancy, *Madison and Jefferson* (Random House, 2010).

Chaldecott, John A., *Justus Erich Bollmann and His Platinum Enterprises Activities in North America and Europe before the Year 1816*, Platinum Metals Rev., 1981, 25, (41), 163-172.

Chandler, David L., *The Jefferson Conspiracies: A President's Role in the Assassination of Meriwether Lewis* (William Morrow & Co., 1994).

Clark, Daniel, *Proofs of the Corruption of Gen. James Wilkinson* (Books for Libraries Press, 1970; originally published 1809).

Côté, Richard N., *Theodosia -- Theodosia Burr Alston: Portrait of a Prodigy* (Corinthian Books, 2003).

Davis, Matthew L., *Memoirs of Aaron Burr,* 2 vols. (Harper & Brothers, 1836; Reprint De Capo Press, 1971).

Davis, Matthew L., *Private Journal of Aaron Burr,* 2 vols. (Harper & Bros., NY, 1838; Reprint Literature House/Gregg Press, 1970).

Drexler, Michael J. and White, Ed, *The Traumatic Colonel: The Founding Fathers, Slavery, and the Phantasmatic Aaron Burr* (New York University Press, 2014).

Feldman, Jay, *When the Mississippi Ran Backwards: Empire, Intrigue, Murder, and the New Madrid Earthquakes* (Free Press, 2005).

Fitch, Raymond E., ed., *Breaking with Burr: Harman Blennerhassett's Journal, 1807* (Ohio University Press, 1988).

Fleming, Thomas, *The Duel: Alexander Hamilton, Aaron Burr and the Future of*

America (Basic Books, 1999).

Flores, Dan I., *Jefferson & Southwestern Exploration: The Freeman & Custis Accounts of the Red River Expedition of 1806* (University of Oklahoma Press, 1984).

Gilligan, Stephen G., *Therapeutic Trances: The Cooperation Principle in Ericksonian Hypnotherapy* (Brunner/Mazel, 1987).

Goebel, Julius, Jr. & Smith, Joseph H., eds., *The Law Practice of Alexander Hamilton* (Columbia University Press, 1964-1980, 5 vols.).

Gordon-Reed, *Thomas Jefferson and Sally Hemings: An American Controversy* (University Press of Virginia, 1997).

Hamlin, Arthur S., *Gideon Granger* (Granger Homestead Society, Canandaigua, NY, 1982).

Henshaw, Lesley, ed., "Burr-Blennerhassett Documents," *Ohio Historical and Philosophical Society*, Quarterly Publications, volumes 7-9 (1912-14) http://ia700407.us.archive.org/24/items/annualreporthis00corwgoog/annualreporthis 00corwgoog.pdf.

Isenberg, Nancy, *Fallen Founder: The Life of Aaron Burr* (Penguin Group, 2007).

Karlsen, Carol. F. and Crumpacker, Laurie, eds., *The Journal of Esther Edwards Burr: 1754-57* (Yale University Press, 1984).

Kennedy, Roger G., *Burr, Hamilton, and Jefferson: A Study in Character* (Oxford University Press, 1999).

Kline, Mary-Jo and Ryan, Joanne Wood, eds., *Political Correspondence and Public Papers of Aaron Burr* (Princeton University Press, 1983, 2 vols).

Koch, Adrienne, *Jefferson and Madison:The Great Collaboration* (Oxford University Press, 1950).

Koch, Adrienne & Peden, William, eds., *The Life and Selected Writings of Thomas Jefferson* (Random House, 1944, 1972, 1993; Modern Library Edition, 1993).

Levy, Leonard W., *Jefferson and Civil Liberties: The Darker Side* (Harvard University Press, 1963; Elephant Paperback, 1989).

Linklater, Andro, *An Artist in Treason: The Extraordinary Double Life of General James Wilkinson* (Walker Pub. Co., 2009).

Lipscomb, Andrew A., and Bergh, Albert, eds., *The Writings of Thomas Jefferson* (Thomas Jefferson Memorial Assn., 20 vols., 1903).

Lomask, Milton, *Aaron Burr: The Years from Princeton to Vice President: 1756-1805* (Farrar, Straus, Giroux, 1979). (Lomask 1.)

Lomask, Milton, *Aaron Burr: The Conspiracy and Years of Exile: 1805-1836*

(Farrar, Straus, Giroux, 1979). (Lomask 2.)

Malone, Dumas, *Jefferson and His Time, 6 vols.* (Little, Brown, 1948).

McCaleb, Walter F., *The Aaron Burr Conspiracy* (Wilson Erickson, 1936).

Parton, James, *The Life of Aaron Burr* (1858).

Peterson, Merrill D., ed., *Thomas Jefferson: A Reference Biography* (Charles Scribner's Sons, 1986).

Plumer, William, *Memorandum of Proceedings in the United States Senate: 1803-1807* (Everett S. Brown, ed.) (McMillan Co., 1923).

Robertson, David, tr., *Reports of the Trials of Colonel Aaron Burr* (Hopkins & Earle, 1808; Reprinted by De Capo Press, 1969, 2 vols.).

Rowland, Eron (Mrs. Dunbar Rowland), comp., *Life, Letters, and Papers of William Dunbar* (Press of the Mississippi Historical Society, 1930).

[Sansay, Leonora], *Scarlet Handkerchief* (3 vols., London, 1823).

Schutz, John A., & Adair, Douglas, eds., *The Spur of Fame: Dialogues of John Adams and Benjamin Rush, 1805-1813* (Liberty Fund, Indpls., 1966).

Skeen, C. Edward, *John Armstrong, Jr., 1758-1843* (Syracuse Univ. Press, 1981).

Stewart, David O., *American Emperor: Aaron Burr's Challenge to Jefferson's America* (Simon & Schuster, 2011).

Sturm, Oliver Perry, *The Conspiracy against Aaron Burr* (© 1943 Oliver Perry Sturm and © 2005 Aaron Burr Assn.)

Van Bergen, Jennifer, *Aaron Burr and the Electoral Tie of 1801: Strict Constitutional Construction*, 1 Cardozo Public Law, Policy & Ethics Journal (No. 1, 2003, 91-130).

Van Bergen, Jennifer, *Reconstructing Leonora: Early 19th Century Novelist & Friend of Aaron Burr*, A New World is Possible, January 3, 2010.

Wheelan, Joseph, *Jefferson's Vendetta: The Pursuit of Aaron Burr and the Judiciary* (Carroll & Graf Publishers, 2005).

Zacks, Richard, *The Pirate Coast: Thomas Jefferson, the First Marines, and the Secret Mission of 1805* (Hyperion, 2005).

Selection of Articles

by Jennifer Van Bergen

Repeal the USA Patriot Act
t r u t h o u t | April 1, 2002
http://911research.wtc7.net/cache/post911/legislation/truthout_repealpatriot.htm

Homeland Security Act: The Rise of the American Police State
t r u t h o u t Report, 2,3,4 December 2002
https://ratical.org/ratville/CAH/HSA_RoAPS.html

Bush War: Military Necessity or War Crimes?
(with Charles B. Gittings Jr.)
t r u t h o u t | 14-15 July 2003
https://www.pegc.us/archive/letters/bush_war.pdf

National Security Courts and Torture Warrants
Counterpunch, August 20, 2004
https://www.counterpunch.org/2004/08/20/national-security-courts-and-torture-warrants/

What's Wrong with Torture?
Counterpunch, September 14, 2004
https://www.counterpunch.org/2004/09/14/what-s-wrong-with-torture/

The Bush Administration: A Closed Family System
Counterpunch, November 30, 2004
https://www.counterpunch.org/2004/11/30/the-bush-administration-a-closed-familysystem/

The Unitary Executive: Is The Doctrine Behind the Bush Presidency Consistent with a Democratic State?
Findlaw, Jan. 9, 2006
https://supreme.findlaw.com/legal-commentary/the-unitary-executive-is-the-doctrine-behind-the-bush-presidency-consistent-with-a-democratic-state.html

How Government Forfeitures are Shutting Down U.S.-Based Muslim Charities: Going After Terrorism's Financiers Is the Right Strategy, But the Law Needs Reform
Findlaw, May 1, 2006
https://supreme.findlaw.com/legal-commentary/how-government-forfeitures-are-shutting-down-us-based-muslim-charities.html

FBI Confidential Informant Also Said to be Provocateur
Raw Story, June 8, 2006
https://www.rawstory.com/news/2006/FBI_confidential_informant_also_said_to_0608.html